Fabric, Form and Flat Pattern Cutting

Blackburn
College

Fabric, Form and Flat Pattern Cutting

Second edition

Winifred Aldrich

Book design, photography and computer graphics by James Aldrich

Blackwell
Publishing

© 2007 by Blackwell Publishing
© 1996 Winifred Aldrich and James Aldrich

Editorial Offices:
Blackwell Publishing Ltd, 9600 Garsington Road, Oxford OX4 2DQ, UK
  Tel: +44 (0)1865 776868
Blackwell Publishing Professional, 2121 State Avenue, Ames, Iowa 50014-8300, USA
  Tel: +1 515 292 0140
Blackwell Publishing Asia Pty Ltd, 550 Swanston Street, Carlton, Victoria 3053, Australia
  Tel: +61 (0)3 8359 1011

First edition published 1996
Second edition published 2007

ISBN-13: 978-14051-3620-4
ISBN-10: 1-4051-3620-0

Library of Congress Cataloging-in-Publication Data

Aldrich, Winifred.
    Fabric, form, and flat pattern cutting / Winifred Aldrich ; book design, photography, and computer graphics by James Aldrich. – 2nd ed.
      p. cm.
    Includes bibliographical references.
    ISBN-13 978-1-4051-3620-4 (alk. paper)
    ISBN-10: 1-4051-3620-0 (alk. paper)
    1. Dressmaking–Pattern design.   2. Garment cutting.   I. Title.

TT520.A42 2007
646.4'072–dc22

200604

A catalogue record for this title is available from the British Library

Set in 9 on 10 pt Palatino
by SNP Best-set Typesetter Ltd., Hong Kong

For further information on Blackwell Publishing, visit our website:
www.blackwellpublishing.com

FSC
Mixed Sources
Product group from well-managed
forests and other controlled sources
Cert no. SGS-COC-2953
www.fsc.org
© 1996 Forest Stewardship Council

Contents

Acknowledgements

We have had a great deal of practical help from people and organisations during the production of this book but its realisation would have been impossible without the inspiration and support of the following people:

Mark Cooper, who made up nearly all the designs photographed in this book and helped us to construct the fabric boards.

Dina Furtado, the model for the photographs and the drawings.

Professor Newton of the Nottingham Trent University, who gave me time from other duties to work on this book.

Gillian Bunce of the Nottingham Trent University, see the Introduction.

Christine Smith, Brian Stanley and Dawn Molloy of the Nottingham Fashion Centre, for their assistance and the extensive use of their Fabric Resource Library.

Richard Prescott for his professional advice, high quality photographic printing of the garments and the electronic reproduction of the fabric boards.

Steve Maddox of Colourbase Ltd, for his lighting and technical assistance during the photography of the garment designs.

A group of students attending a course at the Nottingham Fashion Centre who participated in the testing and the revision of my theories.

Alec Aldrich who constructed the testing equipment for the first edition of this book (see Appendix Three). The equipment was used to register the fabric codes associated with the sample garment designs.

Richard Miles of Blackwell Publishing for his great support of my work.

We would also like to acknowledge other companies and people who have assisted us:

Stephen Chalkley of Concept II Research
Len Boxall of Kennet and Lindsell Ltd
Brian Smith of the Nottingham Trent University
Sue Pike of The Nottingham Trent University
Emma Nixey of Nix-E Design
Terry Parkin of TEZ
David Bell of assyst-bullmer

We would like to thank the fabric companies who have supplied us with samples and sample lengths for this book:

A.F. Allen Son (Leicester) Ltd (GB)
Aire Mills (GB)
Andre Cristol (France)
Wm. Becker (Germany)
Bennett Silks (GB)
Bie Barzaghi SRI (Italy)
Borovics (GB)
Guy Birkin Ltd (GB)
J.B. Broadley Ltd (GB)
Carrington Fabrics (GB)
Clarkson Knitting Ltd (GB)
Cloverbrook Fabrics (GB)
Courtaulds (GB)
Crowthers (GB)
Deschamps (France)
Elastic Knitting Ltd (GB)
Evergreen Recycled Fashions (GB)
Gauthier Tissus (France)
Greenwood Mill Inc. (USA)
Haemmerle & Vogel (Austria)
Harris Halpern (Italy)
Harris Tweed Authority (Scotland)
Hurel Jersey (France)
James Hare Silks (GB)
Jean Valette (France)
J.T. Knitting Ltd (GB)
Jacksons Fabrics Ltd (GB)
John England Textiles (Ireland)
Lanificio Rosenstein & Co (Italy)
Lazzati Tessuti Innovati (Italy)
Leathertex (Italy)
Liberty (GB)
Linton Tweeds Ltd (GB)
Maish Felts (GB)
Marioboselli Jersey (Italy)
Mermet (France)
PJT (France)
Plouquet (France)
A. Rowe Ltd (GB)
Scheibler Peltzer GmbH & Co (Germany)
Schwarzschild Ochs Ltd (GB)
Simpson & Kay Ltd (GB)
Singlam Fabrics (GB)
Sofinal SC (Belgium)
Soho Silks (GB)
Textil Santanderina (Spain)
Textile King (GB)
Toray Textiles (GB)
Welbeck Fabrics (GB)
Whaleys (BFD) Ltd (GB)

An acknowledgement of fibre manufacturers and associations who have provided technical information for both the earlier and present editions of this book:

Akzo Nobel Fibres Ltd
Asahi Kasei Fibres Corporation
Bayer plc
The British Leather Confederation
Cargil Dow
Cosejo Espanol de la Piel, Spain
Curtidores Espanoles
Cotton Incorporated
Courtaulds European Fibres
CSIRO
Du Pont USA
Hyosung Corporation
ICF Industries Inc.
The International Wool Secretariat
The Irish Linen Guild
Kelheim Fibres
Kurabo Industries Ltd
Lenzing
Novaceta Group
Nylstar Ltd
Rhone-Poulenc Fibres & Yarns
The Textile Institute
Trevira GmbH & Co KG

Introduction

This second edition of *Fabric, Form and Flat Pattern Cutting* has placed most of the technical information and mechanical measurement procedures of the original book into the Appendices. In the main section of the book, a simpler method of fabric estimation has been introduced, one that will allow students to handle and assess fabrics more directly, and will also encourage tutors to introduce students to its importance at an early stage in their studies. An extra chapter has also been added to assist students with the technical drawing of garments. Whilst elongated and distorted fashion poses are often used in stylistic story boards, fashion illustration and promotion, technical design development for cutting patterns requires that drawings should be proportionate to the human figure. To help students develop this skill, the images of the garment stand and figure poses that have been used throughout the book have been included in Chapter Ten. The technical information on fabric developments has been updated and the relationship between fabric properties and the realisation of 3D CAD images has been included.

Like the original edition, this book is not about fashion, fashion is too transient. This book is an introduction to pattern cutting, it is about understanding the basic material of a fashion designer's trade – fabric.

For many years the range of fabrics available to designers changed slowly. In most decades from the turn of the last century, a new fibre was introduced into the market, but there was time for it to integrate into the current ranges and widen the choice for the designer. During the past decade, new developments have taken place in the use of generic (basic chemical source) fibres and also in the technical engineering of the structure of existing fibres. This has produced an explosion of new fabrics. Many of these have a new appearance and a significantly different handle.

The work of the designer in the clothing industry is extremely varied, it can range from the design of technically based garments in companies with large testing facilities to small high fashion businesses faced with constant innovation and short lead times. Designers now have to become adept at working with changing parameters and the technical demands of particular product groups. More manufacturing is now based abroad but the design of products is seen as the greatest strength of the British Clothing Industry. The relationship between garment cut and fabric potential is probably the most important feature of present design skills.

Many students are overwhelmed by the infinite creative possibilities in fashion and are daunted by rigid technical procedures. This book is an approach to design and flat pattern cutting that is based on the appraisal of the fabric and the body form. I hope that this book astrides the arts and sciences offering students the ability to gain a 'fabric sense' and use it intuitively.

Students develop their skills in different ways. There are many methods of achieving pattern shapes, for example: modelling on the stand, direct measurement, the modification of stored pattern shapes or by block adaptations. Very often it is achieved by a combination of methods. By recognising this diversity it is hoped that this book will help a wider range of students, particularly those who have found the *Metric Pattern Cutting* series too directive. The focus of this book is the relationship of fabric to the body form and this idea can apply to any method of pattern creation.

There is no substitute for working directly on the dress stand for analysing how fabric works with a human body form. It is an essential experience for students when they begin a pattern cutting course. Working in this way offers more opportunity for creating new dimensions of cut. However, most designers working in mass production have the difficult task of transposing 3D mental images into 2D pattern shapes. It can take years of experiencing success and defeat to do this effectively, and the appearance of new fabrics constantly challenges the designer's skill. Knowledge of how fabrics will behave is essential in the speculative cutting of new garment shapes.

Many designers consider colour to be the most important element of fabric and fashion design, therefore knowledge of colour theory is an essential part of a designer's education. But colour and printed textile design have been deliberately ignored in this book, the purpose is to see the garment form clearly without any distractions. It has been a tradition in workrooms to work on initial shapes in cream, white or beige fabrics. Working in this way the focus becomes clear; for many designers it reduces the distractions, and therefore the style lines or modification lines become more apparent. This book will illustrate some forms in black and some in white or beige, this is to provide a reference for students for comparing shapes in opposing tones. The breadth of aesthetic opportunity in the use of texture, pattern and surface decoration is also ignored unless it creates a structure that may affect the basic pattern shape.

Colleges and universities have introduced new modular structures to their courses, these can increase the divisions between fabric knowledge and pattern cutting. Textile knowledge is often taught as a technical module that is distinct from the aesthetic appreciation of fabric. This book does not cover fabric technology in depth, it offers an overview and directs students to where further information can be acquired. Many textile books offer detailed information of fabric properties and mechanical tests for specific fabric properties. These tests are used in industry for comparisons between similar fabrics when assessing their best performance in specific conditions. *Fabric, Form and Flat Pattern Cutting* concentrates on the visual, tactile and structural characteristics of fabrics and the shapes that will be determined by their use.

The method of estimating and categorising fabrics for pattern cutting described in this book was stimulated by the work of Gillian Bunce[1] who developed a classification system for textile repeats. Her work made me consider that it may be possible to find a way of assessing fabrics and pattern cutting techniques in a flexible but effective structure. The method provides a way of determining how a particular characteristic of a fabric will affect the method of cutting a pattern. Five characteristics are isolated: *weight, thickness, shear, drape and stretch*, and demonstrations are given of how they can be estimated and simply coded.

Students can gain valuable knowledge of cutting principles by visiting costume museums and reading about designers. They should approach the subject realising the context in which the designs were developed, the social and technical aesthetic imposed on designers and particularly the fabrics available to them. Fabric technology has produced a range of fabrics that allows new opportunities for experimentation with cutting techniques. New concepts can be explored and old concepts re-examined, sometimes adapting methods, but often marrying them with technologically advanced fabrics to create new structures. The extravagance with which the various cuts and techniques are extended must be seen in relation to the final user of the garment and a moving body form.

Specific information

Although this book can be used alone, where specific detailed methods are required, cross-references to *Metric Pattern Cutting* can be made. A selection of block shapes (size 10 and 12) are included at the end of the book, these can be enlarged on a photocopier for experimental work. Detailed instructions for their construction are available in *Metric Pattern Cutting*. However, this book is concerned with principles rather than specific methods, these ideas can be applied to menswear, children's wear or blocks and patterns from other sources.

The book describes how different types of blocks have been developed from simple flat geometric shapes. To create some continuity amongst many visual ideas, all the designs are shown on one model size 10, 5ft 9″ in height. The size 10 block was lengthened 2 cm in the nape to waist measurement and 3 cm in the sleeve measurement. The same fashion model was used for the photographic figure images and for the drawings. In order to ensure consistency in the proportions of the photographed and drawn designs, Kennett & Lindsell Ltd provided a modified size 10 stand. The flat pattern cutting techniques described in the book include: direct measurements, working on flat grid drafts, and the adaptation of both 'flat blocks' and 'body shaped' blocks. About seventy per cent of the pattern cutting for the designs shown in the book was done in a computer pattern cutting program. A model stand was placed alongside the system to check the proportions of the styles and it was surprising how few modifications had to be made to the computer patterns. No fittings took place on the model, Dina Furtado. The diagrams in the book are scaled down plots of the original garment patterns.

The designs were all made up as unfinished garment toiles working directly in the original fabric. This decision, at the beginning of the project, allowed a true assessment of the fabric's characteristics, and the freedom to experiment and reject ideas if necessary. Only one idea was abandoned as unworkable.

The sample fabric pieces are shown through a grid mount. This is done to give a sense of perspective and to gain an impression of the thickness of the fabric. Some sense of how the fabric may form pleats or gathers has been attempted.

Using CAD to reproduce the blocks

Colleges that have access to CAD programs and printers may be able to use them to reproduce the blocks in full size. Different methods are explained on page 188 and further instructions are given in Appendix Six.

PART ONE: FABRIC ESTIMATION FOR PATTERN CUTTING

1 A technical overview of fabrics

A technical overview

This is not a book on textile technology. This does not mean that technology is considered unimportant. It is essential that all clothing design students understand the basic origin of fibres, the basic fabric structures and the finishes that are available, the importance of the technical performance of the product, the qualities that are required and how to access necessary technical information. Excellent textile books are available for reference. A selection of fabric technology books that are regularly updated are referenced in the bibliography. They are necessary supplementary reading to the brief textile technology section of this book. The pace of developments is so fast that the trade journals are also essential reading for students and designers. The Internet will also provide further information on any fibre, fabric, textile organisation or trade name through the GOOGLE search engine.

I have deliberately chosen the word *fabric*, 'a product of skilled workmanship', instead of the word *textile*. Although the term textile is no longer understood in its original meaning of woven cloth, the word fabric, and its translations, are a simple means of communication between designers that is universally understood. This is important, knowledge of the variety of materials used in the construction of garments is becoming increasingly difficult to understand. Therefore, the word *fabric* in this book will cover a wide range of materials: woven, knitted, interlaced, felted, plastic, leather, in fact any medium used to create garments. Clothing is produced for a wide variety of pursuits; it can range from fantasy and formal wear to highly technical sportswear and hospital surgical wear. Therefore, it is not surprising that the range and combination of materials used in their constructions is almost infinite. However it is not the technical performance of fabrics that is the concern of this book. *The focus is the recognition of the fabric qualities that will have an effect on the final shape of the garment, the qualities that will determine how the designer will cut the garment pattern.*

The explosion of fabrics that is now available is a result of the amount of scientific research into the production of man-made fibres that has taken place during the latter half of the past century, particularly during the last decade. This research, that is increasing at an accelerating rate, has focussed not only on the development of new generic (natural or chemical base group) fibres, but on the modification or blending of existing fibres or the merging of polymers to give fabrics added characteristics. The dimension of character is seen as important in all processes of fabric manufacture; in yarn developments, in new fabric constructions and in new fabric finishes. Some new developments read like science fiction, intelligent fabrics that react and respond to body temperature or static electricity and fabrics which respond to light. Students and designers can be overwhelmed with the complexity of choice now available. Fabrics are frequently being launched as 'the new wonder fabric'. The fibres of most of these new fabrics are not made from new generic fibres, but are blends, mixtures and modifications of fabric structures. Unless a designer is working in a particular field of clothing, the chemical source or the technological structure of the fibre is not the primary interest. The main concerns are the fabric's aesthetic appearance, its performance and handle.

The range of new fabrics available to a designer is immense; it is important that knowledge of their qualities, as well as their technical composition, is absorbed at an early stage of their design education. To drown a student in technical knowledge too early can result in revulsion of anything technical. What is required is a realisation that, when making a product, crucial elements have to be considered about the materials that will be selected. A desire to do this and to develop a personal method of engaging on the task is far more important. The goal is an integration of the many facets of fabric knowledge enabling the designer to make intuitive decisions when handling and comparing a range of fabrics. Chapter One offers a simple basic overview of the main processes involved in the creation of a fabric.

Flexibility and high profile marketing has a greater significance today. Response to new trends and customer awareness is now essential; fibre producers now have sophisticated promotions of their products, and new methods of communication accelerate the demand for a quick response. The problem facing the fibre and fabric manufacturers is the balance between the infinite opportunities that fibre engineering offers and the ability to produce them commercially to the timing of fashion and consumer demand.

The design and selection of fabrics

Designers select fabrics for their ranges as much as twelve months before the garments reach the stores; however, the trend is moving towards a reduction in this time lag. The fibre and fabric producers aiming at the fashion market have to take note of the prediction companies who interpret and capture the future mood of the customer. There is a strong element of risk in this situation. The garments are shown to manufacturing companies at major fabric fairs. Europe has two major fabric fairs, PREMIER VISION and INTERSTOFF, which show spring and autumn collections. Some years ago designers were restricted to buying their fabrics from producers' existing ranges; but today, particularly where large orders are at stake, designers often work in partnership with the fabric producers in the development of fabric ranges, particularly print design. The fabric shows are a vital point of contact between designers and producers; producers gain knowledge of the performance of their previous products in production and during wear, and of future requirements.

Designers working in particular product areas will have their initial parameters defined. They must be assured that the fabric will perform adequately in specific conditions and they will also have to be aware of any technical limitations. Some fabrics are released onto the market before they are fully tested, or they may encounter unforseen conditions (for example, new cleaning processes). As fabrics become more scientifically based and yarn structures are more complex, it is not only students who are perplexed, designers can find themselves overwhelmed with a mass of technical information. The biochemical contents of a waterproof fabric are of marginal interest to a lingerie designer. The information can be obtained as required as the designer becomes immersed in a particular sector of the trade.

The competition from man-made fibre development has led to new efforts to 'improve' the qualities of natural fibres, by biological methods of breeding, by fibre engineering, chemical treatment of fibres and fabrics and by blending with other natural or man-made fibres. The greatest change that has taken place in the textile industry is the reduction in woven fabric production and the increase in knitted fabric production. The variety of constructions available, the speed of production, the competitive pricing and the stretch characteristics of knitting structures make these fabrics very attractive to the middle to low cost retailing area. The finishes that are available to the cloth manufacturer can produce fabrics whose appearance has little relationship to the loom state. Some finishes are applied to garments after they are made up. The changes of shape that occur have to be taken into account when the garment patterns are constructed.

The changing working environment places the designer in a dilemma. Even if one considers that an individual designer will focus on her particular product range and the materials that are appropriate, even in this field the choice is now extensive. Cloth manufacturers strive to produce novel fabrics to tempt the buyers; these fabrics may not have undergone field trials (an assessment of the limitations and the performance of fabrics). Some fabrics fail in wear because they become subject to unforseen conditions.

Buying from fabric swatches is difficult. Small sample lengths may be available, but many producers do not hold large fabric stocks but produce to order and require orders of 500–1000 metres. This is a problem for small companies producing limited ranges. The information usually given on a fabric swatch is:

Quality or Design number .... Width ....
Composition .... Weight ....

Further technical information, for example dimensional stability during wear or laundering conditions, can be gained from the large fabric suppliers who will supply appropriate care labels on the purchase of the fabric. Information from smaller suppliers can be difficult or time consuming to acquire. Large companies have their own laboratories that test garment fabrics, interlinings and trimmings to establish whether they are 'fit for purpose'. Small companies can engage the services of commercial testing laboratories, but this can be expensive and may be disregarded when there is a race to get garment ranges into the stores on time.

The technical information that is available is often not useful or not presented in the form that can be understood by a designer/pattern cutter. Technical testing is aimed at 'fit for purpose' comparisons of fabrics; it is often done within narrow limits for quality control purposes or for staged improvements of a fabric. The understanding of the crucial concepts of 'handle' and 'drape' do not appear to have agreed common meaning between designers, designers and technologists or even amongst technologists themselves.

The world of laboratories and technologists is a great distance away from the world of fashion prediction books and the showbusiness environment of trade fabric fairs. The prediction companies do not see these activities as a part of their remittance. The contradiction between the increased technological base of fabrics and the kind of hype used by public relation, sales promotion and fashion prediction companies leave a gap in the middle ground. This is where practising designers outside the large manufacturing groups have to operate. The environment at trade fairs is frenetic. Building a fashion range requires a speed of fashion reaction that can involve switches of 'fancy' and changes of focus. Bombarded with new fabrics, the designer has to work with intuition and knowledge. The 'technically correct' fabric is not a commercial choice unless it responds to the current mood or reflects the aesthetic style of the range.

Successful co-operation between technologists and designers does occur and long term directions do proceed alongside the turbulent fashion switches of mood that many technologists find perplexing. Many fabrics take years of development, and the process is often an act of faith by research teams as they struggle with the difficulties of production. A fibre or a length of fabric produced in a laboratory is not a finished commercial product and may be impossible to produce in any viable quantity or with consistent quality control.

Fibres

Introduction to fibre classification

A fibre is long compared to its diameter, this enables it to be twisted with other fibres to create a yarn. One can usually expect a finer fibre of the same type to reduce in strength and increase its bending capacity. Halving a fibre's thickness would reduce its breaking strength by a factor of four, making it fragile. Fibres can be divided into two main groups, natural and man-made. But fibres from most groups can be blended to gain the properties of each component fibre.

Natural fibres

Natural fibres come from animal or vegetable sources. All the natural fibres, except cultivated silk, have relatively short fibres (staple) which are combed and twisted to form yarn that is strong enough for use in the manufacture of the fabric. Cultivated silk which is unwound from the silk moth's cocoon can be 2000 metres long and is therefore considered as continuous or a filament fibre.

Man-made fibres

Man-made fibres are produced from chemical solutions that are manufactured into fibres; for example, a chemical liquid can be forced through minute holes and then solidified in air (dry or melt spun) or by chemical (wet spun) processes. They can be used in filament or cut to form staple fibres. A fibre can be produced from a solution that has a natural source (regenerated fibre) or from a solely chemical or mineral source (synthetic fibre).

The fibres classified on page 13 are edited so that they relate to garment production.

Fibre production

Although a garment fabric does not have to begin with a fibre, for example leather or plastic sheeting, the vast majority of fabrics used for making garments have been made from yarns produced from fibres. Therefore, it is logical that the characteristics of the original fibre will be carried through into the finished fabric. These characteristics can, of course, be suppressed or enhanced by the chemical finishes of the yarn or fabric and the structure of the fabric. To appreciate the qualities of fabrics, it is important to understand the characteristics of the basic constituent fibres of the yarns and how they are modified and changed.

As the Far East increases its supply of low-cost, high quantity textiles, European producers' attitudes to fabric production have changed. They are looking for higher value products rather than quantities; this entails the development of more sophisticated fibres and fabrics. It also means great co-operation between industries; the fibre producers, the spinners, the weavers and knitters, the finishers and printers. There is less division between man-made fibres and natural fibres. Fibre marriages in blends can exploit the unique qualities of the natural fibres and the 'structural engineering' of the man-made fibres. Light-weight fabrics that offer good performance in warmth and wear are in demand and most natural fabrics have a limit to their degree of fineness.

Although there may seem to be a bewildering number of new fabrics on the market, the cost of the research and development means that very few new generic fibres are developed. Many so-called new fibres are complex engineering of existing fibres, for example micro-fibres and bi-component fibres (composites of two generic filament fibres i.e. polyester and nylon). Researchers are also constantly attempting to increase or suppress basic characteristics of natural or man-made fibres in order to compete in the market. Whilst the total fibre market volume has increased at a rate of more than 3% over the last twenty years, the largest increase has occurred in man-made fibre production, particularly the synthetics. This has accounted for 82% of the growth in fibre production during the last decade. Figure 1 illustrates the changing share of the market between natural and man-made fibres in the past decade.

Fibre labeling on fabrics

Most garments are made from textile fibres. In 1986 'Textile Products (Indications of Fibre Content), Regulations 1986' came into force. This has meant that all piece fabric or clothing made in new fabrics sold in the European Community has had to be labelled with its percentage fibre content (natural or 'man-made'). The generic (chemical group) name is used on the label to prevent confusion. The regulations are updated as new generic fibres are produced. The generic terms for man-made fibres, and other names which cover natural fibres, are listed in Appendix Five. Manufacturers are supposed to adhere to these when labelling their garments. Fabric swatches and garment labels list the fibres and their percentage under these basic chemical or natural fibre groups: for example, cotton 50% polyester 40% viscose 10%.

Most people are familiar with natural fibres such as wool and cotton; however, man-made fibres present a different problem. Fabrics in one generic group can have radically different appearances; modified fibre structures and blends and finishes increase the confusion, and yet more confusion is added by the brand names for example, 'TREVIRA' (polyester) and 'VILOFT' (viscose), which fibre producers give to their particular products to give them an identity.

Fibre production

production 1995

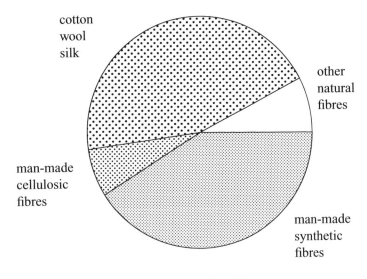

cotton
wool
silk

other
natural
fibres

man-made
cellulosic
fibres

man-made
synthetic
fibres

production 2004

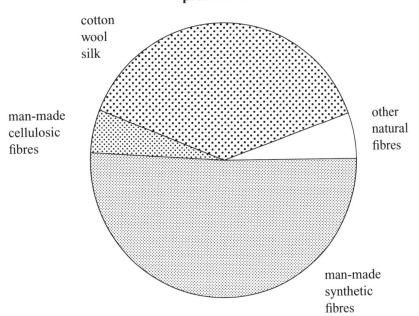

cotton
wool
silk

man-made
cellulosic
fibres

other
natural
fibres

man-made
synthetic
fibres

Figure 1   The sizes of the two circles illustrate the growth in the world production of fibres from 1993–2004. The diagram also illustrates the increasing domination of synthetic fibre production.

The classification of fibres used in garment making

Natural fibres

Natural fibres can be divided into two groups, vegetable and animal, these can be sub-divided again to form the generic groups by which the fibres are labelled (see Fig. 2).

Although frequently blended or woven together, many garments are made entirely from silk, wool, cotton and flax; the other fibres listed are usually mixed with the main fibres to add practical characteristics or aesthetic interest to the fabric. When characteristics are added or suppressed by chemical processes and breeding, the structure of the fibres are not changed. Advances in present gene research are beginning to alter this position. Fabrics made from natural fibres, especially cotton, still hold a strong position in the market, despite the fact that they can be more expensive than a product made from man-made fibres. They are comfortable to wear because of their natural absorbency, and there is great aesthetic appeal in their textures, their dye affinities and their handle.

Man-made fibres

Man-made fibres can be divided into two sub-groups, regenerated fibres and synthetic fibres (see Fig. 3). Regenerated cellulosic fibres are reconstituted by converting natural products such as wood pulp and cotton by solvents into a liquid form for spinning. Synthetic fibres are made from chemical sources. They are mainly petroleum based. However, a new generic fibre polyactide (PLA) is manufactured by producing polyactic acid that is derived from carbon and other elements in the sugars of corn or sugar beet.

Man-made fibres began by copying the characteristics of natural fibres. Originally, man-made fibre lengths were matched to those of existing natural fibres because natural fibres were successful and the new fibres could be processed on existing machinery. These regenerated cellulosic fibres, a chemical reduction of a natural source (wood pulp) created the first man-made fibre (rayon viscose) known as 'artificial silk'. Acetate followed, and more recently the new fibre lyocell has been created. The manufacture of synthetic fibres for the garment industry has now overtaken the production of all natural fibres. Nylon, polyester and acrylic originally displayed unique characteristics that were easy to identify. Until quite recently it was fairly easy to place the fibres of a fabric within a generic group and make certain assumptions about their properties; now, recognition is more difficult.

The appearance, handle and comfort of a fabric are affected by the structure of the fibres. Whilst the length and external surface of the fibre is important, the internal structure also determines the basic properties of a particular fibre. The shape of the fibre can determine the lustre: for example, the filaments of silk are prism shaped and reflect light. The cross-sections of fibres can be changed by varying the holes on the spinneret to match the shape of natural fibres or experiment with new shapes. These can be round, cross-like, triangular, Y-shaped or bean-shaped. The structural shapes of fibres also determine more mechanical properties such as bulk, stiffness and absorbency; for example, circular shaped fibres tend to resist bending, Y-shaped fibres give resilience, hollow fibres are light in relation to their bulk. However, the yarn construction, fabric structure and finish have to be combined intelligently to satisfy aesthetic and practical market demands.

Today man-made fibres are increasingly difficult for the designer to categorise from a chemical perspective. Bi-component fibres combine polymers at very early stages in the production of the fibres and new blends with regenerated fibres have created for the designer or user new 'families' of fabrics more closely related to the product. Designers are becoming less concerned with a fabric's origin than its proven qualities in use and appearance. New technological processes in fibre and yarn construction can be used to create fabrics as varied as gaberdine and synthetic fur to silk-like jerseys from one fibre source (for example polyester). The proliferation of fibre brand names can obscure knowledge of the chemical source of the fabric and can extend the confusion.

Micro-fibres

The name micro-fibre is not a generic term, but there is general agreement amongst producers that it describes a fibre of 1 decitex or less. Silk is the only natural fibre that approaches this degree of fineness and it is the Japanese who have specialised in creating silk-like fabrics with high drape qualities. The exploitation amongst European and American producers has been aimed at underwear fabrics (light-weight but 'full and soft') and weatherwear (light and dense); therefore wind and weatherproof but allowing the escape of perspiration. Most micro-fibres are produced from polyamide and polyester fibres. Many more micro-fibres can be used in a given size of yarn, they offer good draping qualities and a lightweight bulk unmatched by other fibres.

New fibre developments

New fibres have been developed from natural sources; fungi, alginate fibres from seaweed, and chitosan from insect skeletons and crab shells. They have valuable uses in surgical dressings and clothing. The new synthetic generic fibre PLA is produced from sugars in crops such as corn.

The growth of multi-nationals has provided the means to fund expensive synthetic fibre engineering that changes the structures of man-made fibres. New fibres are responding to the sensual demands of touch, sight, smell and hearing. Fibre structures are the source of many new visual effects and can be engineered to mimic natural fibres. New fibre structures have been realised from studies of the natural world, using morphology to copy and create new surfaces. The study of the planes of butterfly wings initiated the creation of fibres that catch the light; the study of the dense but ragged surface of the lotus leaf influenced the structure of SUPER MI-CROFT. Man-made fibres do not have to look like natural fibres, co-polymers with different characteristics and reactions to finishes create new textures with a different aesthetic appeal.

Bioengineering technology is creating fibres which contain natural minerals such as silver, jade and mica. Fabrics produced from these fibres can be flame resistant, antimicrobial and deodorising.

Nano-fibres, produced by electro-spinning, are fundamentally different in scale (one nanometre is one billionth of a metre). They have a large surface area in comparison to their form. Although light-weight and breathable, they are impermeable to biological and chemical agents. Nano-composite fibres can incorporate nano-particles of metals that create a shield from UV rays and other harmful agents. They can also incorporate nano-capsules that react to body temperatures to release drugs or perfume.

Natural fibres

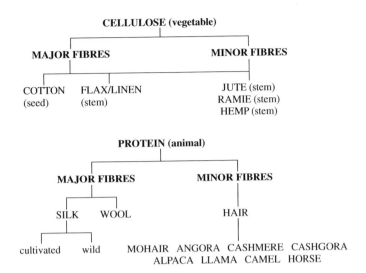

Figure 2 Classification of natural fibres generic terms used in clothing.

Man-made fibres

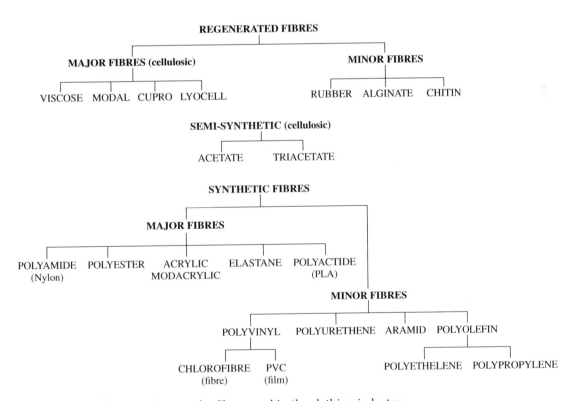

Figure 3 Classification of the generic terms for fibres used in the clothing industry.

Yarns

The fineness of yarn or filament (count) is measured by weight/length. The measurement of the fineness of the yarn is expressed by Denier (grams per 9,000 metres) or more usually Decitex (grams per 10,000 metres). Most fibres for clothing are usually in the range 5–15 decitex, micro-fibres are defined as fibres with a maximum count of 1 decitex.

Staple fibres are short in length and must be twisted to form yarns, they are known as spun yarns and they are usually more soft and textured than those from filaments (continuous fibres). The direction and the amount of twist inserted in the yarn will affect the characteristics of the finished fabric. The fibres are often encouraged to lay in all directions to increase the bulk and texture of the yarn. Complex yarns can be constructed where yarns of varying thickness, crimp and fibre source are spun together. Introducing effects into the yarn such as loops, knots, pile (chenille) or metallic filaments produces fancy yarns.

Filament fibres have a continuity of length and are usually spun with the filaments lying parallel, this makes the yarn more compact and will enhance the fibre's natural lustre and smoothness. Fibres which are destined for smooth fabrics are combed after carding to ensure the fibres lay parallel.

Man-made fibres are chemically created, their reaction to heat and other chemicals offers the opportunity to produce yarns that can be enhanced or textured in ways that are not possible with natural fibres. The use of elastane fibres has given woven fabrics some of the stretch characteristics that could only be achieved by knitted constructions, and stability to knitted constructions. Corespun yarns have a fibrous sheath twisted around a core filament thread; for example, elastane yarns have a core thread of elastane covered with the main fibre. New methods of electro-spinning blend fibres in electro-spin laced mat layers that can be combined with coatings.

Yarns can be single, folded (2 or 3 yarns twisted), or cabled (folded yarns twisted). The direction of twist can be a Z or an S twist. Different twists can be found in the same yarn and are used in different warps and wefts to create different fabric appearances.

Fabrics

Yarns and fibres are woven, knitted, interlaced or pressed into a fabric form. In most situations it is the fabric which the designer confronts when realising the design range. Her first aesthetic reactions will be a major part of the criteria that determines the purchase.

Fabric construction can enhance or subdue the characteristics of a yarn. The complex forms that can be produced from the major means of manufacture (weaving and knitting) now offer bewildering choices; textile designers have to balance the visual and textural qualities with its stability and its 'fitness for purpose'. It can take a close examination of some fabrics to distinguish which manufacturing process has been used. The bonding of fabrics of different manufacture can confuse simple categorisations.

The scale of world production of woven and knitted fabrics has changed. During the last two decades, knitted fabric production has increased at the expense of woven fabric production.

Fabric structures

The principal methods of creating fabric are knitting and weaving. The minor methods, interlacing, embroidered and braided are used in many luxury or hand-crafted fabrics (see Fig. 4). Non-woven fabrics are: felt, many types of interlinings, PVC sheets and some pile fabrics fused onto PVC backing.

Woven fabric

A fabric is considered to be woven if horizontal threads, the weft, are interlaced with vertical threads, the warp. Garments are usually made up with the warp threads running down a garment, and the weft threads running across or at an accurate 45 degree angle (which is known as the bias or crossway) to give increased stretch and draping qualities.

Pattern pieces are always marked with a grain line to ensure the garment is cut correctly.

The yarns can be interlaced in many different ways to create weaves. Classic weaves become easily recognised: plain weaves give horizontal, vertical and chequered effects; twill weaves give diagonal or herringbone structures; jacquard weaves create complex patterns; satin weaves give smooth surfaces and lustre. Different yarns inserted in the warp and weft can give three dimensional rib effects. In pile constructions, yarns in the warp (velvet) or weft (velveteen) give different effects. Many unusual weaves can be created by combining different weaves, or by creating double or double-face fabrics; for example cloque is produced by one set of threads shrinking at a different rate and producing blistering. Matellasse has extra warp threads inserted which produce a quilted effect. When yarn types and colour and print are added to weave constructions, combinations become almost limitless.

The rate of woven cloth production has been increased by the rapier looms which fire (by air or water jet) a number of weft threads across the loom instead of the old shuttle method. Other methods (multiphase or triaxial weaving) have been developed, they offer faster as well as different production methods.

Knitted fabric
Weft-knitted fabric
Weft-knitted fabric is made on machines where the yarn is held by latch needles that move up and down to create rows of interlocking loop stitches across the fabric. Some machines produce flat fabrics, others circular or tubular fabrics. The structure of the fabric is flexible and varies with the gauge (how closely the needles are positioned) of the machine, the type of yarn, and the tension that the yarn is being held whilst it is knitted. Some machines knit shaped

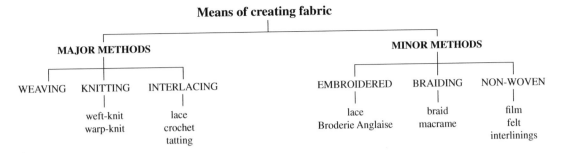

Figure 4 Fabric structures.

garment parts on fully fashioned knitting machines, but most of the production is produced on flat or circular machines. A proportion of the production is in 'body blank' form, the fabric is knitted to the width and length of the body pieces, but minor shaping (necks and armholes) are cut later. The remainder of the fabric production is sold as piece lengths; garment shapes are arranged into lay plans and are cut in a similar manner to cutting woven fabrics. The major problem is that loosely knitted structures can unravel, ladder or distort in handling.

Variations of stitch and patterning; ribbing, inlays, interlock, intarsia and jacquard, create an incredible range of options for the knitwear designer. Weft-knitting can respond to short orders, the machines do not have the complicated setting up of warp threads that is required for woven or warp-knitted fabrics. A strong craft industry of small knitwear businesses, that is design led, has had a strong influence on mass-market design. 'Influence' should not infer copying, copyright battles of the 'David and Goliath' kind have been more successful recently. Designs, which have been bought to be copied in the Far East and then sold cheaply in high street stores, have had to be withdrawn from sale.

Warp-knitted fabrics
Warp-knitting machines create vertical interlocking loop chains. Two yarns are often used together to give the fabric stability. There has been a great increase in warp-knitting; the machines are very fast and produce a large amount of fabric from man-made fine filament yarns. The fabrics are particularly suitable for lingerie, openwork and net effects can be produced on the machines. Raschel machines are taking the place of traditional lace machinery, particularly Leavers lace. Raschel machines can knit complex patterns, but these patterns are limited by the machinery; for example the width of the guide bars that swing the threads across the warp. The use of micro-fibres, particularly TACTEL blended with LYCRA on Raschel machines, produces extremely fine, strong, soft, stretch fabrics for lingerie.

The names of warp-knit fabrics can be confusing, particularly the pile fabrics; the most common are fleece (brushed velour), terry cloths, velvets, corduroys, loop and pile fabrics. Warp-knit fabrics also provide the backing structure for many laminate and flocked pile fabrics. Depending on its use or its aesthetic effect, the pile side may be used on the face or the back of the fabric.

Other developments on Raschel machines have been the 'laying in' of warp or weft threads during the knitting process. Soft staple yarns are used, complex patterning and rigidity in the structure can give a 'woven fabric' look to the fabric which still retains a specified amount of stretch.

Interlaced and embroidered fabrics
Lace machines (for example Leavers or Schiffli) can be compared with embroidery machines where the pattern is laid on a net background. Traditional machine lace making is reducing, and therefore the skills required to use some of the older machinery are no longer available.

Many laces are known by the region where the original handmade lace was made; for example Alencon, Cluny, Chantilly. Pillow lace was constructed over a pillow with many bobbin threads interlaced to form the fabric. Many types of lace designs are now copied on a Raschel machine. Luxury effects are now added to many laces by machine embroidery, ribbonning and beading. Crochet and tatting effects can also be copied. However, hand-worked embroidered laces from the Far East often compete on price, choice and availabilty.

Guipure lace is embroidery made with multi-head embroidery machines. Embroidered fabrics can be made up of 90% surface decoration and 10% backing. Complex structures can be built up incorporating many processes, this makes it difficult to categorise the fabric under a single group, unless under the heading 'constructed textile'.

Barmen machines create a braided heavy lace mainly used in furnishings but the lace appears in fashion ranges when the mood is 'natural'.

16

Fabrics of different structures

Pressing the fibres of fabrics together would seem to be a simple way of making fabric, but until man-made fibres were produced, only wool had the properties that allowed the fibres to felt together to form a mass. This group of fabrics, often referred to as 'non-woven', is used mainly in the garment industry for interlinings. These fabrics often have adhesive backings for fusing to garments. To prevent the pressed web from breaking up, a number of techniques are employed: interlacing the fibres, adhesives, thermal-bonding, stitch-bonding and punching. Improvements in laminating techniques have improved the handle of bonded fabrics. Fibres can be held together by chemical binders, by heat setting one of the fibres. Unexpected handle can be achieved, satin bonded onto a felt-like backing can give designers new opportunities for shapes. New waterproof, breathable membranes have been produced for weatherwear.

Leather and fur are natural non-woven fabrics. Leather can vary from delicate light suede fabrics with soft drape to heavy dense skins (horse). Stretch leather is achieved by bonding a sliver of suede onto a stretch jersey backing.

Simulated suedes and leathers are mainly produced on a warp-knitted backing. PVC is usually considered a non-woven fabric, but in many cases some form of plastic material is sprayed onto a fine web or knitted backing.

Fabric finishes

All fabrics are finished, the simplest form is simply washing, shrinking and pressing, but most fabrics have some form of extra finish, many of which are complex and may be a completion of an earlier process of manufacture (e.g. crepe or stretch fabrics). The finish may be added to improve the aesthetic and tactile quality of a fabric, to enhance or suppress its natural properties, or to add some specific or novel quality. The finish can be permanent or temporary.

White dyed or printed fabrics produced from cellulose fibres have to be bleached. Fabrics made from fibres that have a rough texture can be smoothed by cropping and singeing, by chemical finishes (e.g. mercerising and bio-polishing), or calendering, glazing and engraving. They can have their rough appearance enhanced, the surface is raised by brushing or plucking. Many of these fabrics then have a pile or 'nap' that is usually cut one way with the fibres laying towards the bottom of the garment; however, interesting effects can be created by cutting up and down a napped fabric. Thicker and softer yarns woven on the back of a fabric can be brushed to give an outer flat appearance and a warm fleecy back. Stripe effects can be made by pile finishes on groups of warp yarns.

Fabrics made from filament yarns are usually smooth and lustrous, and many of those made from man-made fibres imitated silk. However, experiments with combinations of fibre and yarn structures and finishes have created a large explosion of new fabrics which respond to unusual finishes and produce unique combinations of qualities (e.g. Tactel, Tencel, and Japanese 'Shingosen' fabrics).

Combinations of many of the above techniques, in particular areas or finishes targeted at particular yarns, can give uneven and sculptural effects to fabrics. Fabrics made from thermoplastic synthetic yarns can achieve similar effects by heat-setting. Coating or bonding fabrics usually produces dramatic change to any fabric; many of the coatings on bondings are thermoplastic and are heat-set.

Most of the processes discussed are those that alter the characteristics that are of interest to the process of pattern cutting. However, many finishes are developed for garments that are used for particular purposes, for example athletic wear requires high absorbency, weatherwear requires waterproofing, and some industrial wear requires chemical and flame proofing. The designer has to consider this kind of parameter when developing a range in a particular product field. A list of finishes, practical and aesthetic, can be found in Appendix Two.

Some finishes (crease resistant, distressed and textured) are completed after the garment is made up. This means that quite complex shrink allowances are required during the development of the pattern, and tight controls are required on the finishing processes.

New fabric developments

New fabrics have been developed in the past by research and development; the difference now is that the research has become so complex and science-based that structures and characteristics are now often defined in terms of numbers, algebraic equations and complex graphs. Computers are now used to create visual shapes to define the geometry and the forces applied to fabric changes.

Many new developments in fabrics are based on the technical structure of the fabric's fibre, see page 12. A number of new finishes are based on micro-encapsulation and nano-technology, these coatings are only 3–5 nm thick and have no effect on the drape or permeability of the fabrics. Finishes that keep garments fresh, self-cleaning and deodorising as well as releasing micro-capsules of perfume are now available. Antimicrobial finishes can come from the release of an agent incorporated within the fibre during finishing, or by providing protective coatings which contain nano-capsules of an antimicrobial agent or nano-silver particles. There are many breathable and waterproof fabrics competing in the market, thus stimulating new features. Micro-fibre technology has produced lighter and softer fabrics that are now resistant to UV rays and fading. Thermocules between layers create a micro-climate that can store excess body heat and then release it as the body cools. Other products store moisture from sweating between the layers, keeping the body dry.

Fabrics which incorporate micro-electronics are often referred to by the terms 'smart fabrics' or 'intelligent fabrics'. They are produced by using conductive fibres or coatings. The fabrics can contain sensors that can monitor changes in athletes' performances and actions, or organ and skin functions in hospital patients. Clothing can have integrated controls for music systems such as iPods or phones for entertainment and alarm systems for the vulnerable.

The term techno-fabric is used loosely and covers almost anything from a fabric with a superficial shine to a high performance fabric with artificial intelligence or to new experimental materials that can interact with the human body.

A brief overview of special features of fibres, fabric construction and finishing in particular clothing use is shown in Fig. 5 on the opposite page. The features are described in more detail in Chapter Three, which illustrates the fabrics of individual fibre categories.

USE	DEVELOPMENTS
ATHLETICS AND SPORTSWEAR	fibres that speed up evaporation without cooling the body too quickly fibres that warm muscles or react to body temperature nano-fibres that incorporate minerals to have deodorising properties 'second skins' for streamlined racing membranes that swell and absorb moisture from sweating, keeping the body dry
WEATHERWEAR	sheath and core fibres that increase absorbency micro-pore and breathable 'wicking' membranes for wind and waterproof clothing spacer fabrics with air pockets between two fabric layers body heat stored between fabric layers, released as the body cools thermal bonding for double fabrics ceramic interlinings that store heat
PROTECTION	nano-fibres produce light-weight breathable fabrics that protect against fire and chemicals protection against ultraviolet rays nano-particles of metals provide antimicrobial fibres and finishes
APPEARANCE	'shape memory finishes' provide the retention of pleats, crinkles, etc., after washing invisible nano-coatings give stain resistance, e.g. against coffee, wine and oil split filaments create mock suedes and leathers thermochromatic fabrics can change colour on contact to body or external heat
DECORATION	soft flexible metallic yarns and transfers new coatings and laminates new fibres which incorporate gemstones
ELECTRONICS IN CLOTHING	sensors that can measure performance or organ function built in music and alarm systems
MISCELLANEOUS	fibres containing nano-capsules that contain perfume which react to body heat fabrics with deodorising properties

Figure 5 A brief overview of fibre and fabric developments for particular use.

Fabric production

Fabric widths
Fabrics are produced in piece lengths which vary in length and width. The piece length is decided by the weight and bulkiness of the fabric. The width will vary from 72 cm (Harris Tweed) to circular jersey fabric which can be as wide as 180 cm. Light-weight fabrics have mainly been woven 90–114 cm in width; but companies, who produce large quantities, are demanding wider fabrics to gain greater efficiency in their garment lays. Woollen fabrics and tweeds are generally woven at 150 cm width. The width of the fabric is crucial to the garment designer. Costing negotiations frequently require modifications to a design, the final cut of the garment may be determined by the width of the fabric.

Fabric weights
Fabric weights are given in two ways; weight per running metre or weight per square metre. The latter is the most useful when comparing different qualities. Fabric swatches do not always state the type of weight, therefore the designer or technologist may have to re-weigh a sample piece. Very light-weight fabrics have to be made from strong fibres or specially processed fibres and tend to be more expensive than medium-weight fabrics. Heavy-weight fabrics are usually expensive because of the quantity of yarn used. Exceptions to these generalisations can be found and hard wear or strength may not be characteristics of principal concern for the design.

Fabric thickness
The thickness of a fabric is dependent on a large number of variables; the fibre structure, the yarn structure and finish, the fabric structure and finish, surface decoration, fabric bonding or lamination. Double-faced fabrics can be made by interweaving two layers of woven cloth, or in knitting, using the front and back needles. A great improvement in bonding techniques has led to many combinations of fabrics being bonded: to give strength to a weak or flexible structure; to 'sandwich' insulating fabric to create reversible cloths; to bond weatherproof membranes; to create a particular handle or three dimensional appearance.

Ecology

Ecology is a branch of science that deals with human beings' relationship with their environment. For many decades textile and clothing technology has centred on the comfort and protection of the human body; but a greater concern is now emerging – that of the survival of the environment itself. This has had serious implications for the textile industry. The major threats to the environment and human life come from resource depletion, pollution and global warming. Textile and garment production increases the threats in the following ways:

Vegetable fibres – crop growth – **pesticides**
Animal fibres/skins – cleaning – **pollution**
Man-made fibres – **resource depletion/energy use/pollution**
All fibres – fabrics – production – **energy use/pollution**
All fibres – fabrics – dyeing finishing – **energy use/pollution**
Garment production – **energy use/pollution**
Retailing – **energy use**
Discarding clothes – **resource depletion/pollution**

The greatest pollution in textile production or leather processing is produced from scouring, bleaching, dyeing, printing, finishing and tanning. New laws are now in place which affect all areas of the textile/garment production cycle. These differ from country to country. UK and EEC regulations, such as the Pollution Prevention and Control (PPC), and ISO 14000 (environmental quality standards) and ISO 14064 (greenhouse gas emissions) are increasing pressure and imposing costs in order to clean up the industry's pollution and emissions. Western European fibre producers have already spent vast amounts of money on meeting standards, they publicly support a 'green' image, but their concern is that their competitors in other areas of the world are not subject to the same controls. During the production process, the energy used and the carbon emissions produced are incurring increasing costs; they are therefore becoming a new focus of a company's attention. Company and farming associations are advising on ways of improving methods, attempting to adhere to these whilst remaining commercial. Many companies are prepared to flout laws that are not strictly enforced or the penalties are insignificant on the balance sheet.

The wearing of natural fibres can appear to be ecologically responsible, but much of the cotton grown uses large amounts of pesticides on the crops and the effluent from the chemicals used in its processing, finishing, bleaching and dyeing are pollutants. Ecologically sound 'green cotton' is only a very small percentage of total production. As waste disposal and recycling becomes critical, the advantage of natural fibres and the new synthetic fibre PLA is that they are degradable. There is increasing interest in biodegradable fibres and sustainable fibres such as soya bean protein fibres.

Although more supermarkets are seeing the success of offering organic produce or FAIRTRADE products, the shopper's enthusiasm does not appear to have spread yet to clothing. Many consumers may wish to be supportive of environmental issues but lack information. Marketing hypes and unbalanced or badly researched articles and information confuse the public. But, companies can see marketing advantages in appearing ecologically sound, and public relations and information are now crucial marketing strategies of the manufacturers and retailers. Some major retailers such as M&S, Oasis and Debenhams have launched organic cotton ranges and others have applied to the Soil Association for licenses for leather and wool products, but these sales initiatives are only a tiny percentage of their total turnover.

When Courtaulds produced the first Tencel fibres, it claimed that the plant had been built to cause minimum environmental damage. Effluent has always been a particular problem for sizing, dyeing and finishing plants. More than half of clothing produced is re-used. It is sold through the charity shops and also exported overseas to poorer countries. This saves water, energy and pollution. However, as new clothing prices have reduced quite dramatically over the last decade, more clothing is going for recycling. It is becoming harder for recycling companies to make a profit and textiles get less support in this area than other sectors of industry. Clothing made from natural fibres can be broken down and re-spun, but a number of companies that produced recycled yarn from discarded clothing have found it uneconomic and have ceased trading. There can be a reluctance to use recycled fabrics unless they appeal aesthetically to the designer and the buyer. Other products produced from recycled rags such as paper or household cloths have been more successful. However, recycling is not limited to natural fibres, Malden Mills in the USA, use recycled polyester film to produce fleece fabrics.

There are an increasing number of young designers and fashion students who are specialising in eco-fashion. But, the overriding focus of many designers is still the visual aspect of design and not the eco-consequences of producing the fabric or the trims. A concern for the environment places designers as educators of society. Some design labels, for example ESPRIT, try to be socially and environmentally responsible. However, their in-house *Ecollection* range had to be discontinued in 1998 as it was not financially viable. There has to be a strong commitment by any company to pursue ideals, but there has also to be a demand from the public. A consistent eco-position may be hard to pursue economically. Fashion itself depends on the public discarding garments in favour of the new season's range. This concept pays scant acknowledgement to ecological concerns and frustrates the fabric technologists not familiar with transient fads. Short-lived fashion trends aimed at tempting the consumer can mask a serious long-term problem for the clothing industry.

PART ONE: FABRIC ESTIMATION FOR PATTERN CUTTING

2 A categorisation for designers and pattern cutters

Measuring fabric characteristics

The background

Designers should be aware that a major consideration in any design decision is the 'fitness for purpose'. In particular sectors of industry, other considerations may override the 'ideal' design decisions; for example, cost or availability of fabric. In sportswear, absorbency and perspiration control are principal property requirements. It is important that a designer discovers the type of relevant tests that are required for a product's viability (see Appendix Four). However, this book is concerned with those characteristics of a garment which affect its visual form.

The visual appearance of any garment is directly affected by the characteristics of the fabric in which it is made. Selecting the correct material for a design is a difficult problem for a designer when an artefact is made from materials that are solid, rigid and stable, but the problems are immense for garment designers working with the infinite variety of shapes and fabrics used in the textile industry. Mathematics, textile chemistry, physics, mechanics, structural engineering and other fields of science have been used in order to create theories that could be applied. Journals are prolific with papers showing graphs and calculations to support methods of analysis, and expensive equipment has been devised to measure the properties of fabrics. Many large textile and garment producers use these tests (see Appendix Four) especially when comparing similar fabrics for their advantages for a particular product range.

Some computer programs use these theories in their attempts to create realistic three dimensional (3D) models of fabric. The aim is to realise a virtual image of a garment during the pattern cutting process (see page 28). However, as discussed on page nine, the selection of a fabric by a designer usually comes at a much earlier stage in the creation of a range. Computer programs at this stage are more useful for decisions such as colour and pattern. Determining the suitability of a fabric for the *shape* of a design at the concept stage will still rely on human discrimination.

Fabric characteristics: a practical categorisation

There are enormous problems in defining and measuring some fabric characteristics, this does not mean that it should not be attempted. However, the methods of assessment described in the book are used solely for the purpose of pattern cutting, they are done to give a 'sense of visual and tactile order'. Flat pattern cutting is successful when a designer's intuitive knowledge of a fabric can generate a 3D mental image of the *fabric shape* that will be produced by the flat pattern. Industrial pattern cutting has to be done with speed and this human mental facility is faster than any computer system, it can be instantaneous. It has been noted that the reliance on calculators has reduced

the ability in students in a variety of disciplines to 'estimate', the ability of visual estimation is one that clothing designers cannot afford to lose. The techniques in this book may help designers to strengthen their intuitive sense of integrating form and fabric. To illustrate this point the photographs opposite show that a very simple circular shape in basic fabrics (rayon jersey, light–medium-weight calico, heavy cotton twill) behaves quite differently when cut at different lengths and scales. Overlapping shapes at different angles in fabrics of complicated and uneven structures provide problems of infinite complexity that require refinements embedded within the process of cutting, it is not simply a procedure of prediction and modification. The photographs also demonstrate the false images that can be created by working in quarter or half-scale.

Five requirements: **WEIGHT, THICKNESS, SHEAR, DRAPE, STRETCH** for the initial selection of pattern cutting methods have been recognised in this book as crucial. This does not dismiss aesthetic qualities that impact on the senses; for example, colour, subtle textures and tactile experiences or fashion and cultural influences. But these, with the practical considerations of product type and 'fit for purpose', are different elements of the design process.

Weight, thickness, shear, drape, stretch

The relationship of these five characteristics to pattern shapes will be discussed in detail in the pattern cutting sections. Some simple examples may illustrate the changes to the types of garments worn today and how their cut will be principally determined by the fabric.

There is a limit to the amount of heavy cloth (WEIGHT) anyone wishes to carry on their body. Historically, heavy cloth was associated with warmth; but lighter cloths, wadded fabric (THICK), knitted pile (THICK AND HIGH STRETCH) or windproofed bonded fabrics (THIN AND LOW STRETCH), have replaced many heavy woollen cloths. Each of these latter fabrics are likely to require different stylistic and practical pattern cutting methods.

Fabrics that allow distortion of the warp and weft threads (SHEAR) usually have good draping qualities, but they will cause problems if they do not recover their shape, particularly as they come under body strains. But many new fabrics made from micro-fibres have HIGH SHEAR and also high recovery.

Fabrics with little drape or stretch have to have any body shape achieved through cut, whilst a small amount of elastane (HIGH STRETCH) in a fabric can give a garment some internal shape in wear.

These are simple illustrations, but many decisions are in 'grey areas' where defining the limits are not easy. The pattern cutting section will develop basic and more complex shapes and illustrate how fabrics with particular characteristics are likely to behave in those forms.

Figure 6   Three different fabrics cut in circular shapes of varying lengths and scales.

The fabric characteristic scale for pattern cutting

The term 'characteristic' is used because it is a descriptive term. In many textile books the words 'characteristic' and 'property' are used as if they can be interchanged. The latter should be used to relate to a fundamental chemical or biological property and in the context of broad design and garment shape decisions, the term characteristic is far more useful.

The pattern cutting method or block chosen for the development of a style should start with an analysis of the fabric. When the selection of fabrics was limited and style conventions influenced design, methods of cut were predictable. The increased availability of very different fabric ranges during the last decade needed a new approach. The five principal fabric characteristics which should be assessed before deciding the method of pattern cutting or the choice of pattern block are: **WEIGHT, THICKNESS, SHEAR, DRAPE, STRETCH.** They are assessed across a five point scale 1 2 3 4 5.

Opposite ends of each characteristic are as follows:

WEIGHT	Light-weight	1...5	Heavy-weight
THICKNESS (visual)	Thin	1...5	Thick
SHEAR	High-shear	1...5	Low-shear
DRAPE (visual)	High-drape	1...5	Low-drape
STRETCH	High-stretch	1...5	Low-stretch

Note that two are judged as a visual characteristic and therefore could be termed a 'visual measurement'. These terms are explained in the next section.

It is not argued that this method should replace or compete with other forms of technological measurement; instead, it is a different way of approaching the problems of translating 3D forms from 2D pattern templates.

Whilst it is recognised that other characteristics will play some part and would give subtle variations to the stark divisions offered, STRENGTH, SMOOTHNESS (friction), and COMPRESSION are secondary considerations. The weave structure (open or closed) should be examined. Open weave fabrics are often associated with shear, but many of the very closely woven micro-fibre fabrics can have shear characteristics.

The five-point fabric scale

The most accurate way of assessing fabrics is to use a full size circle of cloth, see page 21. However, the analysis in this book is made using only the fabric swatch piece (most fabric swatch pieces are on cards approx. A4 in size). This means that a square of 20 cm can be cut from the swatch. The sample swatch may be all that is available to a designer before purchasing a sample length.

Each fabric illustrated in the book will have a reference number attached for each characteristic. High numbers represent heavy, thick, low-shear, low-drape and low-stretch fabrics. Low numbers represent light, thin, high-shear, high-drape and high-stretch. Fabrics are quite likely to have a mixture of characteristics. The fabrics used in the illustrated garments are coded in the following way, for example:

Fabrics used in the illustration

		We	Th	Sh	Dr	St
1	Cotton voile	1	1	1	3	4

This means that the sample fabric is light-weight, thin, high-shear, medium-drape and medium–low stretch.

The measurements recorded in this book were taken using simple but specially devised equipment (see Appendix Three). However, even simpler methods of achieving a similar result are shown on the following pages. Any student could take fabric measurements by these methods. If students begin to assess fabrics in this manner, in quite a short time they should be able to intuitively code a fabric for comparison quite quickly. This helps the process of visualising a fabric's capability to produce certain shapes, and therefore compare and select fabrics.

Because the fabrics were so diverse (the scale would have been distorted if any statistical procedure had been imposed) the divisions between the categories 1–5 have had to be taken across an even spread across the majority of the fabrics. Extremely thick fabrics were not allowed to distort the group.

It is possible for others to disagree with my divisions and devise their own. This is not a mathematical scheme to be imposed, but a method that could be used across the whole range of fabrics, or adapted for a particular fabric group. Within narrow fabric groupings, the use of a statistical method (centiles) could be practical, agreement of the category divisions could then be made.

Throughout the book, there are no rules that dictate which fabrics should be used for particular blocks or pattern shapes, but visual examples are given which demonstrate what is likely to happen when they are realised in fabrics with different characteristics.

Special note 1. The 20 cm sample piece of woven fabric should be cut accurately along the warp and weft threads, and along the wales of knitted fabrics. The fabric piece should be checked to determine that it is perfectly square before the tests are carried out.

Special note 2. The order of the fabric characteristics is set for appreciation for pattern cutting. However, if only one 20 cm square fabric sample is available, the least distortion to the fabric will occur if the tests are made in the following order: **drape, thickness, weight, shear, stretch.**

Special note 3. The scale is a comparison across all fabrics and is not a comparison within a particular fabric group (e.g. shirtings).

Weight

The weight of a fabric is important, large amounts of heavy fabric can be uncomfortable to wear, but weight in a fabric will help to make graceful vertical folds and will 'swing' dramatically. There has been a general movement to lighter weight cloths, but some manufacturers are finding some resistance where customers attach weight to fabric quality, especially in wool fabrics. Often it is the reverse. Lighter wool fabrics are often made from higher-grade fibres or yarns and can be more difficult to weave. Light fabrics with low-drape and low-shear (example: cotton organdy) often give sharp crisp outlines but often crumple in use. This feature has been enhanced by many of the crinkle finishes available. Light fabrics with high levels of drape and stretch (example: single jersey) give wonderful body fitting and drape lines. Compact, closely woven medium-weight fabrics with high-drape and medium–high shear are excellent for crossway cutting (example: crepes or some micro-fibre fabrics).

Weight information is usually recorded by the square metre and to the nearest gm, although some fabric ranges give 5 gm intervals. In most cases, the weight will be listed on the fabric swatch or is available from the manufacturer. European manufacturers generally list the weight per running metre. To convert grams per metre length to grams per metre square: divide the weight by the fabric width and multiply by 100. Some UK manufacturers may still show the weight in ounces. To convert oz weight to gm weight: multiply the oz weight by 33.91.

Some domestic scales (see the photograph below) will measure in 1 gm intervals, this would be adequate for the type of broad categorisation that students may wish to undertake for themselves when calculating from a 20 cm square of fabric. Very accurate scales are required for more rigorous tests (example: British Standards). These scales are usually available in university textile departments.

Method for student practice

If the weight is not listed on the fabric swatch, weigh a 20 cm square piece of fabric (Fig. 7), then multiply the weight by 25 to calculate weight per square metre.

The categories shown below were decided by judging that any fabric over 450 gm should be described as 'heavy', and then five divisions were created.

The weight characteristic scale (in grams)

1 Light	2 Light–medium	3 Medium	4 Medium–heavy	5 Heavy
0–79.9	80–179.9	180–299.9	300–449.9	450+

Equipment used for weighing the fabrics recorded in this book

The fabrics used and recorded in the book were weighed (20 cm square) on an accurate TANITA Cal-Q-Scale which calculated to 0.1 gm. See Appendix Three, page 212.

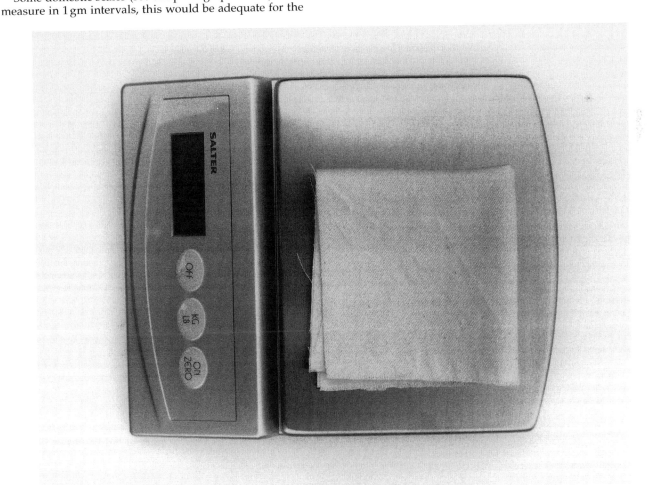

Figure 7 Measuring weight. A method suitable for student practice. A 20 cm square of fabric measured on a domestic scale that records in 1 gm intervals.

Thickness

Fabric thickness is so variable that each fabric has to be judged individually. Fabrics that appear thick can be highly compressible, other fabrics have uneven thickness that may be unevenly distributed. Very close fitting garments will require extra ease allowances unless the fabric has stretch and recovery qualities. Most thick garments are adapted from the easy fitting blocks. Particular pattern cutting techniques have to be used where there is gathered or pleated fullness to reduce the bulk. Thick fabrics with low-drape and low-shear characteristics can give exaggerated and stable geometric outlines. Extravagant but soft shapes can be achieved with fabrics that are thick and have high-drape qualities.

Fabric thickness is extremely difficult to measure. Technical laboratories measure it under pressure, it is recorded with a 'load' reference which flattens the fabric. This is useful for the making up of fabrics; but for pattern cutting a visual measurement which does not distort the fabric is more useful. When comparing fabrics that are very textured or are unevenly woven or knitted, a measurement can record the thinnest and thickest points and take an average measurement.

Method for student practice

Place the 20 cm square of fabric between two blocks (Fig. 8). Use a linen tester (a magnifying glass marked in millimetres and used in thread counting) to determine the thickness of the cloth. Linen testers are available from MORPLAN, a major supplier to the clothing trade.

The categories shown below were decided by judging that any fabric over 5 mm thick should be described as 'thick', and then five divisions were created. For illustrations of a wider range of fabrics see Appendix Three, page 212.

The thickness characteristic scale (in mm)

1	2	3	4	5
Thin	Light–medium	Medium	Medium–thick	Thick
0–0.4	0.5–0.9	1–2.4	2.5–4.9	5+

Equipment used for measuring the thickness of fabrics recorded in this book

The fabrics used in the book were hung vertically and scanned on an A4 SHARP flat-bed scanner. See Appendix Three, page 212.

Figure 8 Measuring thickness. A method suitable for student practice. A 20 cm square of fabric placed between blocks and measured with a magnifying glass marked in mm.

Shear

The amount the fabric shears (distorts in the warp and weft; see diagram) can be measured. Shear can be an advantage or disadvantage and the amount is important. The amount of recovery after strain is important. Closely woven fabrics with a high-shear characteristic (for example, micro-fibre silk-like fabrics or some crepe weave fabrics) are very stable when used in crossway cutting. Open-weave high-shear fabrics distort if under strain. Many complicated luxury fabrics, particularly fabrics in linen, silk and viscose have this characteristic. Fabrics will tailor more satisfactorily if there is some shear quality, it allows the tailor to shape the garment; however, too much shear becomes a problem.

Method for student practice

Create a card scale for measuring shear and stretch. Draw a horizontal line at the bottom of the card. Draw two lines at right angles to this line 16 cm apart. Mark the right vertical line and horizontal line in 0.5 cm intervals for 10 cm as shown opposite. Draw a third vertical line at the end of the scale.

Tape the 20 cm square of fabric onto the underside of two rulers using 2 cm of cloth on each ruler. Place the first ruler firmly at the left-hand start of the scale. Move the second ruler under tension in a vertical (shear) direction along the marked scale. The shear measurement is the amount that the fabric shears before ripples appear on the surface of the cloth. The amount can be measured on the vertical line of the scale. The amount of recovery can also be measured.

The categories shown below were decided by judging that any fabric with shear over 5 cm should be described as 'high shear', and then five divisions were created.

The shear characteristic scale (in cm)

1	2	3	4	5
High shear	High–medium	Medium	Medium–low	Low-shear
5+	4.9–3.5	3.4–2	1.9–0.5	0.4–0

Percentages

The percentage shear can be calculated by the following equation.

$$\frac{\text{amount sheared}}{\text{original length}} \times 100 \quad \text{e.g.} \quad \frac{2\,\text{cm}}{20\,\text{cm}} \times 100 = 10\%$$

Equipment used for measuring the fabric shear recorded in this book

A special piece of equipment was constructed that held the fabric under tension between two bars. A photograph of it in use is shown in Appendix Three, page 213.

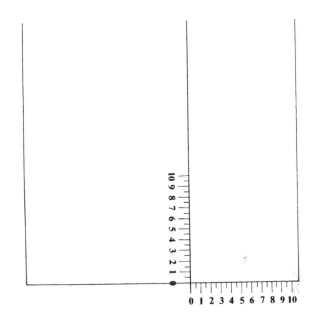

Fabric shear

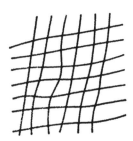

Figure 9 Measuring shear. A method suitable for student practice. The card scale and a 20 cm square of fabric taped to two rulers and the amount of shear measured on the scale.

Drape

Drape is the ability of a fabric to hang in soft folds and to fit around a figure, particularly in movement, without creating angular distorted creases and buckles. The strain is often across the fabric, thus good draping is needed across the fabric falling from flared shapes. The drape test done for these experiments concentrated on a crossway hanging test as this is a good guide to a fabric's potential to drape. Drape is a characteristic valued in many fabrics, it is only a part of that elusive quality 'hand'. 'Hand' is a combination of many qualities that will differ in different fabrics and this, I believe, is not measureable.

A simple assessment of the drape of a fabric, cut on the straight grain, can be made by holding a gathered sample piece vertically. The increased drop that would result from the weight of a larger piece of fabric would have to be taken into account. The difficulty of assessing how fabric may behave in circular cut is demonstrated on page 21. Asymmetrical shapes, crossway cutting and the effects of joining different curve shapes would add further complexity. The drapeometer test (BS 5058, see Appendix Four), which drapes a 30 cm circle of cloth over a circular disk, has little relationship to the hang of clothing. The new simple visual test, using a 20 cm sample piece, is only given as guide across the five categories.

Method for student practice

On a piece of thick white card mark a central point at the top. Mark a central line. Draw two lines at 45° each side of the line. Divide the area each side of the line into five sections. Mark them 1–5. Drive a nail or large drawing pin through the top point. Hang the corner of the 20 cm square of fabric onto the point at the top centre. The drape category can then be recorded.

The drape characteristic scale

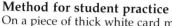

1	2	3	4	5
High-drape	High-medium	Medium	Medium-low	Low-drape

A low-shear fabric will hang as a flat shape on the board; therefore, in pattern cutting terms, low-drape means virtually no drape. Note the difference in the two fabrics shown in Fig. 10.

Equipment used for measuring the fabric drape recorded in this book

The equipment described for student practice was used for the fabric codes recorded in this book.

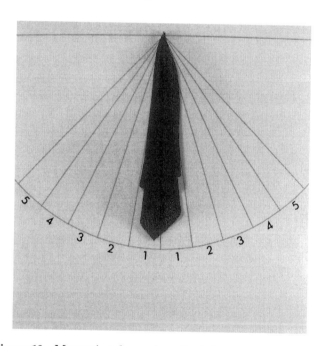
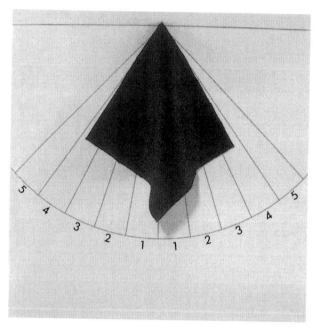

Figure 10 Measuring drape. A method of measuring drape suitable for student practice. The left fabric records 1 (high-drape). The right fabric records 4 (medium–low drape).

Stretch

Stretch characteristics in fabrics offer the opportunity to cut close to the body without complex body shaping. Quite simple shapes will fit closely to the body. Knitted fabrics may stretch but their recovery can be weak. The introduction of a small amount of elastane can make a remarkable difference to its stability. The introduction of elastane into woven and knitted fabrics has penetrated a large sector of the market, but there is still some resistance to the rather 'unnatural' hang of some of the garments. The amount a fabric will stretch can be measured; the instrument below will measure the maximum stretch horizontally, followed by the stretch vertically. However, these practical amounts are of little use if the fabric appears visually unpleasant at very high stretch or near the stretch limits of the fabric. The basic pattern cutting shape has to be based on a basic 'visual stretch' measurement. On body fitting garments or other garments, the designer has to decide the amount of stretch that is visually acceptable and then has to cut the garment pattern accordingly. This is the 'visual stretch' that is recorded in the work in this book.

Method for student practice

Use the card scale created for measuring shear and stretch (see the diagram on page 25). Tape the 20 cm square of fabric onto the underside of two rulers using 2 cm of cloth on each ruler. Place the first ruler firmly at the left-hand start of the scale. Move the second ruler under tension in a horizontal direction along the marked horizontal scale. The 'visual stretch' measurement in the weft direction is the amount that the fabric stretches before it begins to distort the fabric unpleasantly. The amount can measured on the horizontal line of the scale. The amount of recovery can also be measured.

The categories shown were decided by judging that any fabric which had a visual stretch of more than 5 cm should be described as 'high-stretch', and then five divisions were created.

The stretch characteristic scale (in cm)

1	2	3	4	5
High-stretch	High–medium	Medium	Medium–low	Low-stretch
3.5+	3.4–2.5	2.4–1.5	1.4–0.5	0.4–0

Close body fitting garments

Four other measurements can be taken on the scale when cutting close body fitting garments in stretch fabrics.
(1) The horizontal visual 'action' stretch (visually acceptable stretch when the body is in action).
(2) The vertical (warp) stretch of bi-stretch fabrics.
(3) The decrease in measurement of the fabric vertically when the fabric is stretched horizontally.
(4) The amount of recovery after the fabric has been stretched.

Percentages

The percentage stretch can be calculated by the following equation.

$$\frac{\text{amount stretched}}{\text{original length}} \times 100 \quad \text{e.g.} \quad \frac{2\,cm}{16\,cm} \times 100 = 12.5\%$$

Equipment used for measuring the fabric stretch recorded in this book

A special piece of equipment was constructed that held the fabric under tension between two bars. A photograph of it in use is shown in Appendix Three, page 213.

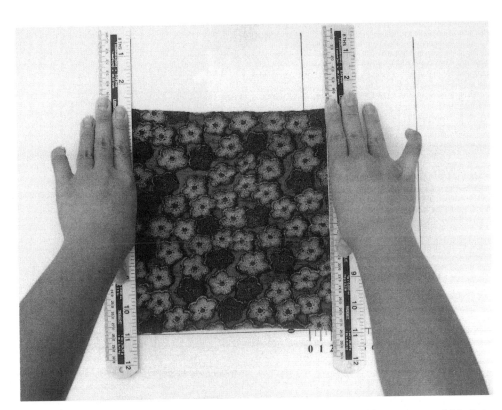

Figure 11 Measuring 'visual stretch'. A method suitable for student practice. A 20 cm square of fabric taped to two rulers and the amount of 'visual stretch' measured on a card scale.

Fabric properties and 3D CAD images

A number of CAD software companies – for example Browzwear, assyst-bullmer, Optitex and Lectra – have developed software that creates the realisation of virtual garments in high resolution. Garment pattern pieces are joined together to create a 3D CAD image of a garment worn by a virtual model figure that will demonstrate how the garment will look when finished. The mannequin's skin, face and hair can be customised. The shape and size of the figure can be determined by the input of manual or body-scanned measurements. These virtual figures can revolve, change poses and perform many human movements.

In most companies many garment samples of designs are made up but then discarded. CAD suppliers claim that 3D CAD realisation could reduce this apparent waste of time and materials because decisions could be made at an early stage in the design cycle. A further purported advantage is that the fit and stress of the garment can be measured technically.

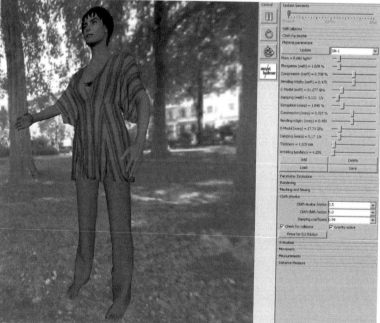

The companies have developed their programs in such a way as to emphasise different functions. Companies will select the software that responds to their priorities. For example, a design emphasis may focus on the manipulation of colour, shape and printed pattern in the development of a design range, whilst other companies may be more concerned with the fit, or the garment stress of body movements in sportswear, industrial wear or military activities.

However, the common denominator in all the programs is the realisation of how the fabric will determine the image of the garment. This requires the input of the measurements related to the mechanical properties of the fabric, and the majority of program developers are using The Kawabata Evaluation Systems for Fabrics (KES-F TEST). This is described in Appendix Four. It is usually large companies that invest in these CAD systems and they have access to fabric testing laboratories that conduct these tests.

An example of the fabric properties required can be seen in Figure 12: mass, elongation, compression, bending rigidity, E-modal, damping, thickness, wrinkling tendency.

The images show how the garment shape changes when different property values are input into the system. Some systems allow designers to use the sliders interactively to examine how a change of fabric will affect the design.

Students of CAD will find that an intuitive knowledge of fabric behaviour, so necessary for their manual pattern cutting, will also be invaluable in any technological future.

Figure 12 Notice how the shape of the garment is changed as the values for compression and bending rigidity are altered. Photographs reproduced with permission of assyst-bullmer.

PART ONE: FABRIC ESTIMATION FOR PATTERN CUTTING

3 A categorised range of fabrics

The arrangement of the fabric groups

Fabric illustrations arranged by fibre

The double-spread pages are arranged by fibre groups and they are listed above. One page is devoted to fabrics with some elastane content. All of the other fabrics illustrated do not contain elastane fibres; therefore, the stretch rating of these fabrics refers to the stretch that is given by the fibre, the structure or the finish of the fabric.

Fabric illustrations arranged by structure

The fabric illustrations, on most of the pages, are arranged in the following grid format:

The three columns represent:
column one: light and light–medium-weight
column two: medium-weight
column three: medium–heavy and heavy-weight.

The four rows represent:
row one: woven structures (open)
row two: woven structures (close)
row three: knitted structures
row four: miscellaneous.

Open structures are usually associated with high-shear characteristics and close structures with low-shear, but this is not always the case. Many micro-fibre close structures can have medium-shear characteristics. Also, some open structures have laquered or other finishes that stabilise the fabric and are not readily apparent.

Three pages where this arrangement of fabrics does not take place are:
Non-textile fabrics: leather, film
Man-made fibres/natural polymer: lyocell. This is a new generic fibre and therefore the range of fabrics is limited.
Man-made fibres/synthetic polymer: minor fibres and coatings.

Abbreviations

(warp) = warp-knitting
(weft) = weft-knitting
The full names corresponding to the fibre abbreviations can be found in Appendix Five.

The majority of garment lays in mass production are cut with the warp grain of the fabric running vertically through the garment. Although many fabric lays have the patterns laid up and down the cloth, some fabrics can only be cut one way: for example fabrics with a nap (raised surface finish), one-way printed designs, one-way woven checks and stripes, and many knitted fabrics. Cutting in one way can place restrictions on the shapes of the patterns; angular shapes do not interlock easily and make a poor utilisation of the fabric.

Fabrics do not have to be cut with the warp running vertically. As fabrics are now available in widths of 160–180 cm the length of the pattern is often not the main concern. It is usually assumed that the strong yarns will be in the warp and the softer decorative yarns in the weft. It is a sensible practice to ensure that the strongest yarns are placed where there is likely to be directional strain within the garment but many weft yarns are quite adequate for general wear. Many novelty woven fabrics have weft stripes and these are often used vertically because they are more flattering to the figure.

Although the right side of the fabric is the side with the 'finished' surface, the wrong side of a fabric can have the right aesthetic appeal and using the right and wrong side of a fabric in one garment can give co-ordination. Modified fabrics are often used in individual designs or small ranges: threads are added or removed, the surface is decorated, cut away or overlaid.

Non-textile fabrics: film, leather

The characteristic scale in this book was developed for textile structures produced from the fibres described on the following pages. However, the scale can be used as a first stage when designing with some films and leathers. Developing complex shapes with these materials usually requires further explorations and the use of special techniques.

Film

Many sheets of film can be made into clothing. Designers are experimenting with synthetic materials and metals that can be shaped into garment forms. This area of work is a craft or art form in which the creator has to experiment and learn about the materials and their limits.

Leather

Whilst the UK still produces some quality leather in its tanning industry for clothing, shoes and accessories, its production has reduced dramatically. Spain and Italy are still renowned for their fashion and quality. However, since environmental restrictions have come into force in Europe, production is being moved to less developed areas of the world where restrictions are more lax.

Clothing leather is available in a wide range of weights and handle. Nappa leather can be printed to resemble the skins of exotic animals that are under threat of extinction. Antique, distressed, metallic, printed, decorated and waterproof finishes are now major factors in the market. This is the result of the high fashion focus on shoes, bags and accessories.

Technological developments are improving the quality of leather. Enzyme technology has improved the handle and finish of sheepskins and lambskins, and hydrophobic emulsifiers not only soften leather but also offer waterproofing qualities and intense dye shades. 'Stretch suede' has been created by bonding suede splits onto LYCRA jersey. Some lambskin nappa leathers and suede are more drapeable than many woven fabrics. The main limits, for pattern cutters working with leather, are the uneven thickness that can occur and the size of the skins.

Fur

A very effective campaign against fur some twenty years ago almost decimated the industry. But there has been a strong revival in the use of fur in high fashion by a number of the couturiers and this has created some conflicts. Their sales are high in very cold countries where fur and sheepskin are essential 'weather' clothing. A competing environmental argument has also been offered that fur is degradable whilst many of the synthetic furs are not.

Working with fur is a very specialised skill, creating larger shapes from small animal skins of varying texture, thickness, handle and colours cannot be associated with mainstream pattern cutting and is not covered in this book.

The fabrics shown on the opposite page and listed below demonstrate the Fabric Characteristic Scale described on page 22. The series of five numbers after each fabric name shows their rating from 1–5 on each characteristic.

LIGHT-WEIGHT	1 . . . 5	HEAVY-WEIGHT
THIN	1 . . . 5	THICK
HIGH-SHEAR	1 . . . 5	LOW-SHEAR
HIGH-DRAPE	1 . . . 5	LOW-DRAPE
HIGH-STRETCH	1 . . . 5	LOW-STRETCH

The fabrics illustrated are grouped with heavier fabrics in the right hand column but, because of their character, the fabrics do not all conform to the general groupings of the book.

1. Suede (calf)
Weight	medium	3
Thickness	thin–medium	2
Shear	medium–low	4
Drape	medium–low	4
Stretch	medium	3

2. Suede (pig)
Weight	medium	3
Thickness	medium	3
Shear	medium–low	4
Drape	medium–low	4
Stretch	medium–low	4

3. Foil transfer (calf)
Weight	medium–heavy	4
Thickness	thin–medium	2
Shear	low	5
Drape	low	5
Stretch	low	5

4. Flexible opaque film
Weight	medium	3
Thickness	thin	1
Shear	low	5
Drape	low	5
Stretch	low	5

5. Nappa leather (lamb)
Weight	heavy	5
Thickness	medium	3
Shear	medium–low	4
Drape	medium	3
Stretch	medium–low	4

6. Chamois (calf)
Weight	medium–heavy	4
Thickness	medium	3
Shear	medium–low	4
Drape	medium	3
Stretch	medium–low	4

7. Foil/embossed (calf)
Weight	medium–heavy	4
Thickness	thin–medium	2
Shear	low	5
Drape	low	5
Stretch	low	5

8. Transparent film
Weight	medium	3
Thickness	thin	1
Shear	low	5
Drape	low	5
Stretch	low	5

9. Hide (cow)
Weight	heavy	5
Thickness	medium	3
Shear	low	5
Drape	low	5
Stretch	low	5

10. Lambskin with fleece
Weight	heavy	5
Thickness	thick	5
Shear	low	5
Drape	low	5
Stretch	low	5

11. Embossed (calf)
Weight	medium–heavy	4
Thickness	medium	3
Shear	low	5
Drape	low	5
Stretch	medium–low	4

12. Rigid opaque film
Weight	medium–heavy	4
Thickness	medium	3
Shear	medium–low	4
Drape	low	5
Stretch	medium–low	4

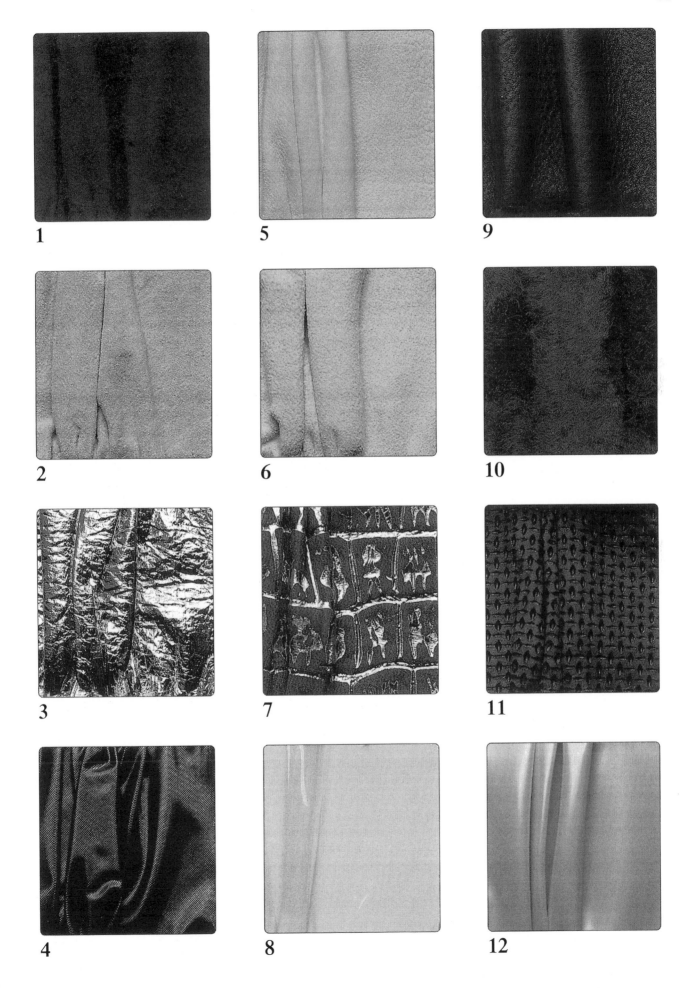

1

5

9

2

6

10

3

7

11

4

8

12

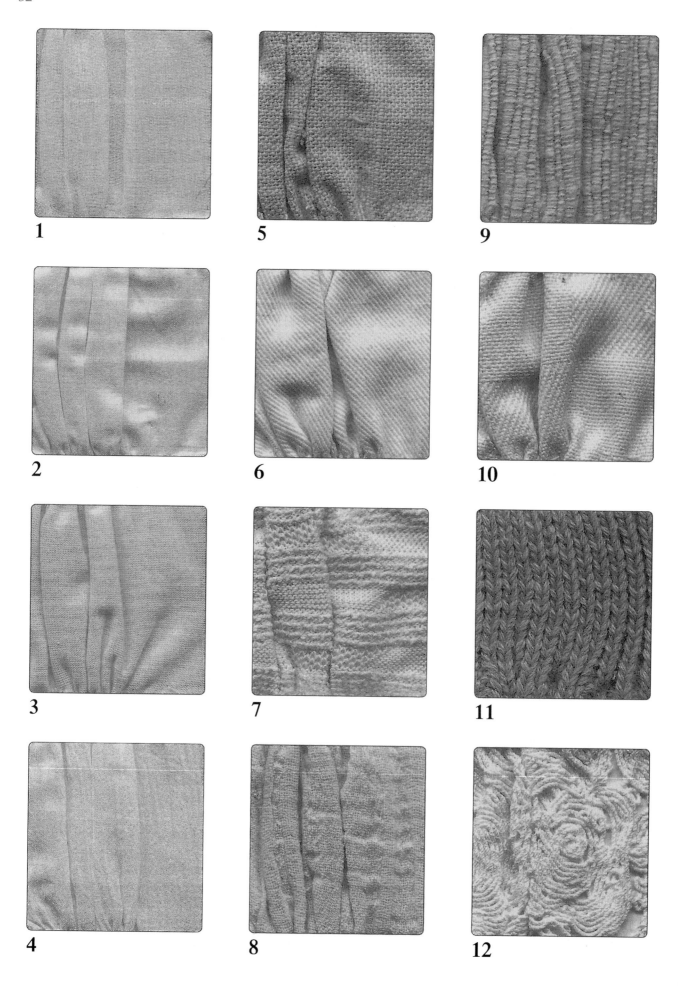

1

5

9

2

6

10

3

7

11

4

8

12

Natural fibres: cotton

One of the earliest fibres used by man, cotton had the largest production total of any fibre until 2003–04 when it was just overtaken by polyester production. However, its price and the continuing popularity of denim has helped it to retain its importance in the market. Part of the fluctuation in fabric production is related to fashion trends.

Cotton grows inside the seed pod of plants from the Gossypium family. The seed pod or boll can contain up to 150 000 fibres. The fibre is flat, twisted and ribbon-like, and can be up to 65 mm in length. The finest comes from the West Indies (Sea Island Cotton) and Egypt. America, the largest cotton exporter, produces strong fibres which are continuing to increase in length and strength (PIMA-7 is an even longer, stronger cotton) and India produces short coarse fibres. The main properties of the fibre are its strength and absorbency. Competition from man-made fibres has driven the new finishing developments in natural fibres.

Examples of new developments

New breeds of cotton varieties with longer, stronger and finer fibres and cotton grown with inherent colouring of soft muted shades does not require dyeing.
PROCESS 2000: a curing process that can keep garments wrinkle free or conversely in their distressed finish when washed. Other 'shape memory' finishes allow processes such as pleating to reappear after washing.
Waterproofing by silicone encapsulation of the cotton fibre.
BIOPOLISHING: a finishing process for cellulosic textiles that gives the fabrics softness, smoothness and reduces pilling. Silicon finishes are creating softer handles.
TOUGH COTTON: a cotton with a 20% better tensile and tear strength but still preserves its drape and handle.

SPINNAIR: a hollow core cotton, creates softer, lighter fabrics for underwear and baby wear.
DOUBLE DRY: an example of a cotton with a high-tech finish that can compete with the synthetics in moving moisture away from the body, yet retaining the innate qualities of a natural fibre.
GENE TECHNOLOGY: research outcomes that can influence the number of fibres produced on a cotton seed, the length of fibres or the production of novel fibres.

Fabric ranges

The fabric ranges produced in cotton are enormous, they offer: feather-light cotton voiles, silky poplins, fine embroidered fabrics and laces; soft fluid jerseys to heavy knits; basic medium cloths from piques to the denims, heavy-ribbed and canvas workwear cloths; thick, soft, brushed and pile fabrics, flannels, corduroys, velveteens, moleskin, terry cloths and fleeces.

The fabrics shown on the opposite page and listed below demonstrate the Fabric Characteristic Scale described on page 22. The series of five numbers after each fabric name shows their rating from 1–5 on each characteristic.

LIGHT-WEIGHT	1 . . . 5	HEAVY-WEIGHT
THIN	1 . . . 5	THICK
HIGH-SHEAR	1 . . . 5	LOW-SHEAR
HIGH-DRAPE	1 . . . 5	LOW-DRAPE
HIGH-STRETCH	1 . . . 5	LOW-STRETCH

The fabrics illustrated are:
column one   light and light–medium-weights;
column two   medium-weights;
column three   medium–heavy and heavy-weights.

1. Voile
Weight	light	1
Thickness	thin	1
Shear	high	1
Drape	medium	3
Stretch	medium–low	4

2. Lawn
Weight	light–medium	2
Thickness	thin	1
Shear	high	3
Drape	medium	3
Stretch	medium–low	4

3. Single jersey (weft)
Weight	light–medium	2
Thickness	thin	1
Shear	medium	3
Drape	high–medium	2
Stretch	medium	3

4. Crinkle finish
Weight	light	1
Thickness	thin	1
Shear	high–medium	2
Drape	medium	3
Stretch	medium	3

5. Slub: 'peasant'
Weight	medium	3
Thickness	thin–medium	2
Shear	medium	3
Drape	low	5
Stretch	medium–low	4

6. Denim twill
Weight	medium	3
Thickness	thin–medium	2
Shear	medium–low	4
Drape	low	5
Stretch	medium–low	4

7. Patterned (weft)
Weight	medium	3
Thickness	medium	3
Shear	high–medium	2
Drape	medium	3
Stretch	medium	3

8. Double cloth
Weight	medium	3
Thickness	medium	3
Shear	high	1
Drape	medium–low	4
Stretch	medium	3

9. Slub: bark weave
Weight	heavy	5
Thickness	medium–thick	4
Shear	medium	3
Drape	medium–low	4
Stretch	medium	3

10. Block weave
Weight	medium–heavy	4
Thickness	thin–medium	2
Shear	medium–low	4
Drape	low	5
Stretch	medium–low	4

11. Rib (weft)
Weight	heavy	5
Thickness	med–thick/thick	4/5
Shear	high–medium	2
Drape	medium–low	4
Stretch	high–medium	2

12. Guipure lace
Weight	medium–heavy	4
Thickness	medium	3
Shear	high	1
Drape	medium–low	4
Stretch	medium	3

Natural fibres: flax (linen), hemp, jute, ramie, bamboo

Flax is believed to be the earliest fibre used by man. Its production, although small compared with cotton, is rising. Grown mainly in Russia, Ireland and the Low Countries, heavy investment has taken place in the industry and 'fashion attitudes' to linen have changed. Seen as a rather boring classic, then as an expensive fashion statement, it then became hot 'ecology' high street fashion with a variety of finishes imposed on it. Its outstanding qualities have yet to be explored fully by designers, but knitted structures and blends and mixtures with other fibres add qualities that enhance its rough textured appearance yet give it subtle stretch and drape dimensions that the fibre lacks in its natural state.

Flax is a bast fibre produced in the stem of the plant and is largely pure cellulose fibre; other coarser bast fibres (hemp, jute and ramie) are mainly used in blends and mixtures for 'natural' fashion appeal. Flax is the strongest and least elastic of the natural fibres; the fibres vary from 6–60 cm in length and are highly absorbent. The fibres are cylindrical in shape with swellings at intervals. The contrast of its rough texture yet lustrous appearance is very appealing, and linen has gained a perverse affinity to its natural creasing qualities.

Examples of new developments

Soft, washed and distressed and creased finishes are now available, air-blowing finishes relax the fabric and improve the handle and draping qualities. This contrasts with high-glaze finishes. New yarns and weaves in ramie, hemp, jute, bamboo and linen mixtures are now available. A new eco-friendly fibre has been created by OJO in Japan by producing hemp as paper that is then sliced into fine strips and twisted into threads, to be blended with other fibres. A new ultra-fine yarn is in development using flower stems.

Upmarket alternatives to cotton are being produced, waxed linen for weatherwear, and linen denims, twills and chambrays for casual wear. Gossamer fine voiles and muslins have also been produced.

Fabric ranges

The fabric ranges produced in linen are extending, they offer: light open weaves and fine embroidered fabrics; classic linens in all weights; fashion fabrics in a wide variety of weaves, knits and finishes; linen tweeds.

The fabrics shown on the opposite page and listed below demonstrate the Fabric Characteristic Scale described on page 22. The series of five numbers after each fabric name shows their rating from 1–5 on each characteristic.

LIGHT-WEIGHT	1 . . . 5	HEAVY-WEIGHT
THIN	1 . . . 5	THICK
HIGH-SHEAR	1 . . . 5	LOW-SHEAR
HIGH-DRAPE	1 . . . 5	LOW-DRAPE
HIGH-STRETCH	1 . . . 5	LOW-STRETCH

The fabrics illustrated are:
column one   light and light–medium-weights;
column two   medium-weights;
column three   medium–heavy and heavy-weights.

1. Gauze
Weight	light	1
Thickness	thin	1
Shear	high	1
Drape	medium–low	4
Stretch	medium–low	4

2. Slub
Weight	light–medium	2
Thickness	thin	1
Shear	medium–low	4
Drape	low	5
Stretch	medium–low	4

3. Pointelle (weft)
Weight	light–medium	2
Thickness	medium	3
Shear	high	1
Drape	medium	3
Stretch	medium	3

4. Spaced weft
Weight	light–medium	2
Thickness	thin	1
Shear	high–medium	2
Drape	medium–low	4
Stretch	low	5

5. Creased finish
Weight	medium	3
Thickness	thin–med/med	2/3
Shear	high	1
Drape	medium–low	4
Stretch	medium–low	4

6. Twill suiting
Weight	medium	3
Thickness	thin–medium	2
Shear	high–medium	2
Drape	low	5
Stretch	medium–low	4

7. Striped tuck (weft)
Weight	medium	3
Thickness	thin–med/med	2/3
Shear	medium–low	4
Drape	high–medium	2
Stretch	medium	3

8. Distorted weft: crinkled finish
Weight	medium	3
Thickness	med/med–thick	3/4
Shear	high	1
Drape	medium	3
Stretch	high–medium	2

9. Contrast yarn
Weight	medium–heavy	4
Thickness	thin/thin–med	1/2
Shear	high	1
Drape	low	5
Stretch	low	5

10. Canvas
Weight	medium–heavy	4
Thickness	medium	3
Shear	medium–low	4
Drape	low	5
Stretch	low	5

11. Racked rib (weft)
Weight	heavy	5
Thickness	medium–thick	4
Shear	medium	3
Drape	medium	3
Stretch	medium	3

12. Patterned (weft)
Weight	heavy	5
Thickness	med/med–thick	3/4
Shear	medium	3
Drape	medium–low	4
Stretch	medium	3

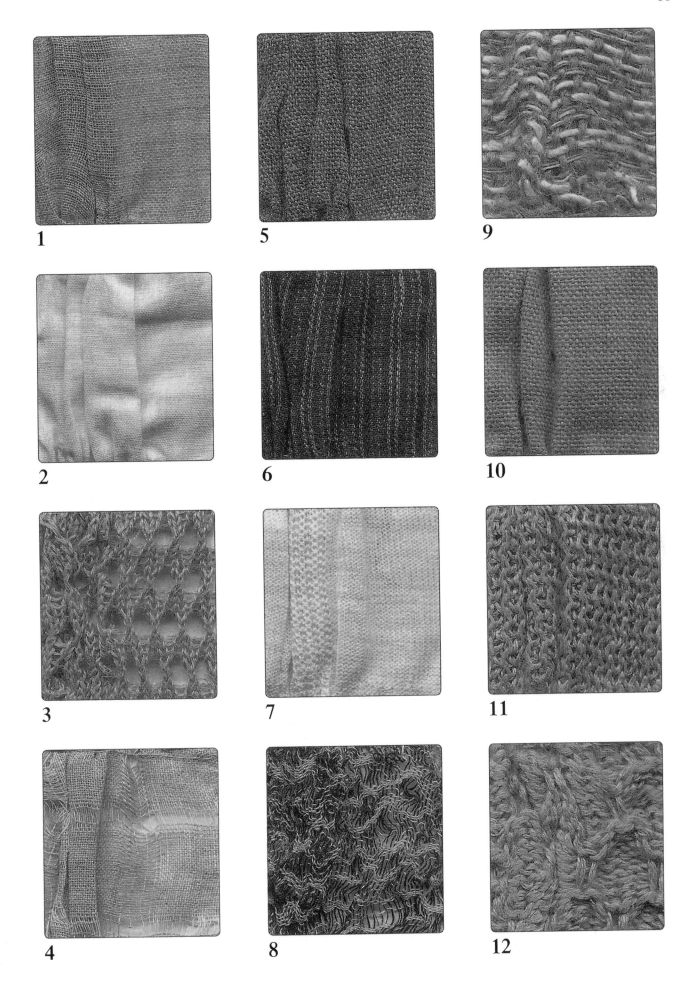

1

5

9

2

6

10

3

7

11

4

8

12

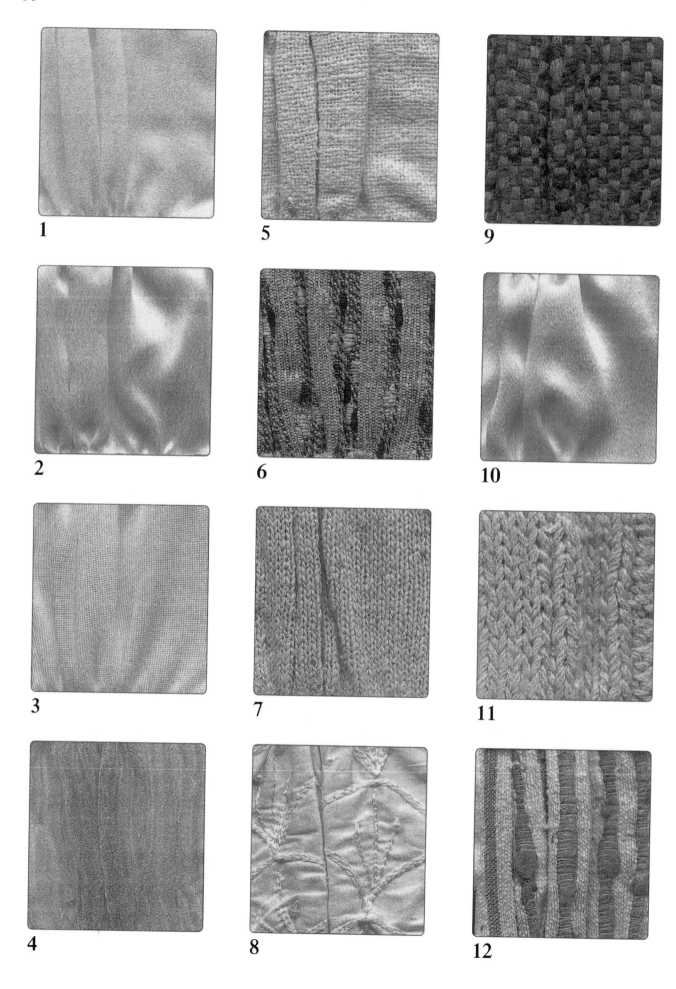

1

5

9

2

6

10

3

7

11

4

8

12

Natural fibres: silk

The production of silk has fluctuated but increased. China is the largest producer of raw silk, but its quality is variable and supplies unstable. Silk is often sold at below its production price in order to obtain hard currency. India has become a major producer of raw silk and of finished fabrics at competitive prices. High quality silk fabric production remains in the traditional areas of Italy and France. Silk fashion promotions and the availabilty of inexpensive silk has driven silk into High Street Fashion.

Silk is unwound from the cocoon of the silkworm. The caterpillar of the Bombyx Mori moth spins the cocoon around itself to change into a chrysalis. The unwound silk strands consist of two filaments held together by a gum. De-gummed filaments are smooth, semi-transparent and triangular in cross-section. Tussah or wild silk is produced from a number of different but similar species of silk worm and the silk is coarser and more irregular. Large quantities of waste silk are produced during the reeling process. This is combed and spun to produce spun silk for use in pile, knitted, and many textured woven fabrics. Silk is lustrous, strong, absorbent and has excellent draping qualities. However, silk can be damaged or distorted by heat and water. New developments have focussed on these weaknesses.

Examples of new developments

Shape memory yarn with thermo-set properties allows crinkle and pleated finishes which are retained after washing. Researchers mapped the genes responsible for spider silk in 1989. But, until recently, some of its characteristics such as its stretch when wet and the difficulty of producing it in any quantity, were impeding its development. However, many of the problems are now being resolved. The fibres are 10–100 times smaller in diameter than human hair but can be woven into light-weight supple fibres that are stronger than KEVLAR.

Fabric ranges

Classic silk fabrics associated with particular names (e.g. habutae, dupion, shantung) are listed in the glossary. The wide fabric ranges currently presented have extended beyond the luxury and classic markets to produce: decorative sheer fabrics and laces; light-weight shirtings and dress fabrics; crepes, rich textured silks and brocades; soft fluid jerseys to textured knits; silk tweeds and rich pile fabrics.

The fabrics shown on the opposite page and listed below demonstrate the Fabric Characteristic Scale described on page 22. The series of five numbers after each fabric name shows their rating from 1–5 on each characteristic.

LIGHT-WEIGHT	1 . . . 5	HEAVY-WEIGHT	
THIN	1 . . . 5	THICK	
HIGH-SHEAR	1 . . . 5	LOW-SHEAR	
HIGH-DRAPE	1 . . . 5	LOW-DRAPE	
HIGH-STRETCH	1 . . . 5	LOW-STRETCH	

The fabrics illustrated are:
column one   light and light–medium-weights;
column two   medium-weights;
column three   medium–heavy and heavy-weights.

1. Georgette
Weight	light	1
Thickness	thin	1
Shear	high	1
Drape	medium	3
Stretch	medium–low	4

2. Sandwashed satin
Weight	light–medium	2
Thickness	thin	1
Shear	medium	3
Drape	high	1
Stretch	medium–low	4

3. Single jersey
Weight	light–medium	2
Thickness	thin–medium	2
Shear	medium–low	4
Drape	high	1
Stretch	medium	3

4. Lurex: crinkle finish
Weight	light–medium	2
Thickness	thin/thin–med	1/2
Shear	medium	3
Drape	medium–low	4
Stretch	medium	3

5. Slub/spun: bourette
Weight	medium	3
Thickness	thin–medium	2
Shear	high	1
Drape	medium	3
Stretch	medium–low	4

6. Slub/lurex stripe
Weight	medium	3
Thickness	thin–medium	2
Shear	medium–low	4
Drape	low	5
Stretch	medium–low	4

7. Snarl single jersey (weft)
Weight	medium	3
Thickness	medium	3
Shear	medium–low	4
Drape	high–medium	2
Stretch	medium	3

8. Embroidered
Weight	medium	3
Thickness	thin/thin–med	1/2
Shear	low	5
Drape	medium–low	4
Stretch	low	5

9. Tweed
Weight	medium–heavy	4
Thickness	medium	3
Shear	high	1
Drape	medium–low	4
Stretch	medium–low	4

10. Satin
Weight	medium–heavy	4
Thickness	thin–medium	2
Shear	medium	3
Drape	medium–low	4
Stretch	low	5

11. Rib (weft)
Weight	heavy	5
Thickness	medium–thick	4
Shear	medium	3
Drape	low	5
Stretch	high–medium	2

12. Coarse slub: stripe
Weight	medium–heavy	4
Thickness	thin–med/med–thk	2/4
Shear	medium	3
Drape	medium	3
Stretch	medium–low	4

Natural fibres: wool, hair

Wool and hair fibres are only a small proportion of world production, but they are unique fibres with characteristics that defy mimicry. 90% of animal fibres produced are wool; hair fibres, longer and finer than wool (e.g. cashmere, vicuna, alpaca, mohair) are usually blended with other fibres in high quality textiles. Australia is the largest producer, New Zealand, South Africa and Russia are also significant. Wool has to fight the price competition of man-made fibres and their increasing versatility. The International Wool Secretariat promotes wool by research and development and establishing quality trade marks, for example the Woolmark symbol.

Although wool and hair have the same chemical structure (keratin), they differ in their physical properties. Shorter coarse fibres, less than 32 mm are spun in a random form for woollen yarn; longer finer fibres are laid parallel and spun with a high twist to produce worsted yarns. The fibre is cylindrical, with a scaly surface, a high crimp and a fibrous internal structure. This gives it the unique natural qualities of warmth, elasticity, drape, and the contradictory qualities of being water repellant yet absorbent. Its notoriety for shrinkage has been the focus of much research and development.

Examples of new developments

Current priorities for transeasonal, easy care, light-weight, drapable fabrics have produced super light-weight COOL WOOL. The handle can be changed to be dry, soft, lustrous. Practical finishes include: shrink resistance (the IBSEN process reduces it by 50%); chemical and heat-setting for pleat retention; stain, water and flame resistant finishes. CASHGORA is a new natural fibre produced by crossing feral goats with angora bucks. It is not as lustrous as cashmere but has a soft delicate handle. Although wool promotes its unique features, it is also competing with man-made fibres by creating very light-weight wools, using finishes that improve washability, and combining with LYCRA to provide extra stretch and stability.

Fabric ranges

The fabric ranges are extensive, they include: light-weight georgettes and laces; fine soft draping woven woollen cloths; soft fluid jerseys to heavy knits; rustic cloths and jacquard weaves; hard wearing worsted suitings and gaberdines; heavy woollen coatings and tweeds of immense range and character; brushed and pile fabrics with interesting surface textures.

The fabrics shown on the opposite page and listed below demonstrate the Fabric Characteristic Scale described on page 22. The series of five numbers after each fabric name shows their rating from 1–5 on each characteristic.

LIGHT-WEIGHT	1...5	HEAVY-WEIGHT
THIN	1...5	THICK
HIGH-SHEAR	1...5	LOW-SHEAR
HIGH-DRAPE	1...5	LOW-DRAPE
HIGH-STRETCH	1...5	LOW-STRETCH

The fabrics illustrated are:
column one   light and light–medium-weights;
column two   medium-weights;
column three   medium–heavy and heavy-weights.

1. Gauze
Weight	light	1
Thickness	thin	1
Shear	high–medium	2
Drape	medium	3
Stretch	low	5

2. Fine worsted
Weight	light–medium	2
Thickness	thin	1
Shear	high	1
Drape	medium	3
Stretch	medium–low	4

3. Pointelle (weft)
Weight	light–medium	2
Thickness	medium	3
Shear	low	5
Drape	high–medium	2
Stretch	medium	3

4. Raschel lace
Weight	light–medium	2
Thickness	medium	3
Shear	medium	3
Drape	high–medium	2
Stretch	medium	3

5. Light Harris Tweed
Weight	medium	3
Thickness	medium–thick	4
Shear	high	1
Drape	medium–low	4
Stretch	medium–low	4

6. Wool/cashmere
Weight	medium	3
Thickness	medium	3
Shear	medium–low	4
Drape	medium	3
Stretch	medium–low	4

7. Mohair rib (weft)
Weight	medium	3
Thickness	medium–thick	4
Shear	medium	3
Drape	medium	3
Stretch	high–medium	2

8. Boucle
Weight	medium	3
Thickness	thin/medium	1/3
Shear	high–medium	2
Drape	high–medium	2
Stretch	high–medium	2

9. Herringbone tweed
Weight	medium–heavy	4
Thickness	medium	3
Shear	high–medium	2
Drape	medium–low	4
Stretch	medium–low	4

10. Melton
Weight	heavy	5
Thickness	heavy	5
Shear	medium	3
Drape	low	5
Stretch	medium–low	4

11. Patterned (weft)
Weight	medium–heavy	4
Thickness	medium–thick	4
Shear	high-medium	2
Drape	medium	3
Stretch	high–medium	2

12. Felted wool/cashmere
Weight	heavy	5
Thickness	medium–thick	4
Shear	medium–low	4
Drape	medium–low	4
Stretch	medium–low	4

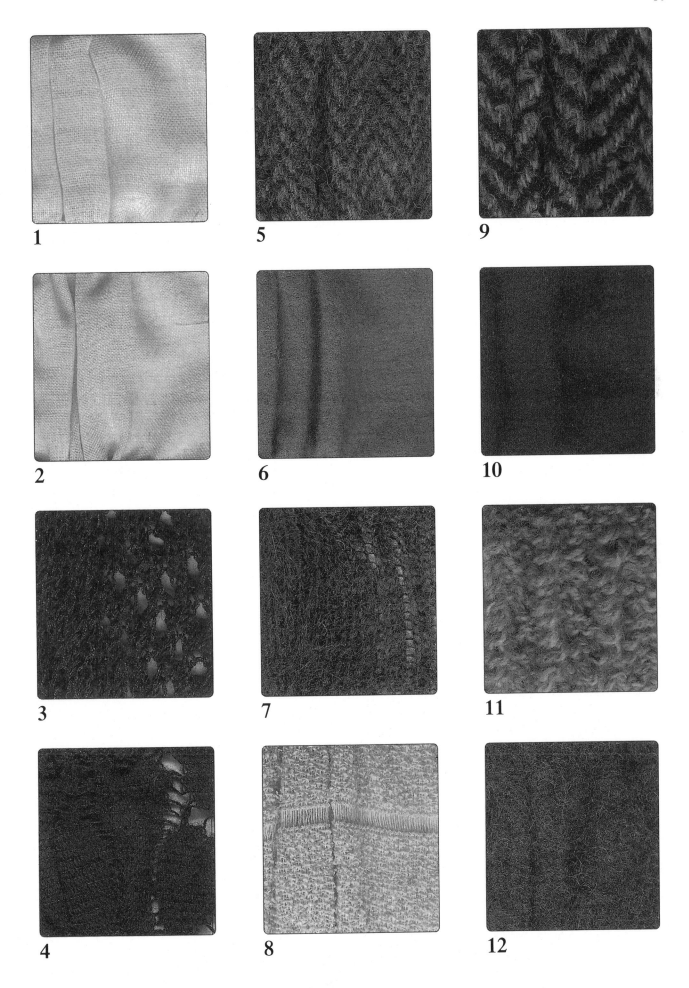

1

2

3

4

5

6

7

8

9

10

11

12

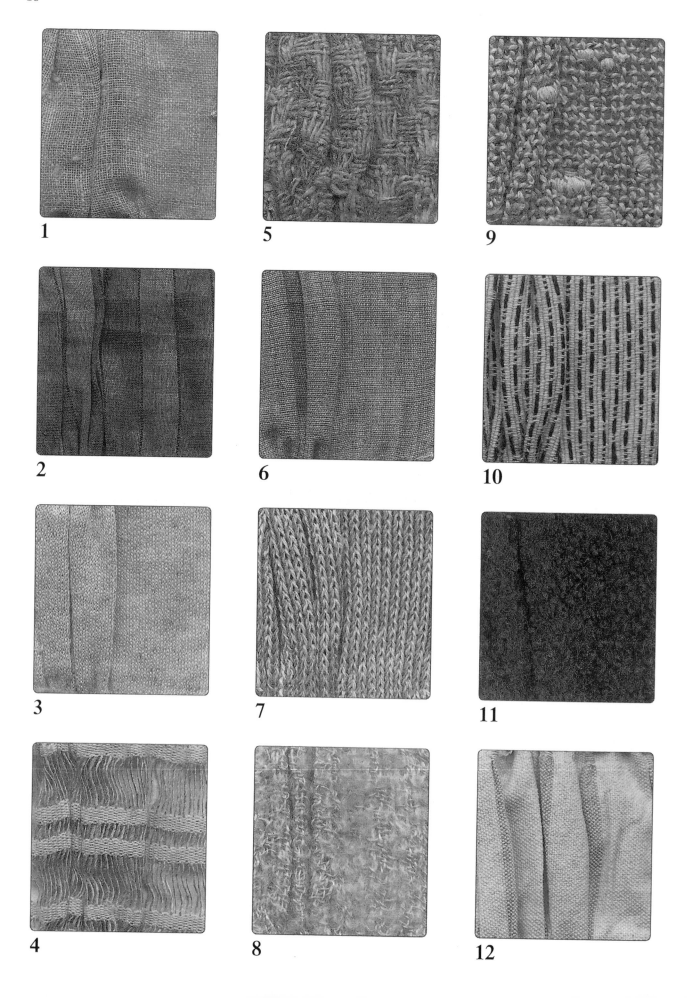

1

5

9

2

6

10

3

7

11

4

8

12

Natural fibres: blends and mixtures

Examples of mixed fibre fabrics, with cotton warps and woollen wefts, have been found in ancient Peruvian textiles, and the Egyptians in the first century used linen warps and wool wefts. Nowadays woven and knitted fabric manufacturers produce many fabric blends and mixtures. A fibre lacking a property could be supplemented with a fibre that has this quality. Vyella, a cotton/wool fabric has a historical pedigree. However, in some cases blends were undertaken to lower the price and 'blend' became associated with cheaper quality. A reversal has now occurred; for example, a high quality fibre such as silk is often added to give a luxury image to wool and to add characteristics to fibres of existing quality. Linen gives wonderful aesthetic qualities and strength to wool/linen blends and mixtures. Fabrics are available that may contain three or even four natural fibres. The use of ramie, hemp and jute can give 'character' to many cotton knits. Elastane (largest producer LYCRA) yarns are described on page 54, but it should be noted here that many natural fabrics now have added elastane. The tendency of natural fabrics to distort, unless held by high-twist yarns or firm weave or knitted structures, can be stabilised by adding elastane yarns.

Examples of new developments

Many new blends and mixtures are taking place in order to create unusual fabrics such as a blend of bamboo and cashmere that offers the bright features of bamboo yet the soft delicacy of cashmere; boucle and chenille yarns are being spun with animal hair to give new surface appeal.

LUNAFA is a new cotton fibre with a wool core. It produces washable fabric that is soft, smooth and warm but also has great moisture absorption characteristics. FANON is a new blend of cotton and cashmere.

Fabric ranges

Blended fabrics usually have a dominant fibre which is a high percentage of the total content. The fabric ranges produced in mixtures and blends can generally reproduce many of the fabrics produced by that dominant fibre. Blending with other fibres can extend a fabric's range by improving the practical qualities and extending the aesthetic possibilities.

The fabrics shown on the opposite page and listed below demonstrate the Fabric Characteristic Scale described on page 22. The series of five numbers after each fabric name shows their rating from 1–5 on each characteristic.

LIGHT-WEIGHT	1 . . . 5	HEAVY-WEIGHT
THIN	1 . . . 5	THICK
HIGH-SHEAR	1 . . . 5	LOW-SHEAR
HIGH-DRAPE	1 . . . 5	LOW-DRAPE
HIGH-STRETCH	1 . . . 5	LOW-STRETCH

The fabrics illustrated are:
column one   light and light–medium-weights;
column two   medium-weights;
column three   medium–heavy and heavy-weights.

1. Slub gauze
58% linen 42% silk
Weight	light–medium	2
Thickness	thin–medium	2
Shear	medium	3
Drape	medium–low	4
Stretch	medium–low	4

2. Fine slub stripe
80% ramie 20% silk
Weight	light–medium	2
Thickness	thin	1
Shear	medium	3
Drape	medium–low	4
Stretch	medium–low	4

3. Single jersey (weft)
50% silk 50% linen
Weight	light–medium	2
Thickness	light–medium	2
Shear	medium–low	4
Drape	high	1
Stretch	medium	3

4. Open leno weave
60% linen 40% cotton
Weight	light–medium	2
Thickness	thin/thin–med	1/2
Shear	medium	3
Drape	high–medium	2
Stretch	medium–low	4

5. Recycled basket weave
35% hemp 35% cotton 20% wool
10% mixed fibres
Weight	medium	3
Thickness	medium–thick	4
Shear	high	1
Drape	medium–low	4
Stretch	medium–low	4

6. Crinkled finish (weft)
80% linen 20% cotton
Weight	medium	3
Thickness	thin–medium	2
Shear	medium	3
Drape	medium	3
Stretch	low	5

7. Weft
70% cotton 20% viscose 10% silk
Weight	medium	3
Thickness	medium–thick	4
Shear	medium	3
Drape	high–medium	2
Stretch	medium	3

8. Boucle
57% linen 43% wool
Weight	medium	3
Thickness	medium–thick	4
Shear	high–medium	2
Drape	medium	3
Stretch	medium	3

9. Knop
60% silk 40% cotton
Weight	medium–heavy	4
Thickness	medium	3
Shear	high	1
Drape	medium	3
Stretch	medium–low	4

10. Novelty dobby weave
64% linen 36% cotton
Weight	medium–heavy	4
Thickness	thin–medium	2
Shear	medium	3
Drape	low	5
Stretch	low	5

11. Curled pile (weft)
60% wool 40% viscose
Weight	heavy	5
Thickness	thick	5
Shear	medium	3
Drape	medium	3
Stretch	medium	3

12. Creased finish
84% cotton 16% linen
Weight	medium–heavy	4
Thickness	thin–medium	2
Shear	medium–low	4
Drape	low	5
Stretch	low	5

Man-made fibres/regenerated cellulosic polymer: viscose, modal, cupro

Viscose rayon, the oldest of the man-made fibres (cellulose filaments were produced in France in the late nineteenth century), lost its lead as the primary man-made fibre produced to polyester, but it is probably the most widely used man-made fibre. New methods of production are now producing fibres that are helping it to regain its popularity, particularly in blends. The word 'rayon' is rarely used; historically it implied cheapness, whilst for many younger buyers the name 'viscose' has no link and is now associated with many quality fabrics. Fibre manufacturers are promoting particular facets and improvements to their fibres and awarding brand names to manufacturers who attain quality standards.

Viscose rayon is made from regenerated natural sources, cotton linters (waste cotton) or wood pulp. The cellulose is dissolved, forced through a spinnaret and wet spun as staple or filament fibre. The shape of the fibre structure can be changed and methods of spinning, inserting crimp and texture can make the fibre resemble the natural cellulosic fibres, cotton and silk. The fibre's greatest disadvantage is its weakness when wet, but modified rayons (MODAL and CUPRO) and new finishing processes have reduced this problem. The colour fastness remains and the fabrics stay smooth and soft even after repeated washings. Modified rayons are often blended with cottons to improve the surface of the fabric. MICROMODAL yarns can be spun ultra-fine for delicate clothing, 10000 metres of yarn weigh only a single gram.

Examples of new developments
Viscose is a manufactured fibre, this allows the development of fibres with their own character; for example, hollow fibres. These new fibres and new finishing techniques have produced fabrics with good draping

qualities, bulk and better crease resistance. VILOFT has an engineered cross-section which traps pockets of air, which not only gives fabrics a soft handle and thermal properties but achieves a technically advanced capillary action that draws moisture away from the skin and through the fabric.

Fabric ranges
Because of its versatility, fabric ranges produced in viscose are extensive; once used mainly in the lower price dress and underwear trade as a cheaper substitute for cotton or silk. Its present versatility means that it is now used across all price ranges and in many different weights, weaves, knits, blends, mixtures and textures.

The fabrics produced from cupro fibres have a silk-like appearance, drape well and are mainly of dress weight, whilst fabrics manufactured from modal fibres have some similarity to cotton.

The fabrics shown on the opposite page and listed below demonstrate the Fabric Characteristic Scale described on page 22. The series of five numbers after each fabric name shows their rating from 1–5 on each characteristic.

LIGHT-WEIGHT	1 . . . 5	HEAVY-WEIGHT
THIN	1 . . . 5	THICK
HIGH-SHEAR	1 . . . 5	LOW-SHEAR
HIGH-DRAPE	1 . . . 5	LOW-DRAPE
HIGH-STRETCH	1 . . . 5	LOW-STRETCH

The fabrics illustrated are:
column one   light and light–medium-weights;
column two   medium-weights;
column three   medium–heavy and heavy-weights.

1. Seersucker
Weight	light	1
Thickness	thin	1
Shear	medium	3
Drape	high–medium	2
Stretch	medium–low	4

2. Cupro jacquard
Weight	light–medium	2
Thickness	thin	1
Shear	high–medium	2
Drape	high–medium	2
Stretch	medium–low	4

3. Gimp plain (weft)
Weight	light–medium	2
Thickness	thin–medium	2
Shear	medium–low	4
Drape	high	1
Stretch	medium	3

4. Colorific-patterned
Weight	light–medium	2
Thickness	medium	3
Shear	medium	3
Drape	high–medium	2
Stretch	medium–low	4

5. Boucle: leno weave
Weight	medium	3
Thickness	medium	3
Shear	high	1
Drape	high–medium	2
Stretch	medium–low	4

6. Velvet
Weight	medium	3
Thickness	medium	3
Shear	medium–low	3
Drape	high–medium	2
Stretch	medium–low	4

7. Double jersey (weft)
Weight	medium	3
Thickness	thin–medium	2
Shear	medium–low	4
Drape	high–medium	2
Stretch	high–medium	2

8. Printed velvet
Weight	medium	3
Thickness	medium	3
Shear	medium	3
Drape	high–medium	2
Stretch	medium–low	4

9. Cord embroidered
Weight	heavy	5
Thickness	medium/thick	3/5
Shear	high–medium	2
Drape	high–medium	2
Stretch	medium–low	4

10. Braid embroidered
Weight	heavy	5
Thickness	med/med–thick	3/4
Shear	low	5
Drape	low	5
Stretch	low	5

11. (Weft)
Weight	medium–heavy	4
Thickness	medium	3
Shear	medium	3
Drape	medium	3
Stretch	medium	3

12. Purl patterned (weft)
Weight	heavy	5
Thickness	medium–thick	4
Shear	medium–low	4
Drape	high–medium	2
Stretch	medium	3

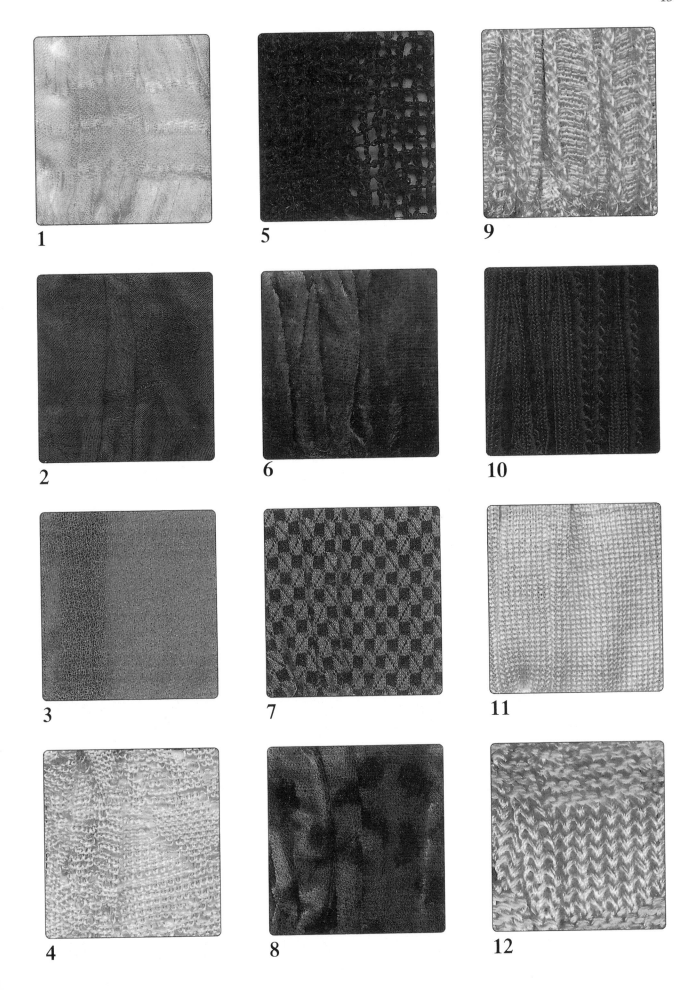

1

2

3

4

5

6

7

8

9

10

11

12

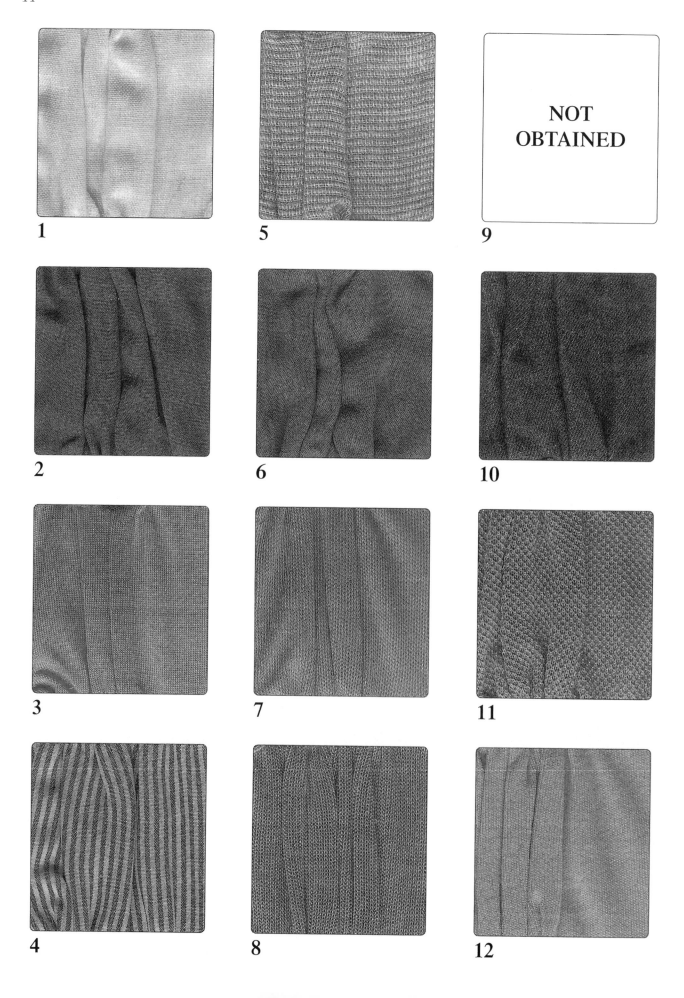

1

5

NOT OBTAINED

9

2

6

10

3

7

11

4

8

12

Man-made fibres/regenerated cellulosic polymer: lyocell

Lyocell is a fairly new generic cellulosic fibre. Whilst Courtaulds have been the first to go into commercial scale production, Lenzing are also producing the fibre and there were some disputes about patents of some of the original research and processing techniques. Lenzing retain the generic name LYOCELL; Courtaulds started marketing the fibre under the name of TENCEL, but Lenzing, through agreement, now have the rights to be sole producers. By 2004 its growth had doubled and further plants are coming on stream under licence in China which should further increase the production. It has the fastest growth rate amongst the cellulosic fibres.

Lyocell has immense strength, yet its 'hand' is soft and lustrous with draping qualities. It is a 100% cellulosic fibre derived from wood pulp; its production is made in an environmentally sympathetic process. Wood pulp cellulose is dissolved in amine oxide; after extrusion the fibre is cut to produce staple. The solvent is removed by washing and re-used, thus reducing the effluent to a minimum. The strongest cellulosic fibre, its strength is good in its dry state and its wet state (85% of its dry state). This strength property compares well with many polyesters and its high modulus allows good stability after washing. The fibre swells 40% when wet, the molecular structure is the key characteristic, abrasion in the wet state causes the fibre to fibrillate (fibrils appear on the surface but remain attached to the fibre). This quality allows the fabric engineer to develop interesting aesthetic finishes. Although Tencel can be dyed and finished with treatments that are applied to other cellulosic fibres, care is required, as it can behave differently. Lyocell has dye affinity, but control of the fibrillation is crucial; problems of uneven dyeing can occur. Lyocell also has good washability and moisture absorbtion. Jeans manufacturers, wishing for a soft finish, find it attractive. Most of the jean fabrics produced at the moment are finally finished in the garment state.

Fabric ranges

The total fibre production is low and many of the present fabrics are experimental in character, but the possible ranges are wide. They presently include crepes, twills, poplins, denims, velvets, chambrays and many knitted fabrics.

The fabrics shown on the opposite page and listed below demonstrate the Fabric Characteristic Scale described on page 22. The series of five numbers after each fabric name shows their rating from 1–5 on each characteristic.

LIGHT-WEIGHT	1...5	HEAVY-WEIGHT
THIN	1...5	THICK
HIGH-SHEAR	1...5	LOW-SHEAR
HIGH-DRAPE	1...5	LOW-DRAPE
HIGH-STRETCH	1...5	LOW-STRETCH

The fabrics illustrated are:
column one   light and light–medium-weights;
column two   medium-weights;
column three   medium–heavy and heavy-weights.

1. Plain weave
Weight	light–medium	2
Thickness	thin–medium	2
Shear	medium–low	4
Drape	low	5
Stretch	medium–low	4

2. Raised finish
Weight	light–medium	2
Thickness	thin–medium	2
Shear	high–medium	2
Drape	high–medium	2
Stretch	medium–low	4

3. Single jersey
Weight	light–medium	2
Thickness	thin	1
Shear	medium–low	4
Drape	medium	3
Stretch	medium	3

4. Shirting
Weight	light–medium	2
Thickness	thin	1
Shear	medium	3
Drape	high–medium	2
Stretch	medium–low	4

5. Weft rib weave
Weight	medium	3
Thickness	thin	1
Shear	high–medium	2
Drape	low	5
Stretch	low	5

6. Twill
Weight	medium	3
Thickness	thin	1
Shear	medium	3
Drape	high–medium	2
Stretch	medium–low	4

7. Double jersey (weft)
Weight	medium	3
Thickness	thin–medium	2
Shear	medium–low	4
Drape	high	1
Stretch	high–medium	2

8. Rib (weft)
Weight	medium	3
Thickness	thin–medium	2
Shear	medium–low	4
Drape	high–medium	2
Stretch	high	1

9. Not obtained
Weight	
Thickness	
Shear	
Drape	
Stretch	

10. Denim
Weight	medium–heavy	4
Thickness	thin–medium	2
Shear	medium–low	4
Drape	medium–low	4
Stretch	medium–low	4

11. Tuck (weft)
Weight	medium	3
Thickness	medium	3
Shear	low	5
Drape	high–medium	2
Stretch	high–medium	2

12. Brushed jersey (weft)
Weight	medium	3
Thickness	thin–medium	2
Shear	low	5
Drape	high–medium	2
Stretch	high–medium	2

Man-made fibres/semi-synthetic cellulosic polymer: acetate, diacetate, triacetate

Acetate, a chemically modified cellulosic fibre was commercially developed in the 1920s. A lustrous fibre, it became known as 'artificial silk'. Like viscose, the fibre's popularity was undermined by the appearance of polyester, triacetate being the major casualty. Renewed interest in acetate and diacetate has come from the increase in lingerie (body suits and slip dresses) being worn as outerwear and from the tremendous increase in blends.

Acetate, like viscose, is also produced from cotton linters (waste cotton) or wood pulp; however, the cellulose is dissolved in acetic acid and when forced through a spinnaret, it is dry spun. Because of its production process, it is the only cellulosic that is thermoplastic and is therefore often considered to be a semi-synthetic. Its thermoplasticity means that embossed, crinkled or pleated fabrics can be heat-set and permanent. The fibre allows wide variations in the filament (its shape, thickness, lustre and texture) and this feature can produce a wide range of novelty and decorative fibres. The distinguishing qualities of acetate are its low level of absorbtion, its drape and its heat-setting (thermoplastic) properties. Diacetate and triacetate demonstrate higher levels of these qualities and have a greater stability and crease resistance.

Examples of new developments

The improvement in the technical qualities of acetate, its finer filaments and its better performance during the weaving process have increased renewed interest in the fibre.

Fabric ranges

Acetate fabric ranges are extensive in woven and knitted fabrics: low absorbency makes it attractive for swim and weatherwear; its drapability and lustre is used in luxury fabrics (e.g. crepes, velvets and satins); its variability allows it to create crisp and embossed fabrics (e.g. taffetas and brocades). It is also widely used for lining fabrics.

The fabrics shown on the opposite page and listed below demonstrate the Fabric Characteristic Scale described on page 22. The series of five numbers after each fabric name shows their rating from 1–5 on each characteristic.

LIGHT-WEIGHT	1...5	HEAVY-WEIGHT
THIN	1...5	THICK
HIGH-SHEAR	1...5	LOW-SHEAR
HIGH-DRAPE	1...5	LOW-DRAPE
HIGH-STRETCH	1...5	LOW-STRETCH

The fabrics illustrated are:
column one   light and light–medium-weights;
column two   medium-weights;
column three   medium–heavy and heavy-weights.

1. Spaced leno weave

Weight	light–medium	2
Thickness	thin–medium	2
Shear	high–medium	2
Drape	medium–low	4
Stretch	low	5

2. Faille

Weight	light–medium	2
Thickness	thin	1
Shear	low	5
Drape	low	5
Stretch	low	5

3. Single jersey (weft)

Weight	light–medium	2
Thickness	medium	3
Shear	medium	3
Drape	high	1
Stretch	high–medium	2

4. Jacquard

Weight	light–medium	2
Thickness	medium	3
Shear	medium	3
Drape	low	5
Stretch	medium–low	4

5. Satin stripe: crinkle

Weight	medium	3
Thickness	thin–medium	2
Shear	high	1
Drape	high–medium	2
Stretch	medium	3

6. Woven cloque

Weight	medium	3
Thickness	medium	3
Shear	medium	3
Drape	medium–low	4
Stretch	medium–low	4

7. Lurex purl (weft)

Weight	medium	3
Thickness	medium	3
Shear	medium–low	4
Drape	high–medium	2
Stretch	medium	3

8. Laquered/patterned (weft)

Weight	medium	3
Thickness	medium	3
Shear	medium–low	4
Drape	high–medium	2
Stretch	medium	3

9. Not obtained

Weight		
Thickness		
Shear		
Drape		
Stretch		

10. Heat-set crushed velvet

Weight	medium–heavy	4
Thickness	medium	3
Shear	medium–low	4
Drape	medium	3
Stretch	low	5

11. Transfer (weft)

Weight	heavy	5
Thickness	medium–thick	4
Shear	high	1
Drape	high–medium	2
Stretch	medium	3

12. Racked rib (weft)

Weight	medium–heavy	4
Thickness	medium	3
Shear	medium–low	4
Drape	high–medium	2
Stretch	medium	3

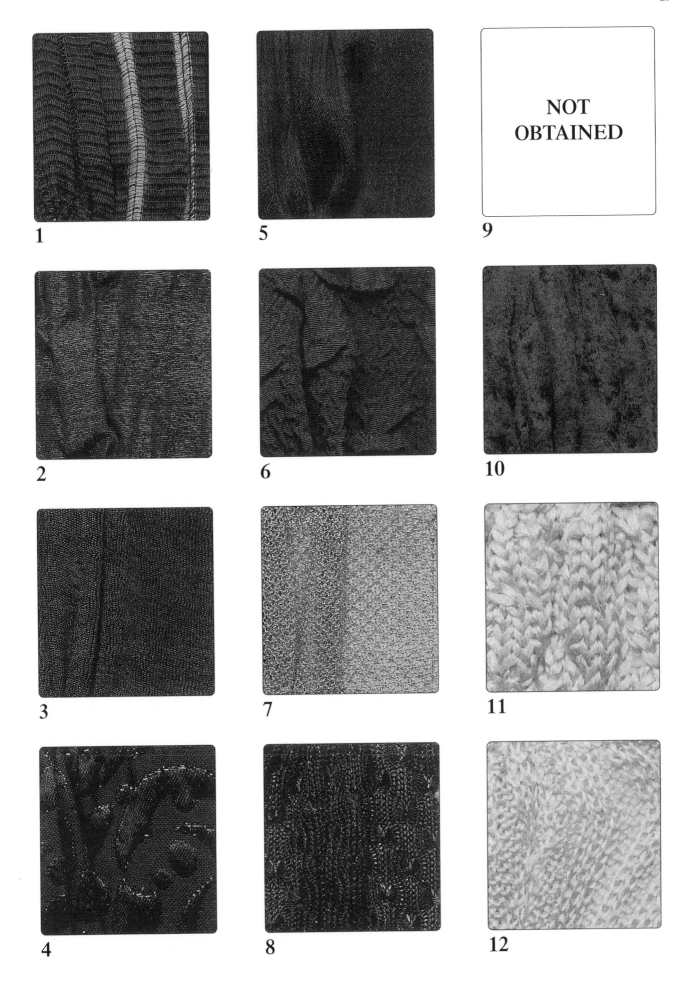

1

5

9

NOT OBTAINED

2

6

10

3

7

11

4

8

12

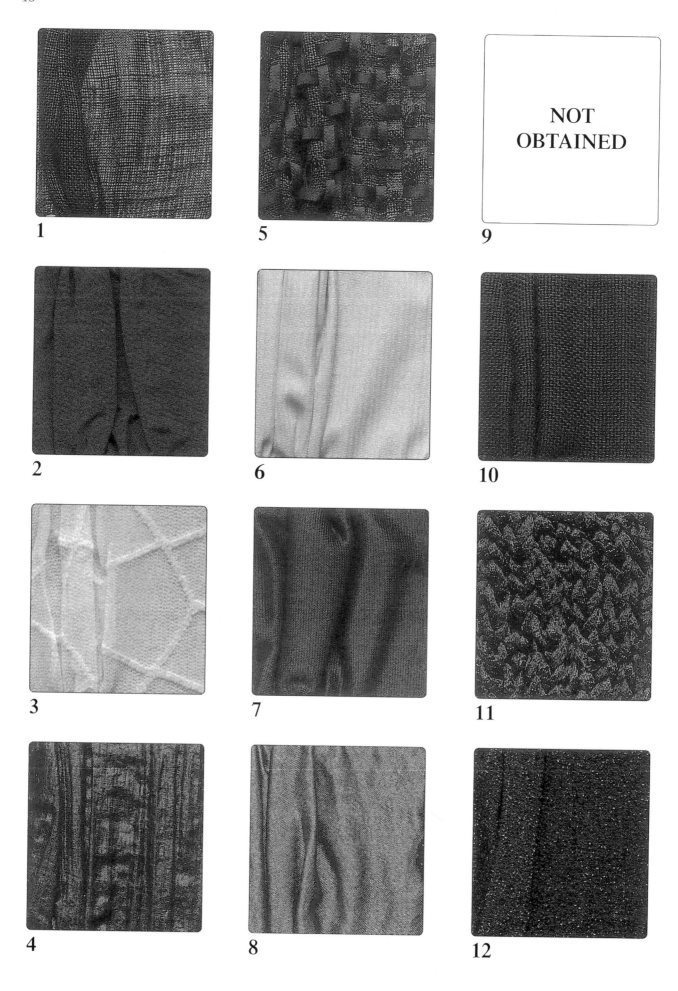

48

1

5

9 NOT OBTAINED

2

6

10

3

7

11

4

8

12

Man-made fibres: synthetic polymer: polyamide

Polyamide (nylon), the first commercial synthetic fibre, went into production in 1939. Nylon's unique strength, stability and fineness gave a truly new dimension to fabrics, particularly in hosiery, underwear and weatherwear. It is still principally identified with these areas of clothing, but the advent of new types of fibre structure, particularly micro-filament yarns are immensely extending its range.

DuPont's aquisition of ICI fibres and the TACTEL brand name transformed nylon from a functional to a fashionable fibre. The TACTEL collection and promotion is centred on comfort; instead of concentrating on technology, it is focussing on the fabrics and the garments. The marketing for new nylon products has had to overcome preconceived ideas about the unsympathetic nature of the fibre. The new fibre collections range from active hard-wearing outdoor wear to soft luxurious lingerie. The MERYL range from NYLSTAR is a direct competitor of INVISTA's TACTEL; its focus is also on the fashion market and specialisms in high-tech fabrics.

Coal is the original source for the chemical base of nylon. The fibre is obtained by melt-spinning; molten material is forced through a spinnaret and solidifies on cooling, making it very responsive to heat-set finishes. The fibre is produced in filament or staple form. Its important qualities are lightness, strength, easy-care and protection. Polyamide fibres, lighter than cotton or polyester, have the highest strength to weight ratio of any natural or man-made fibre.

Examples of new developments

New forms of fibre structure offer breathability that also create fabrics of unusually soft handle, drape and sheen; these revolutionary new fibre structures produce fabric collections that are luxurious but easy-care.

The polyamide range of fibres includes: antistatic fibres; hollow fibres that are light but insulating; rectangular fibres that give an added sheen to fabrics; SKINLIFE yarn that has permanent bacteriostatic properties for underwear, sportswear and paramedical fabrics; MERYL micro-fibre yarns lead the field in the 'seamless' technology of garments. Their micro-fibre range also includes fibres with UVA and UVB protection. Other polyamide fibres coated in silver have antimicrobial properties and these are being blended with other yarns.

Fabric ranges

Nylon is constructed in most fabric forms and blends: delicate sheers and laces; strong, light fabrics for weatherwear and protection, light-weight and bulked fabrics for comfort and athletics; knitted fabrics of wide variations; micro-fibre fabrics with silky or peachbloom finishes; luxury fabrics, satins, crepes and taffetas, deep pile fabrics and fake furs.

The fabrics shown on the opposite page and listed below demonstrate the Fabric Characteristic Scale described on page 22. The series of five numbers after each fabric name shows their rating from 1–5 on each characteristic.

LIGHT-WEIGHT	1 . . . 5	HEAVY-WEIGHT
THIN	1 . . . 5	THICK
HIGH-SHEAR	1 . . . 5	LOW-SHEAR
HIGH-DRAPE	1 . . . 5	LOW-DRAPE
HIGH-STRETCH	1 . . . 5	LOW-STRETCH

The fabrics illustrated are:
column one   light and light–medium-weights;
column two   medium-weights;
column three   medium–heavy and heavy-weights.

1. Gauze
Weight	light–medium	2
Thickness	thin	1
Shear	medium–low	4
Drape	low	5
Stretch	low	5

2. TACTEL cotton look
Weight	light–medium	2
Thickness	thin	1
Shear	medium	3
Drape	medium	3
Stretch	medium–low	4

3. Raschel (warp)
Weight	light	1
Thickness	thin–medium	2
Shear	medium–low	4
Drape	high–medium	2
Stretch	high	1

4. Schreinered finish
Weight	light–medium	2
Thickness	thin	1
Shear	low	5
Drape	low	5
Stretch	medium–low	4

5. Woven ribbon
Weight	medium	3
Thickness	medium	3
Shear	medium–low	4
Drape	low	5
Stretch	low	5

6. Bedford cord
Weight	medium	3
Thickness	thin	1
Shear	low	5
Drape	low	5
Stretch	low	5

7. Locknit satin warp
Weight	medium	3
Thickness	thin	1
Shear	medium–low	4
Drape	high–medium	2
Stretch	medium	3

8. Satin creased finish
Weight	medium	3
Thickness	thin	1
Shear	medium–low	4
Drape	medium	3
Stretch	medium–low	4

9. Not obtained
Weight	
Thickness	
Shear	
Drape	
Stretch	

10. Plain weave CORDURA
Weight	medium–heavy	4
Thickness	medium	3
Shear	medium	3
Drape	low	5
Stretch	low	5

11. Transfer (weft)
Weight	heavy	5
Thickness	medium–thick	4
Shear	medium	3
Drape	medium	3
Stretch	high–medium	2

12. Lurex crimp (warp)
Weight	medium–heavy	4
Thickness	medium	3
Shear	low	5
Drape	high–medium	2
Stretch	high–medium	2

Man-made fibres/synthetic polymer: polyester

Polyester, first produced in the 1940s, is the man-made fibre with the highest production level. Sharing many of the qualities of polyamide it is cheaper to produce and much research has been focussed on its development.

Polyethelene, produced from oil, is used for the chemical base of polyester. The fibre is obtained by melt-spinning; molten material is forced through the spinnaret and solidifies on cooling. This makes it very responsive to heat-set finishes. The fibre is produced in filament or staple form. It has many similarities to nylon in its strength, quick drying, heat-setting and easy-care qualities. It also has greater stability than nylon; however, it is not as dense.

Examples of new developments

Polyester micro-fibre fabrics are ultra-fine filaments packed in high-density. They create: unique light-weight fabrics with soft handle, such as TREVIRA MICRONESSE; fabrics that are impermeable to wind and weather but allow wicking (air and moisture escape); and fine fleece fabrics with a velvety nap for comfort and performance. The polyester membrane SYMPATEX can be bonded to almost any fabric, it makes it weatherproof yet allows wicking to take place. Hollow fibres such as THERMOLITE and COOLMAX are constructed from filaments with channel structures that move perspiration to the outer surface. They dry quickly and give warmth, breathability and wicking to thermal garments. Instead of a supplementary finishing process, TREVIRA's antimicrobial additives are embedded

in the fibre and are permanent. They have also developed a new fibre, XPAND with two-thirds the expansion function of elastane.

Fabric ranges

Polyester fabrics can be found in virtually every type of fabric range: delicate sheers and laces; strong, light fabrics for weatherwear and protection, light-weight and bulked fabrics for comfort and athletics; knitted fabrics of wide variations; micro-fibre fabrics with silky or peachbloom finishes; luxury fabrics, satins, crepes and taffetas, suitings, deep pile fabrics and fake furs.

The fabrics shown on the opposite page and listed below demonstrate the Fabric Characteristic Scale described on page 22. The series of five numbers after each fabric name shows their rating from 1–5 on each characteristic.

LIGHT-WEIGHT	1 ... 5	HEAVY-WEIGHT
THIN	1 ... 5	THICK
HIGH-SHEAR	1 ... 5	LOW-SHEAR
HIGH-DRAPE	1 ... 5	LOW-DRAPE
HIGH-STRETCH	1 ... 5	LOW-STRETCH

The fabrics illustrated are:
column one   light and light–medium-weights;
column two   medium-weights;
column three   medium–heavy and heavy-weights.

1. Chiffon crinkle finish

Weight	light	1
Thickness	thin	1
Shear	high–medium	2
Drape	high–medium	2
Stretch	medium–low	4

2. Peachskin micro-fibre

Weight	light–medium	2
Thickness	thin–medium	2
Shear	high–medium	2
Drape	high	1
Stretch	low	5

3. Lurex (warp)

Weight	light–medium	2
Thickness	medium	3
Shear	medium	3
Drape	high–medium	2
Stretch	medium	3

4. Leavers lace

Weight	light–medium	2
Thickness	thin–med/med–thk	2/4
Shear	medium–low	4
Drape	high	1
Stretch	medium	3

5. Heat set crinkle georgette

Weight	medium	3
Thickness	thin	1
Shear	high	1
Drape	medium	3
Stretch	high–medium	2

6. Herringbone suiting

Weight	medium	3
Thickness	thin–medium	2
Shear	medium–low	4
Drape	medium–low	4
Stretch	medium–low	4

7. Fleece (weft)

Weight	medium	3
Thickness	thick	5
Shear	medium	3
Drape	medium–low	4
Stretch	medium	3

8. Handmade Torchon lace

Weight	medium	3
Thickness	thin/medium	1/3
Shear	medium–low	4
Drape	medium	3
Stretch	medium–low	4

9. Ribbon weft insertion

Weight	medium–heavy	4
Thickness	medium	3
Shear	medium–low	4
Drape	low	5
Stretch	low	5

10. Twill suiting

Weight	medium–heavy	4
Thickness	thin–medium	2
Shear	medium	3
Drape	medium–low	4
Stretch	medium–low	4

11. Rib (warp)

Weight	heavy	5
Thickness	medium–thick	4
Shear	low	5
Drape	low	5
Stretch	low	5

12. Heat embossed velvet

Weight	medium–heavy	4
Thickness	medium	3
Shear	medium	3
Drape	medium	3
Stretch	low	5

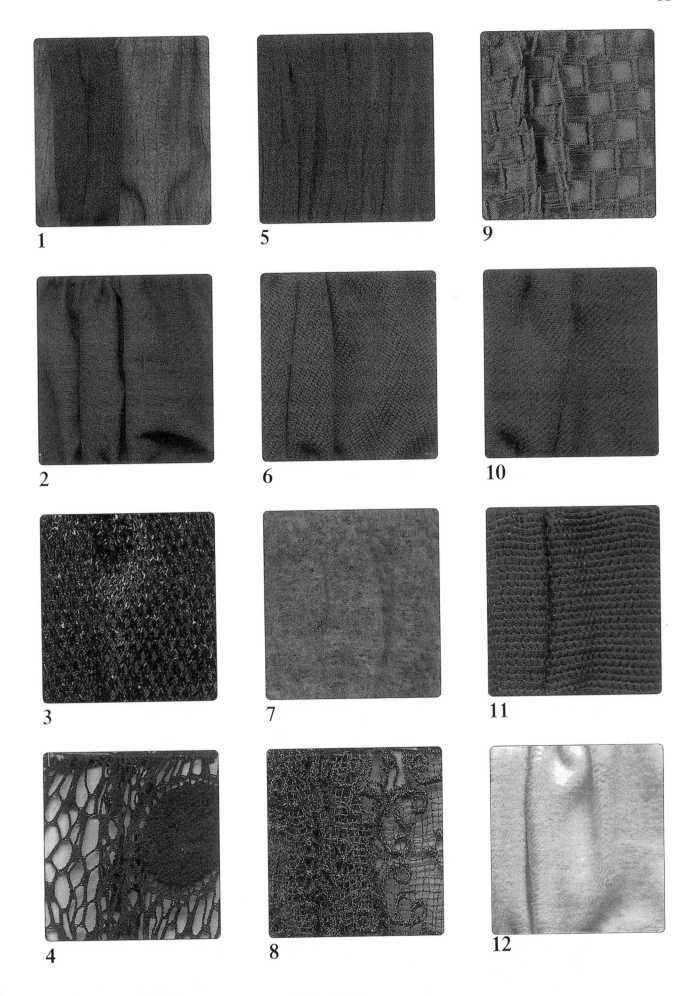

1

5

9

2

6

10

3

7

11

4

8

12

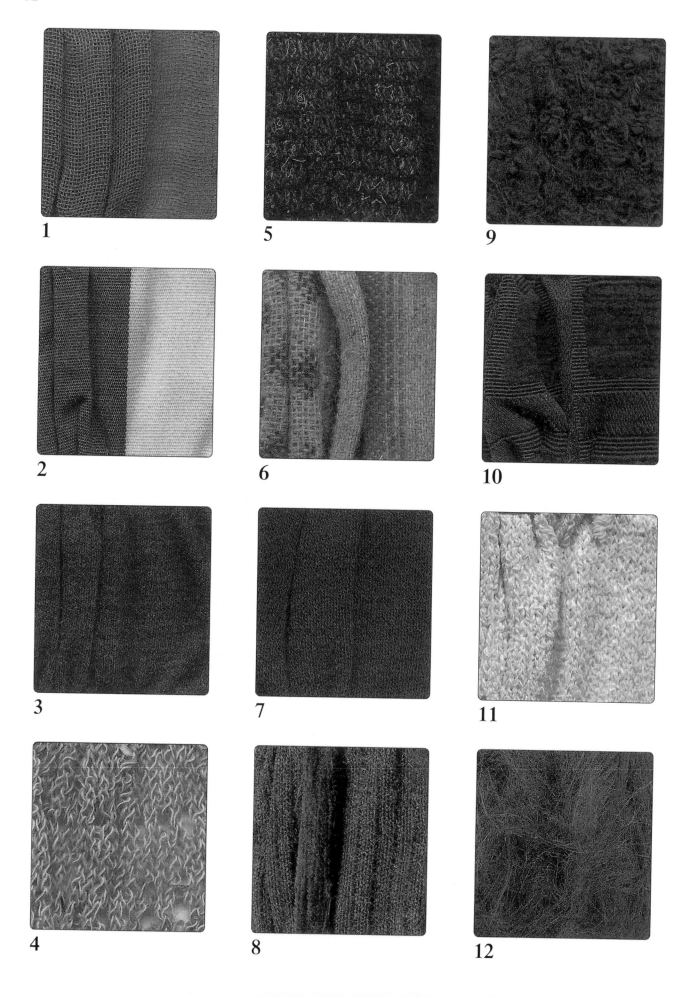

1

5

9

2

6

10

3

7

11

4

8

12

Man-made fibres: synthetic polymer: acrylic

Commercial production of acrylic fibres began in 1950. Many of the fibres sold today are co-polymers and are placed in the group modacrylics. An inexpensive fibre, it was accepted quickly by the knitting industry. Although it had problems with dyeing, its washability and high bulk yarns made it a fierce competitor for wool. Its use in woven fabrics is principally in blends where it adds softness, texture or bulk. Many of the fabrics illustrated are therefore blends and mixtures. The fibre has also developed a strong market in flocking, particularly in the manufacture of fur fabrics.

Created from a derivative of natural gas and air, acrylic fibres are dry-spun to produce filament fibres, or wet-spun for staple fibres; the latter form the major part of the production. Acrylic fibres have a good capacity for crimping and are used to produce bulky yarns. The fibres have a low absorption level and dry easily, good insulation, strength, easy-care and protection qualities. The fibres are heat sensitive and can easily be damaged or distorted, particularly when wet. The development of modacrylics has improved some of these problems, and gained the advantage of flame retardent properties. As other fibre technology has produced many of the qualities of acrylics with superior performance, its production has dropped from 20% of synthetic fibre production in 1970 to 8% in 2004. The fibre is now mainly produced in India and the Far East.

Examples of new developments
Neochrome fibre is dyed during the production of the fibre on a continuous on-line dyeing system which dyes and fixes during the extrusion process. This method offers an unlimited range of shades and dyes and consistency.

Bi-component fibres can give very high crimp and textural effects, they are mainly produced in staple for knitting.

Fabric ranges
Light-weight and bulked fabrics for comfort and warmth, knitted fabrics in most weights and in many textures, deep pile fabrics, flocked fabrics and fake furs.

The fabrics shown on the opposite page and listed below demonstrate the Fabric Characteristic Scale described on page 22. The series of five numbers after each fabric name shows their rating from 1–5 on each characteristic.

LIGHT-WEIGHT	1 ... 5	HEAVY-WEIGHT
THIN	1 ... 5	THICK
HIGH-SHEAR	1 ... 5	LOW-SHEAR
HIGH-DRAPE	1 ... 5	LOW-DRAPE
HIGH-STRETCH	1 ... 5	LOW-STRETCH

The fabrics illustrated are:
column one   light and light–medium-weights;
column two   medium-weights;
column three   medium–heavy and heavy-weights.
The codes used for some of the man-made fibres listed can be found on page 216.

1. Twist
60% acrylic 40% acetate
Weight	light–medium	2
Thickness	medium	3
Shear	medium	3
Drape	medium	3
Stretch	medium–low	4

2. Stripe weave
Weight	light–medium	2
Thickness	thin	1
Shear	high–medium	2
Drape	low	5
Stretch	high–medium	2

3. Single jersey (weft)
Weight	light–medium	2
Thickness	medium	3
Shear	medium–low	4
Drape	high–medium	2
Stretch	high–medium	2

4. Pointelle (weft)
Weight	light–medium	2
Thickness	med/med–thick	3/4
Shear	low	5
Drape	high–medium	2
Stretch	medium–low	4

5. Novelty weave
45% acrylic 25% PE 30% wool
Weight	medium	3
Thickness	medium–thick	4
Shear	medium–low	4
Drape	medium–low	4
Stretch	medium–low	4

6. Tapestry
60% acrylic 40% wool
Weight	medium	3
Thickness	medium	3
Shear	medium–low	4
Drape	medium–low	4
Stretch	medium–low	4

7. Double jersey (weft)
50% acrylic 50% wool
Weight	medium	3
Thickness	medium	3
Shear	medium–low	4
Drape	medium	3
Stretch	high–medium	2

8. Satin stripe weave
38% PE 35% PAN 17% CV 10% wool
Weight	medium	3
Thickness	medium	3
Shear	high–medium	2
Drape	medium	3
Stretch	medium–low	4

9. Boucle
60% acrylic 30% viscose 10% wool
Weight	medium–heavy	4
Thickness	medium–thick	4
Shear	high	1
Drape	medium	3
Stretch	medium–low	4

10. Jacquard blister weave
60% acrylic 40% polyester
Weight	medium–heavy	4
Thickness	medium–thick	4
Shear	medium–low	4
Drape	low	5
Stretch	medium–low	4

11. Transfer (weft)
50% acrylic 50% viscose
Weight	medium–heavy	4
Thickness	medium	3
Shear	medium–low	4
Drape	high–medium	2
Stretch	high–medium	2

12. High pile (warp)
90% acrylic 10% polyester
Weight	heavy	5
Thickness	thick	5
Shear	medium	3
Drape	medium–low	4
Stretch	medium	3

Man-made fibres/synthetic polymer: PLA, elastane

PLA

The source of the new synthetic fibre PLA is corn and sugar beet. Polyactic acid is manufactured from the carbon and sugars that they contain. The fibres are heat set. As pressure grows for the sustainability of natural resources in manufactured textile products, it is seen as a future strong competitor for polyester.

PLA shares many characteristics with polyester, but its producers claim that PLA fibres are superior in softness, stretch and recovery, vibrant colour, and UV and chlorine resistance.

Elastane

DuPont invented LYCRA in 1959, the first elastane fibre, but there are now a number of competitors. As little as 2% elastane fibre content is enough to change the handle, drape and stretch of a fabric whilst retaining the main characteristics of the dominant fibre. Used mainly in sport and body form areas of garment production until the last decade, its high extensibility gave a new fashion element to fabrics as well as adding comfort and stability. The growth of knitted fabrics, and the use of elastane are bringing about great changes in garment pattern development.

The source of elastane is polyurethene. Although most elastane fibres are produced to stretch to three times their length, they can be extended further. Its greatest characteristic is its ability to recover. The elastane fibre is rigid when it is sheathed in fibres that are compatible or match the host fibres by core-twisting or core-spinning. The elasticity is regained during the finishing processes. The fabric can have warp-stretch, weft-stretch or two-way stretch (bi-stretch).

Examples of new developments

Many new developments in elastane fibres have taken place, including an improvement in dimensional stability and the softness of the fibre. Elastane now degrades less in light and resists chemicals such as chlorine. It can now be dyed at higher temperatures to increase its core density. Its whiteness has improved, and INVISTA has launched a new dense black fibre that eliminates the 'grin' which is apparent in black fabrics containing elastane.

Fabric ranges

Because LYCRA is embodied in the host fibre, almost any fabric can have added elastane. The main element of choice for its inclusion is the end use and the aesthetic handle that is required. Some designers still believe that the inherent appearance and feel of natural fabrics are diminished when elastane fibres are added.

LIGHT-WEIGHT	1...5	HEAVY-WEIGHT
THIN	1...5	THICK
HIGH-SHEAR	1...5	LOW-SHEAR
HIGH-DRAPE	1...5	LOW-DRAPE
HIGH-STRETCH	1...5	LOW-STRETCH

The fabrics illustrated are:
column one   light and light–medium-weights;
column two   medium-weights;
column three   medium–heavy and heavy-weights.
The codes for some of the man-made fibres listed can be found on page 216.

1. Spaced weft
95% polyester 3% elastane 2% metal
Weight	light–medium	2
Thickness	thin–med/med	2/3
Shear	medium–low	4
Drape	medium	3
Stretch	medium	3

2. Heat set cloque
87% CA 10% PA 3% elastane
Weight	light–medium	2
Thickness	thin/med–thick	1/4
Shear	medium–low	4
Drape	medium–low	4
Stretch	medium	3

3. Lacquered (warp)
77% polyamide 23% elastane
Weight	light–medium	2
Thickness	thin	1
Shear	low	5
Drape	high–medium	2
Stretch	high–medium	2

4. Raschel lace (warp)
80% acetate 3% elastane
Weight	light–medium	2
Thickness	thin/medium	1/3
Shear	high	1
Drape	high–medium	2
Stretch	high–medium	2

5. Boucle
70% CA 27% PA 3% elastane
Weight	medium	3
Thickness	medium	3
Shear	medium	3
Drape	high–medium	2
Stretch	high–medium	2

6. Suiting
97% wool 3% elastane
Weight	medium	3
Thickness	thin–medium	2
Shear	medium–low	4
Drape	medium	3
Stretch	medium	3

7. Plush stripe (weft)
97% acrylic 3% elastane
Weight	medium	3
Thickness	medium	3
Shear	medium–low	4
Drape	high–medium	3
Stretch	medium	3

8. Raschel (warp)
73% cotton 23% PA 4% elastane
Weight	medium	3
Thickness	thin–med/med	2/3
Shear	medium–low	4
Drape	medium	3
Stretch	high–medium	2

9. Novelty 'couture' ribbon tweed
75% wool 24% PA 1% elastane
Weight	medium–heavy	4
Thickness	medium–thick	4
Shear	medium	3
Drape	high–medium	2
Stretch	high	1

10. Patterned boucle
95% cotton 5% elastane
Weight	medium–heavy	4
Thickness	medium	3
Shear	low	5
Drape	medium–low	4
Stretch	medium–low	4

11. Single rib (weft)
97% cotton 3% elastane
Weight	medium–heavy	4
Thickness	medium–thick	4
Shear	low	5
Drape	medium–low	4
Stretch	high	1

12. Satin faced double cloth
50% PE 47% cotton 3% elastane
Weight	medium–heavy	4
Thickness	medium	3
Shear	low	5
Drape	medium–low	4
Stretch	medium	3

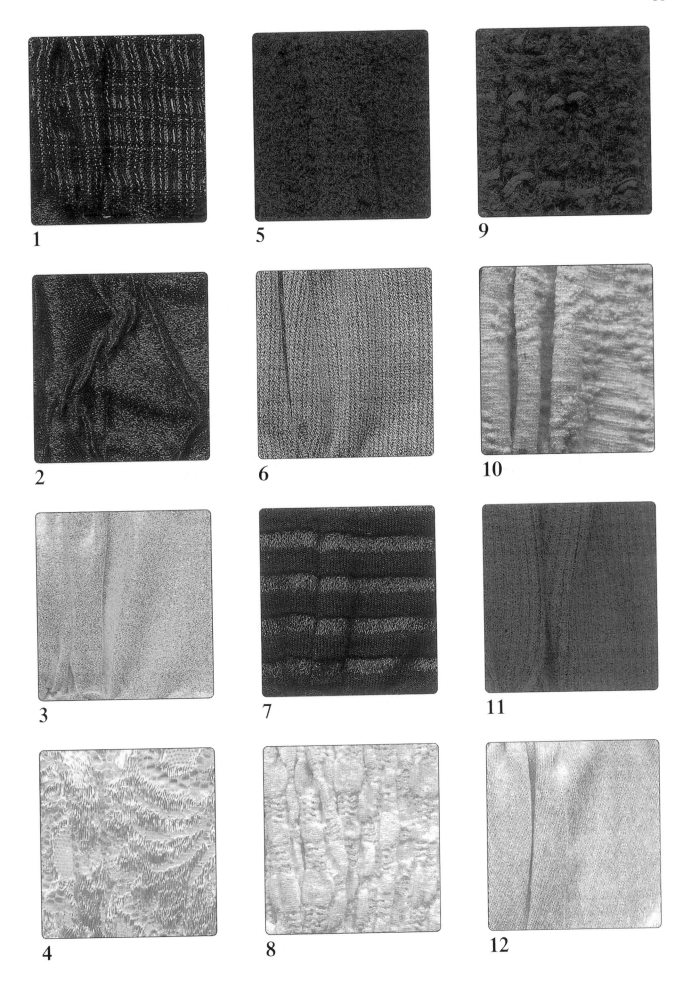

1

5

9

2

6

10

3

7

11

4

8

12

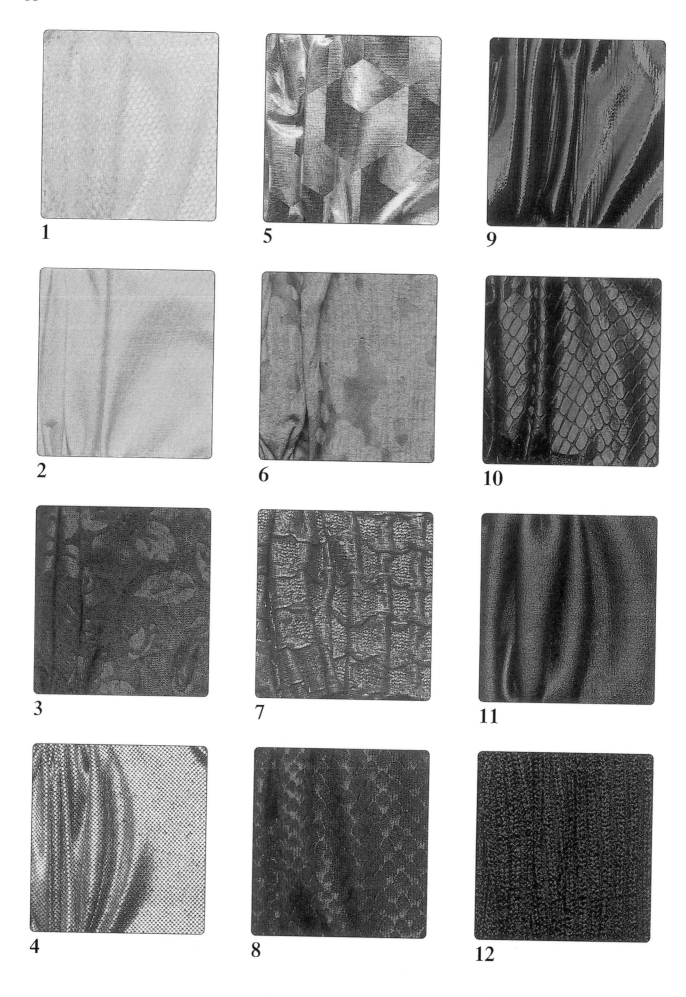

1

5

9

2

6

10

3

7

11

4

8

12

Man-made fibres/synthetic polymer: minor fibres, coatings

The fibres listed below are only a small part of garment fibre production. At present used mainly in blends and laminates, designers are exploring them for new practical and aesthetic end uses.

Polyurethene polyvinylchloride

Many coated and laminated fabrics are created by spraying or bonding plasticised coatings onto fabric backings. Most are impermeable to water and air. Originally, their main use was for waterproof garments, but as other synthetic breathable membranes have been realised, their use is increasingly for fashionable effect. Metal foils sandwiched in plastic film (Lurex) are used in many decorative fabrics.

Chlorofibres, produced from polyvinylchloride, are valued for their inertness to chemicals; their principal garment use is in thermal underwear and sportswear.

Polyethelene

Its source material is made from ethylene; the melt-spun fibres are produced in filament form. First produced in 1938, its extreme strength makes it suitable for ropes and cables. Its shiny hard surface can produce interesting surfaces in knitwear, particularly in mixtures of contrasting textures.

Polypropylene

The most common plastic, its first commercial production started in 1960. The yarn is slit from wider extruded film, most of the production is made in small companies and its bulk use is for industrial carpets and furnishing. The yarn has low elasticity, its use in garments is mainly as knitted fabric. Very durable, light and quick drying it is used mainly for high performance garments and knitted thermal

fabrics. Designers are beginning to use its aesthetic qualities for sheers and special hard shiny effects.

Polyoxamide

Polyoxamide is a new generic name given to one of the first hydrophillic man-made fibres. Its main property is the the absorbtion and transmission of moisture.

Examples of new developments

A number of new finishes are based on micro-encapsulation and nano-technology, these coatings are only 3–5 nm thick and have no effect on the drape or permeability of the fabrics. These finishes keep garments fresh by self-cleaning and deodorising. Many new applications are in development with this new technology.

The fabrics shown on the opposite page and listed below demonstrate the Fabric Characteristic Scale described on page 22. The series of five numbers after each fabric name shows their rating from 1–5 on each characteristic.

LIGHT-WEIGHT	1 ... 5	HEAVY-WEIGHT
THIN	1 ... 5	THICK
HIGH-SHEAR	1 ... 5	LOW-SHEAR
HIGH-DRAPE	1 ... 5	LOW-DRAPE
HIGH-STRETCH	1 ... 5	LOW-STRETCH

The fabrics illustrated are:
column one   light and light–medium-weights;
column two   medium-weights;
column three   medium–heavy and heavy-weights.
The codes used for some of the man-made fibres listed can be found on page 216.

1. Coated net
50% polyamide 50% polyurethene
Weight	light–medium	2
Thickness	thin	1
Shear	low	5
Drape	medium	3
Stretch	low	5

2. Hydrophillic 'PERMATEX'
50% polyester 50% polyurethene
Weight	light	1
Thickness	thin	1
Shear	low	5
Drape	low	5
Stretch	medium–low	4

3. Embossed (warp)
70% polyester 30% polyurethene
Weight	light–medium	2
Thickness	light–medium	2
Shear	low	5
Drape	high–medium	2
Stretch	medium	3

4. Metal transfer
90% polyester 10% metal
Weight	light–medium	2
Thickness	thin	1
Shear	low	5
Drape	high–medium	2
Stretch	medium–low	4

5. Coated (hologram)
68% CV 30% polyurethene 2% metal
Weight	medium	3
Thickness	thin	1
Shear	low	5
Drape	low	5
Stretch	medium–low	4

6. Coated embossed
70% polyester 30% polyurethene
Weight	medium	3
Thickness	thin	1
Shear	low	5
Drape	medium–low	4
Stretch	low	5

7. Metal transfer emboss. (warp)
75% PE 20% polyurethene 5% metal
Weight	medium	3
Thickness	medium	3
Shear	medium–low	4
Drape	medium	3
Stretch	high–medium	2

8. Flocked (weft)
80% viscose 20% polyester
Weight	medium	3
Thickness	thin–medium	2
Shear	medium–low	4
Drape	high–medium	2
Stretch	high–medium	2

9. Coated
68% polyester 32% polyurethene
Weight	medium–heavy	4
Thickness	medium	3
Shear	low	5
Drape	low	5
Stretch	medium–low	4

10. Embossed 'snakeskin'
80% polyester 20% polyamide
Weight	medium–heavy	4
Thickness	thin	1
Shear	low	5
Drape	medium	3
Stretch	medium–low	4

11. Coated (weft)
85% polyester 15% polyurethene
Weight	medium–heavy	4
Thickness	light–medium	2
Shear	low	5
Drape	low	5
Stretch	medium–low	4

12. Rib (weft)
polyethylene
Weight	medium–heavy	4
Thickness	medium	3
Shear	medium	3
Drape	high–medium	2
Stretch	high–medium	2

Man-made fibres: blends and mixtures

The blending of fibres and mixtures of yarns in man-made fabrics is common practice, many high fashion fabrics could only be achieved by the creative marrying of the fibres. Fabrics of unique appearance have been manufactured. Polyamide and polyester give strength and an underlying base to many fabrics, whilst softer and distinctive viscose and acetate fibres offer textural qualities to fabrics. The speed of sampling offered by knitting means that many of these new fabrics are knitted. Close examination of many pile fabrics is now required to determine its construction. Marrying different man-made fibres creates fabrics that use the special characteristics innate in each of the fibres.

Examples of new developments

New fibre structures and multi-filament yarns give soft handle and high-drape. Pile structures and soft filling yarns on nylon or polyester bases are creating new textures. Blending fibres is creating high fashion yarns with new textures; for example, viscose is transformed when it is spun with stainless steel, dyed metal, or is mixed with micro-fibres to create 'natural' soft yarns that are exclusive.

Fabric ranges

The fabric ranges produced in mixtures and blends can generally reproduce those fabrics available in the dominant fibre. Blending with other fibres can extend its range by improving the practical qualities and extending the aesthetic possibilities.

The fabrics shown on the opposite page and listed below demonstrate the Fabric Characteristic Scale described on page 22. The series of five numbers after each fabric name shows their rating from 1–5 on each characteristic.

LIGHT-WEIGHT	1 . . . 5	HEAVY-WEIGHT
THIN	1 . . . 5	THICK
HIGH-SHEAR	1 . . . 5	LOW-SHEAR
HIGH-DRAPE	1 . . . 5	LOW-DRAPE
HIGH-STRETCH	1 . . . 5	LOW-STRETCH

The fabrics illustrated are:
column one   light and light–medium-weights;
column two   medium-weights;
column three   medium–heavy and heavy-weights.
The codes used for some of the man-made fibres listed can be found on page 216.

1. Flocked georgette
80% viscose 20% polyester

Weight	light–medium	2
Thickness	thin/medium	1/3
Shear	medium–low	4
Drape	high–medium	2
Stretch	medium–low	4

2. Plain weave
50% acetate 50% viscose

Weight	light–medium	2
Thickness	thin	1
Shear	high–medium	2
Drape	high	1
Stretch	medium–low	4

3. Devore (warp)
90% modal 10% polyamide

Weight	light	1
Thickness	thin/thin–med	1/2
Shear	medium–low	4
Drape	high–medium	2
Stretch	high–medium	2

4. Raschel lace, cornely embroidered
80% acetate 20% polyamide

Weight	light–medium	2
Thickness	thin/med–thick	1/4
Shear	low	5
Drape	medium	3
Stretch	medium–low	4

5. Fancy yarns: spaced warp and weft
55% CA 30% PAN 20% PE

Weight	medium	3
Thickness	med/med–thick	3/4
Shear	medium	3
Drape	medium	3
Stretch	medium–low	4

6. Satin
50% acetate 50% viscose

Weight	medium	3
Thickness	medium	3
Shear	medium–low	4
Drape	medium	3
Stretch	medium–low	4

7. Rib (weft)
72% viscose 28% polyester

Weight	medium	3
Thickness	thin–medium	2
Shear	medium–low	4
Drape	high–medium	2
Stretch	medium	3

8. Plush (warp)
80% viscose 20% polyamide

Weight	medium	3
Thickness	med/med–thick	3/4
Shear	medium–low	4
Drape	high–medium	2
Stretch	medium–low	4

9. Fancy yarns: spaced warp and weft
80% viscose 20% acetate

Weight	heavy	5
Thickness	medium	3
Shear	high	1
Drape	medium	3
Stretch	medium–low	4

10. Heat-set crushed velvet
65% viscose 35% acetate

Weight	medium–heavy	4
Thickness	medium	3
Shear	medium–low	4
Drape	medium–low	4
Stretch	low	5

11. Purl (weft)
50% viscose 50% acetate

Weight	medium–heavy	4
Thickness	medium	3
Shear	high	1
Drape	high–medium	2
Stretch	medium	3

12. Brushed pile (weft)
60% viscose 40% polyester

Weight	heavy	5
Thickness	thick	5
Shear	medium–low	4
Drape	low	5
Stretch	medium	3

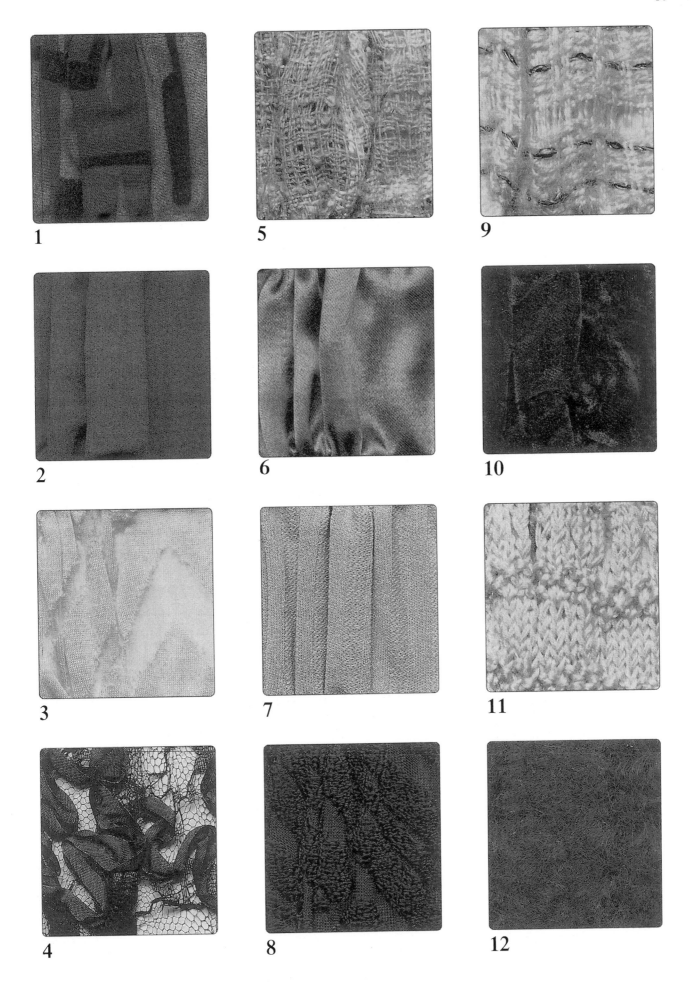

1

2

3

4

5

6

7

8

9

10

11

12

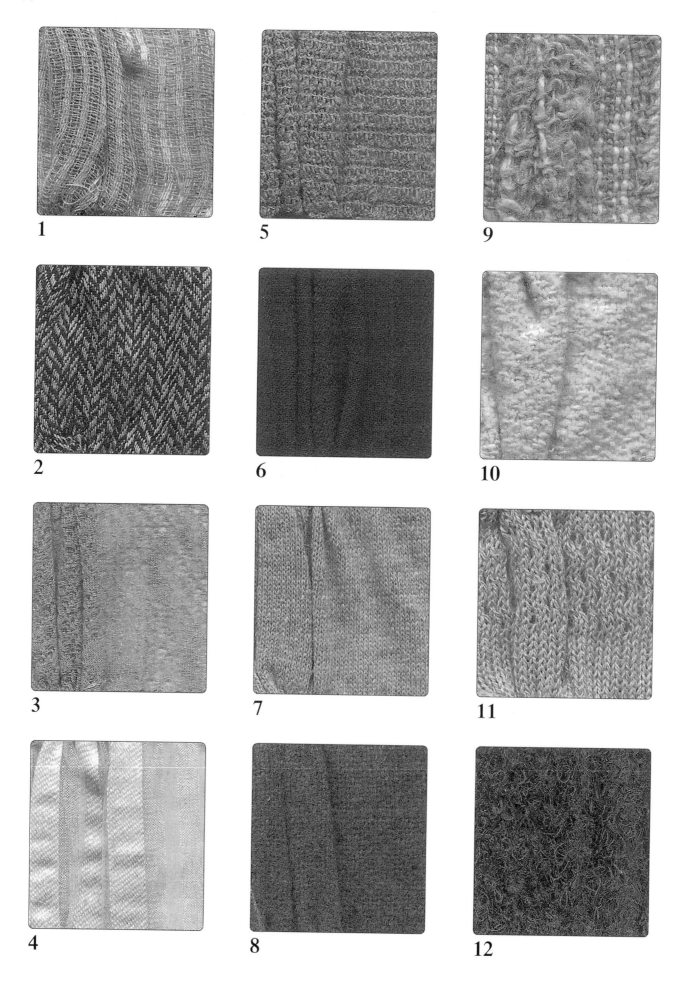

Natural/man-made fibres: blends and mixtures

In early blends the man-made fibre mainly added strength or easy-care qualities to the fabric. Consumers used to see blends as inferior products but now appreciate the range of interesting textures and effects.

1. Recycled open stripe
cotton linen viscose silk

Weight	light–medium	2
Thickness	thin/thin–med	1/2
Shear	high	1
Drape	high–medium	2
Stretch	low	5

2. Recycled satin weave
linen viscose silk

Weight	light–medium	2
Thickness	thin–medium	2
Shear	high	1
Drape	high–medium	2
Stretch	medium–low	4

3. Jacquatronic (warp)
40% modal 40% cotton 20% polyester

Weight	light	1
Thickness	thin	1
Shear	medium–low	4
Drape	medium	3
Stretch	medium	3

4. Stripe weave
90% cotton 10% polyamide

Weight	light–medium	2
Thickness	thin/medium	1/3
Shear	medium–low	4
Drape	medium	3
Stretch	low	5

5. Leno weave
78% linen 12% pa 10% cotton

Weight	medium	3
Thickness	thin–med/med	2/3
Shear	medium	3
Drape	medium	3
Stretch	medium–low	4

6. Suiting
50% cotton 50% modal

Weight	medium	3
Thickness	medium	3
Shear	medium–low	4
Drape	low	5
Stretch	medium-low	4

7. Single jersey (weft)
35% si 30% pa 20% vi 15% ang

Weight	medium	3
Thickness	medium	3
Shear	medium–low	4
Drape	high–medium	2
Stretch	high–medium	2

8. Recycled
50% polyester bottles 50% denim

Weight	medium	3
Thickness	medium–thick	4
Shear	medium	3
Drape	medium	3
Stretch	medium–low	4

9. Washed finish
50% cotton 50% linen

Weight	medium–heavy	4
Thickness	medium–thick	4
Shear	medium–low	4
Drape	medium	3
Stretch	high–medium	2

10. Recycled
polyester cotton polyamide

Weight	heavy	5
Thickness	med/med–thick	3/4
Shear	medium–low	4
Drape	medium–low	4
Stretch	medium–low	4

11. Racked tuck (weft)
60% modal 40% linen

Weight	medium–heavy	4
Thickness	med/med–thick	3/4
Shear	medium	3
Drape	medium	3
Stretch	medium	3

12. Looped (weft)
50% wool 50% viscose

Weight	heavy	5
Thickness	med/med–thick	3/4
Shear	medium–low	4
Drape	medium–low	4
Stretch	high–medium	2

---

1. Twill
55% wool 45% polyester

Weight	light–medium	2
Thickness	thin	1
Shear	high	1
Drape	high–medium	2
Stretch	medium–low	4

2. Shirting
50% polyester 50% cotton

Weight	light–medium	2
Thickness	thin	1
Shear	medium	3
Drape	medium	3
Stretch	medium–low	4

3. (Warp)
50% wool 50% polyester

Weight	light–medium	2
Thickness	medium	3
Shear	medium–low	4
Drape	high–medium	2
Stretch	high–medium	2

4. Stripe blister weave
55% cotton 25% linen 20% viscose

Weight	light–medium	2
Thickness	thin/thin–med	1/2
Shear	medium	3
Drape	medium–low	4
Stretch	medium	3

5. Novelty couture tweed
39% co 29% pa 24% vi 8% wo

Weight	medium	3
Thickness	med/med–thick	3/4
Shear	high	1
Drape	high–medium	2
Stretch	medium–low	4

6. Herringbone suiting
53% wool 47% polyester

Weight	medium	3
Thickness	thin–medium	2
Shear	medium–low	4
Drape	medium	3
Stretch	low	5

7. Rib (weft)
50% cotton 37% mohair 13% viscose

Weight	medium	3
Thickness	medium	3
Shear	high–medium	2
Drape	high–medium	2
Stretch	high	1

8. Brushed lappet weave
80% cotton 20% viscose

Weight	medium	3
Thickness	thin–med/med–thk	2/4
Shear	medium	3
Drape	low	5
Stretch	medium–low	4

9. Recycled tweed
cotton acrylic silk wool

Weight	medium–heavy	4
Thickness	medium	3
Shear	medium	3
Drape	medium	3
Stretch	medium–low	4

10. Astrakhan
50% cotton 50% viscose

Weight	medium–heavy	4
Thickness	med–thick/thick	4/5
Shear	low	5
Drape	low	5
Stretch	low	5

11. Rib (weft)
60% wool 40% polyamide

Weight	heavy	5
Thickness	medium–thick	4
Shear	medium–low	4
Drape	medium	3
Stretch	high–medium	2

12. Double cloth
90% wool 16% polyamide

Weight	medium–heavy	4
Thickness	thin/medium	1/3
Shear	medium–low	4
Drape	low	5
Stretch	medium–low	4

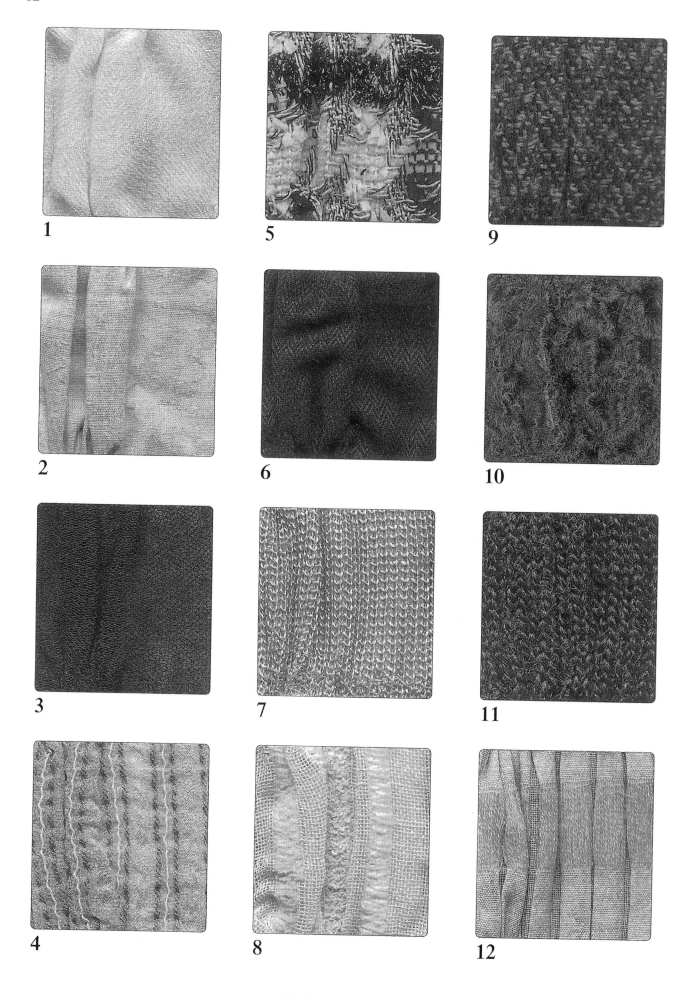

PART TWO: FABRIC AND FORM

4 Fabrics and garment forms

Garment shapes

Most garment shapes created through flat pattern cutting are based on simple shapes that are achieved by simple techniques. More complex shapes can be achieved by combining techniques and inserting the shapes at different points around the body. Appreciation of the shape of the body and its movement is crucial at this point.

Flat pattern cutting techniques can also be used to change the cylindrical forms that are provided by the block shapes.

This chapter considers the covering of the body in simple forms:

(1) using a cylinder of fabric wrapped around the body and suspended from the shoulders (a basic bodice block);
(2) hanging very basic shapes from the cylinder;
(3) creating more complex shapes and combining techniques;
(4) changing the cylindrical shape;
(5) creating overlays;
(6) wrapping and tying fabric shapes;
(7) pleating fabric shapes.

When using any methods, the overriding consideration must be the effect produced by the fabric and its realisation of any creative idea.

Basic information

(1) There are no seam allowances on the blocks or adaptations.
(2) Light thin lines are used to show original block shapes and dotted lines used where there may be confusion or lines are close together.
(3) Heavy lines are used for completed pattern shapes.
(4) Further specific information on adapting from blocks to patterns is available in *Metric Pattern Cutting*.
(5) The definite instructions that are included in the book are to help students understand a sequence of working. Many students learn techniques or principles in isolation; the examples of practice are there to help them to develop their own procedures.

Fabrics and the body structure

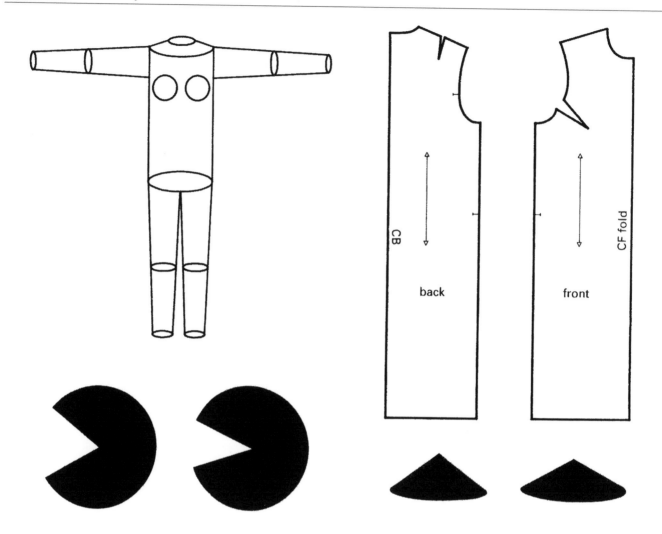

Look at the body shape of humans simply. In the diagram above you see a simple cylinder (the trunk) with other moving cylinders (the limbs) attached. Historically, very simple but effective garments were cut that only took account of these shapes. Of course, the body is far more complicated than this and as you move closer to fit the body all kinds of body shape interference take place. Male, female and children's body shapes are all different; curves and eruptions occur in different places and on a different scale. Because the bust is the most extreme example, a female dress stand is used for demonstrating 3D shapes. Blocks are simple cylindrical basic body shapes, developed by pattern cutters, for different parts of the body. They can be used as initial shapes for design development.

(1) If a fabric has good stretch characteristics, a knitwear block (ref. 1 page 137) without darts can be used **(1)**. The fabric will accommodate the bust and shoulder curves and hang as a vertical cylinder.

(2) Rigid fabrics with little movement will not do this; drag lines appear **(2)**. Therefore 'darting' has to be used. Cut a section (dart) out of a circle and join the lines. The centre of the circle will rise: the greater the section the higher the rise. A dart in a body block has the same effect. The closer the fit the larger the dart has to be. A dart can be 'swung' to other positions (page 196). The bust dart is moved to the armhole for these examples.

(3) The aim is the perfect vertical 'hang' **(3)**. The side seam should be vertical on a balanced shape. The block used for the examples was the Close Fitting Bodice Block (ref. page 202, size 10); it has a back shoulder dart and wide bust dart.

Different fabrics
If, like the example block, a garment pattern shape is close fitting and is used with a fabric with high-shear and without natural stretch and recovery **(4)**, it will easily distort, strain and crease. However quite small amounts of resilience in a fabric allow this narrow shape to work **(5)**.

Very basic geometric forms
The following pages show that almost any geometric shape can be hung onto a firm cylindrical body shape at any point below the bust shaping without it affecting the 'hang'.

Fabrics used in the illustrations

			We	Th	Sh	Dr	St
1	Acrylic	rib weft-knit	3	3	4	2	3
2, 3	Polyester	woven	3	2	4	4	5
4	Silk/linen/ cotton/viscose	woven	3	1/2	1	2	5
5	Polyester (micro-fibre)	woven	2	2	2	1	5

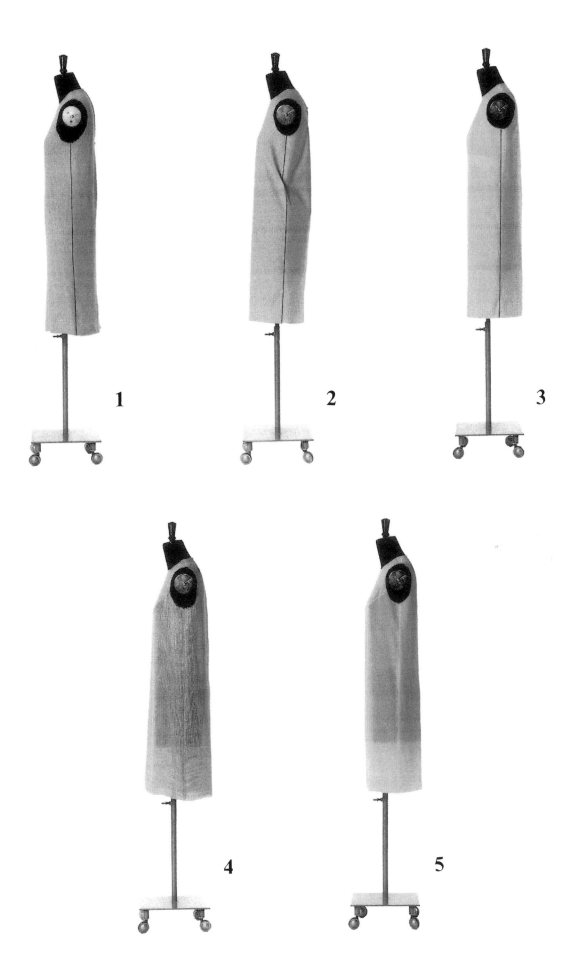

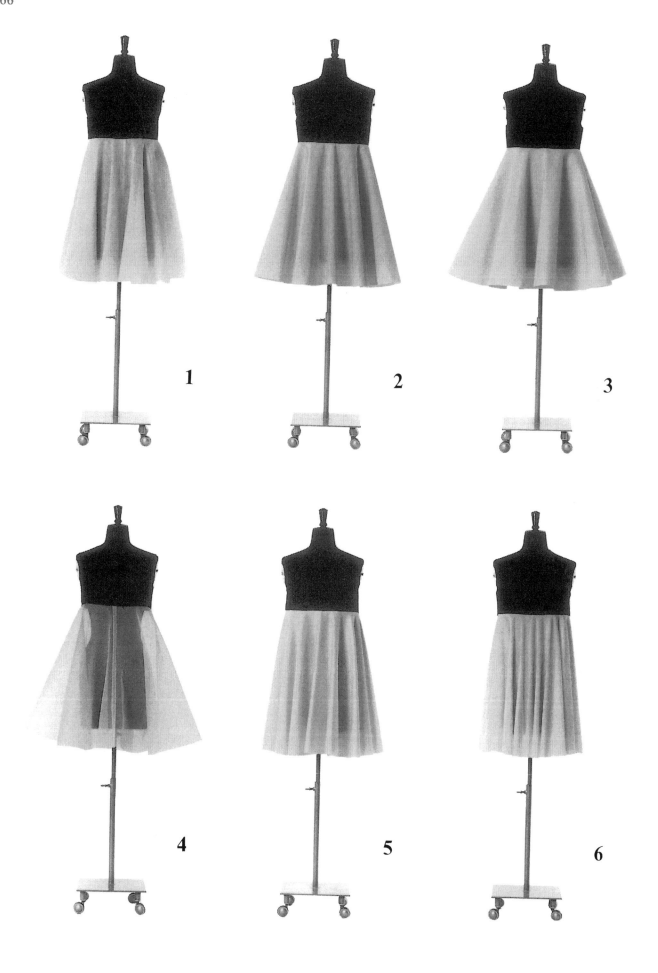

Simple shapes: the circle

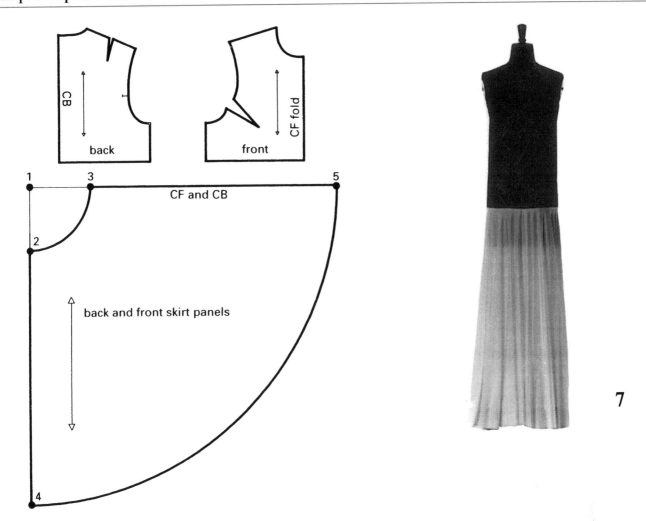

The circle, multi-circles or sections of a circle (e.g. half or quarter circles) can be attached to a simple body shape, be integrated into a garment pattern shape, or be attached to a band or yoke to form a skirt.

This page deals with a circle (length 60 cm) attached to a basic cylindrical body shape (size 10) just below the bust shaping. The measurement of the bodice lower edge is 92 cm.

Constructing a circle

Calculate the radius: divide measurement required by 6.28.
Example: 92 cm (lower edge measurement) divided by 6.28 = 14.968 (round up to 15 cm).
To create a quarter circle section:
Square both ways from 1
1–2 = the radius (e.g. 15 cm) 1–3 = the radius
Draw a quarter circle from 2–3.
2–4 = the length (e.g. 60 cm) 3–5 = the length.
With a metre stick mark out the lower edge of the circle.

Attaching the curved shape to the straight line of the body shape forces the hemline into flutes.

Page 21 demonstrates the importance of recognising that the smaller the inner circle (e.g. if used for a sleeve), the wider the angle of the finished shape created, and there is reduction in the number of flutes. These also change in relation to length: for example, extra length adds extra fabric weight, extra weight narrows the angle and increases the flutes. Other fabric characteristics play a part; fibre and fabric structure and surface finish will

contribute to the final drape and predictions are not always easy to make.

Toile fabrics

Most students use calico of various weights for creating toiles. Calico is cheap and the fabric structure is fairly stable. However, because unbleached calico is usually unfinished, its draping qualities are low and its relationship to many fabrics is tenuous. If the difference in handle is very apparent, alternative cheap fabrics with similar draping qualities should be sought. Calico should never be used to represent knitted fabrics.

NOTE The photographs **(1)**, **(2)** and **(3)** show how light-weight, medium-weight and heavy-weight calico circles look at a 60 cm length. Students should make visual comparisons with other fabrics cut in the same dimensions in photographs **(4)**, **(5)** and **(6)**. Also, compare **(6)** with the longer shape of **(7)**.

Fabrics used in the illustrations

			We	Th	Sh	Dr	St
1	Light-weight calico	woven	1	1	4	4	4
2	Medium-weight calico	woven	2	2	4	4	5
3	Heavy-weight calico	woven	3	2	5	5	5
4	Cotton organdy	woven	1	1	2	4	4
5	Wool	woven	3	2	3	3	4
6, 7	Polyamide (TACTEL)	warp-knit	1	2	5	1	2

Simple shapes: the bell and the balloon

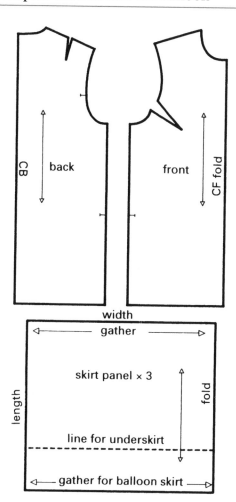

7

Straight lengths of gathered fabric can be attached to a simple body shape, be integrated into any part of a garment pattern or be attached to a band or yoke to form a skirt.

Gathering the length along the top edge creates a bell, gathering along both edges creates a balloon. This page demonstrates the two shapes attached to a basic body shape (size 10) just below below the hipline. The measurement of the bodice lower edge is 92 cm.

The bell
It is usual to cut the length running down the warp because it is usually the strongest yarn. This means that the rectangle has to be cut in sections depending on the width of the cloth.
Main Skirt Sections (example 3 panels); construct a rectangle:
Length = length required.
Width = width of back and front bodice (e.g. 46 cm each).
A single rectangle may be cut with the width running down the warp; this depends on the patterning or structure of the cloth.

NOTE The photographs opposite show the effects of cutting bell shapes of the same dimensions (3× width) in different fabrics. Notice how the amount of fabric that looks acceptable for the polyamide warp-knit **(1)**, has reached the

limit (thickness) in the polyester suiting **(2)** and looks scant in the organdy **(3)**.

The balloon
Main Skirt Sections cut the skirt pattern using the above instructions for the bell.
Underskirt construct a rectangle:
Length = length of main skirt minus 10 cm or required amount.
Width = measurement of lower edge of body section (92 cm).

NOTE The photographs opposite show the effects of cutting balloon shapes in different fabrics and underskirt lengths. Notice the totally different images that are created.

Fabrics used in the illustrations

			We	Th	Sh	Dr	St
1,7	Polyamide (TACTEL)	warp-knit	1	2	5	1	2
2	Polyester suiting	woven	3	3	5	4	5
3	Cotton organdy	woven	1	1	2	4	4
4	Polyamide (TACTEL)	warp-knit	1	2	5	1	2
5	Acetate/cotton	woven/ embroid.	3	2/3	4	4	4–5
6	Wool/mohair	woven	3	4	2	4	4

1

2

3

4

5

6

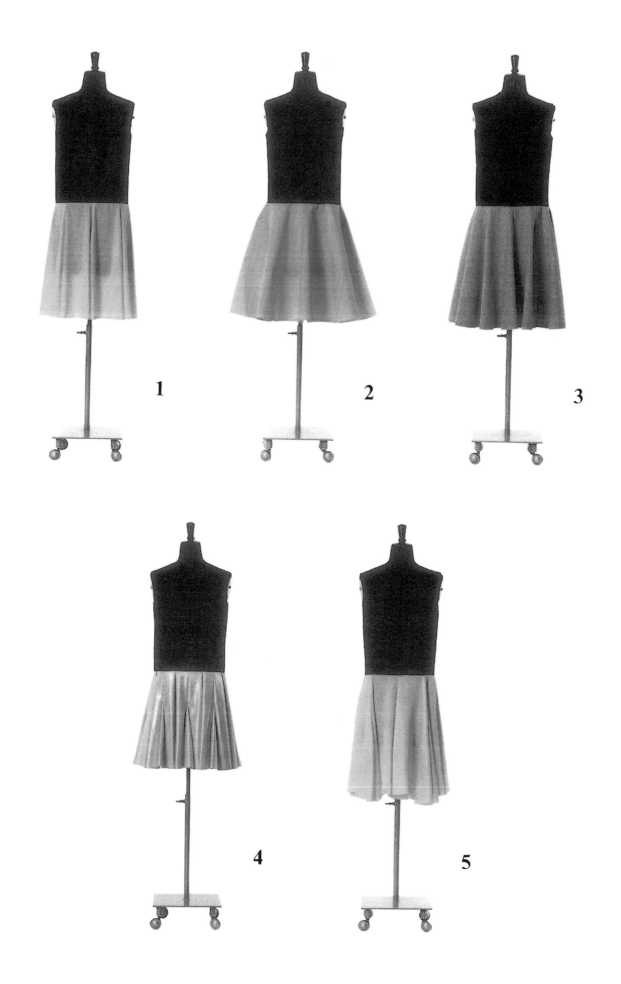

Simple shapes: the triangle

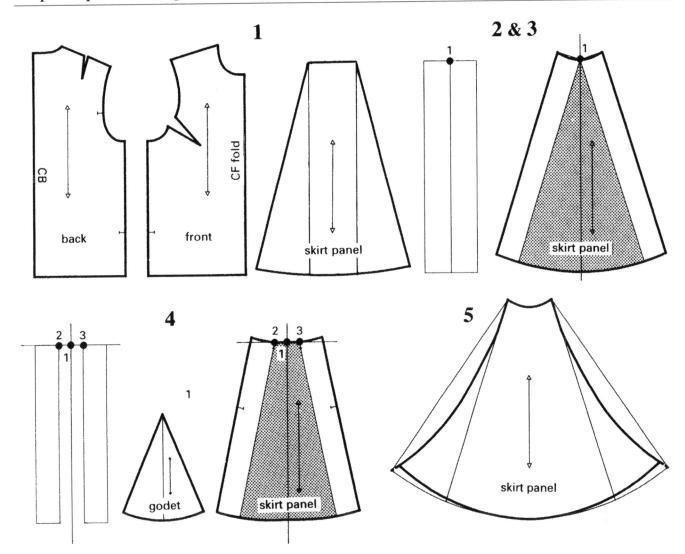

1

2 & 3

4

5

skirt panel

godet

skirt panel

skirt panel

skirt panel

back

front

CB

CF fold

Simple triangular shapes can create a variety of designs.
This page demonstrates the groups of triangles attached to
a basic body shape (size 10) just below the waistline. The
measurement of the lower edge of the bodice is 92 cm.

1   A simple triangle.
Skirt Sections decide the number of gores (e.g. 8).
Construct a rectangle:
Length = the required length.
Width = the measurement of the bodice divided by 8.
Add the required amount of flare to the hem.
Make the diagonal line the same length as the vertical line.
Join lower edge with a curve.

2 and 3   'Cut and spread' shapes (basic method of flare).
Skirt Sections construct a rectangle (ref. 1).
Divide into two equal sections. Cut out the pattern and cut
almost to the top of the centre line at 1.
Lay the pattern piece on the paper.
Open out the slit the required amount equally each side of
the vertical line (e.g. 10 cm).
Draw in new waistline and hemlines with curves.

4   Tucks and godets can change the shapes.
Skirt Sections construct a rectangle (ref. 1).
Cut out and divide into two equal sections.
On a separate piece of paper draw a vertical line with a
horizontal line at the top, mark point 1.

Mark 2 and 3 (positions of the tucks, e.g. 4 cm)
Lay the pattern pieces on the paper at points 2 and 3,
swing out the required amount each side of the vertical
line.
Draw in new waistline and hemlines with curves.
Fold tucks into position before cutting out the waistline.
Triangular godets can be inserted in seams.

5   Extra shaped side flare can be added.
Skirt Sections construct a cut and spread triangle (ref. 2)
but extend the width of the flare (e.g. 15 cm), and draw the
panel line in a curve.

NOTE   The photographs opposite show the effects of
cutting the pattern shapes in different fabrics. Notice how
the skirt hemline will drop in soft fabrics **(5)**. This has to be
remedied by reducing the length of the curve.

Fabrics used in the illustrations

			We	Th	Sh	Dr	St
1	Cotton jersey	weft-knit	2	1	3	2	3
2	Medium-weight calico	woven	2	2	4	4	5
3	Hemp/cotton/wool	woven	3	4	1	4	4
4	Acetate and lurex	woven	2	2	4	3	5
5	Silk (sandwashed)	woven	2	1	3	1	4

Complex 'cut and spread'

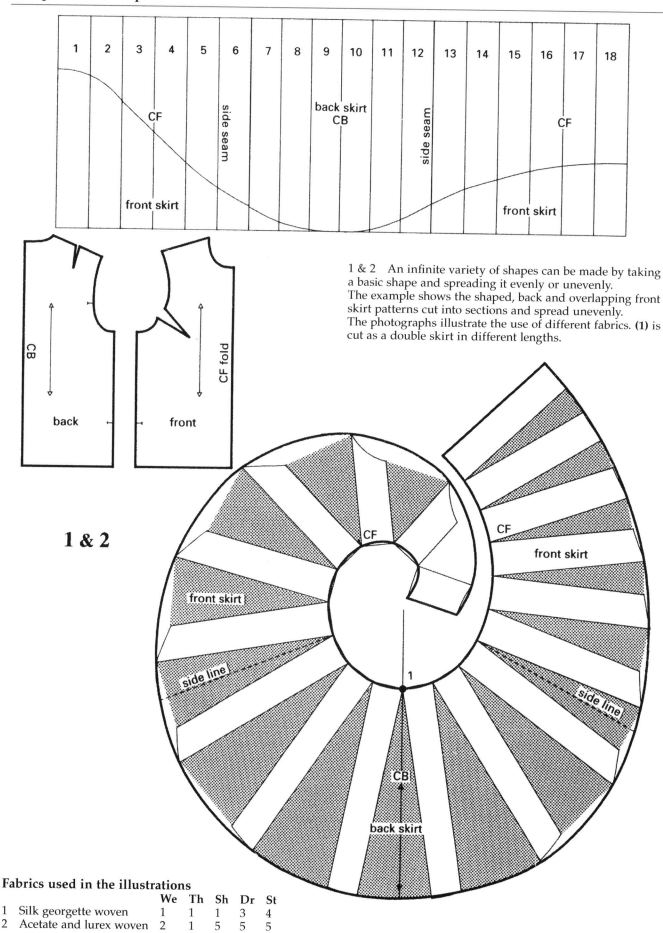

1 & 2 An infinite variety of shapes can be made by taking a basic shape and spreading it evenly or unevenly.
The example shows the shaped, back and overlapping front skirt patterns cut into sections and spread unevenly.
The photographs illustrate the use of different fabrics. (1) is cut as a double skirt in different lengths.

1 & 2

Fabrics used in the illustrations

		We	Th	Sh	Dr	St
1	Silk georgette woven	1	1	1	3	4
2	Acetate and lurex woven	2	1	5	5	5

1

2

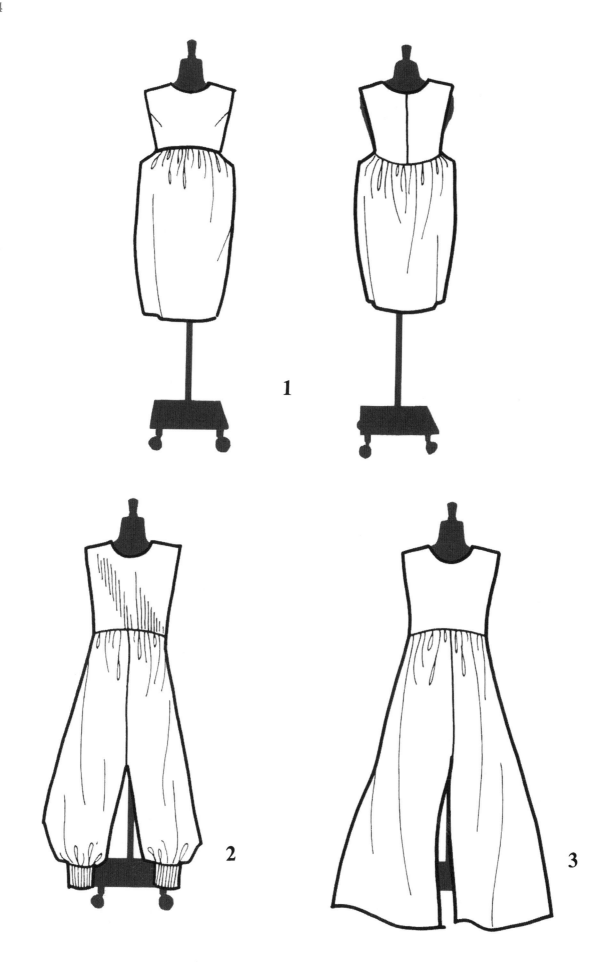

1

2

3

Combining techniques and block shapes

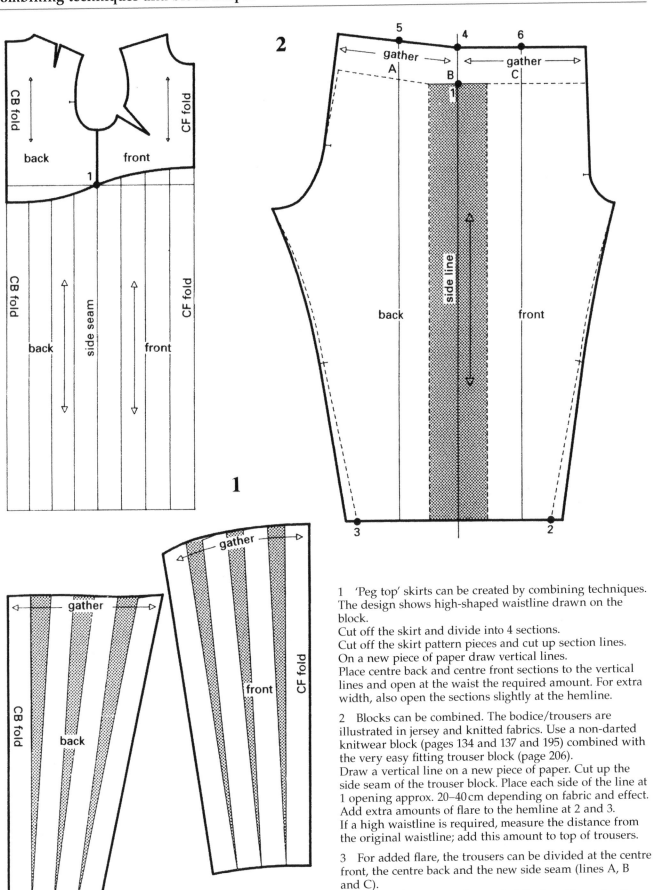

2

1

1 'Peg top' skirts can be created by combining techniques. The design shows high-shaped waistline drawn on the block.
Cut off the skirt and divide into 4 sections.
Cut off the skirt pattern pieces and cut up section lines.
On a new piece of paper draw vertical lines.
Place centre back and centre front sections to the vertical lines and open at the waist the required amount. For extra width, also open the sections slightly at the hemline.

2 Blocks can be combined. The bodice/trousers are illustrated in jersey and knitted fabrics. Use a non-darted knitwear block (pages 134 and 137 and 195) combined with the very easy fitting trouser block (page 206).
Draw a vertical line on a new piece of paper. Cut up the side seam of the trouser block. Place each side of the line at 1 opening approx. 20–40 cm depending on fabric and effect. Add extra amounts of flare to the hemline at 2 and 3.
If a high waistline is required, measure the distance from the original waistline; add this amount to top of trousers.

3 For added flare, the trousers can be divided at the centre front, the centre back and the new side seam (lines A, B and C).
Cut up the lines, cut and spread at the hem lines pivoting from points 4, 5 and 6.

Overlays

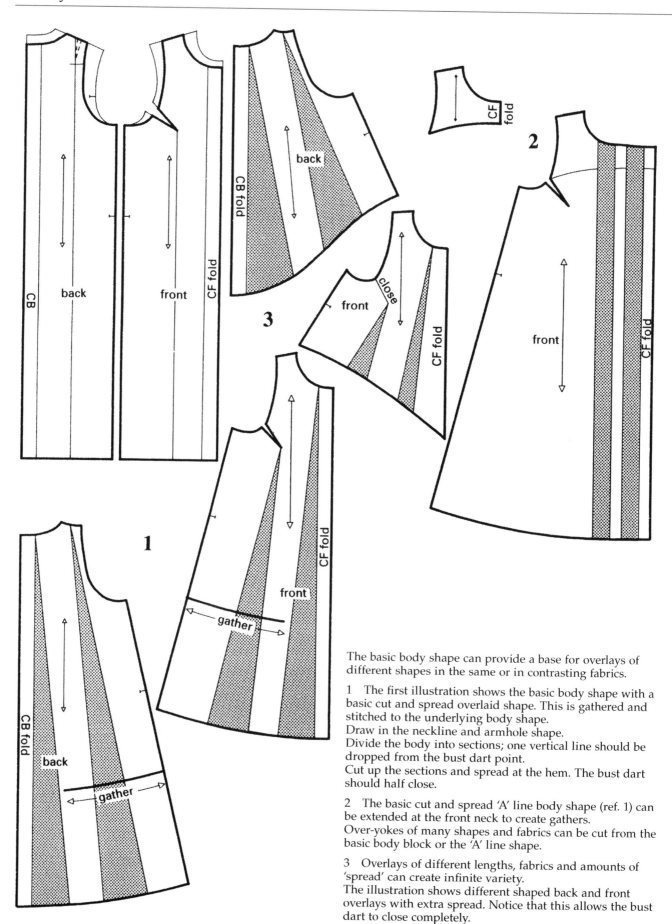

The basic body shape can provide a base for overlays of different shapes in the same or in contrasting fabrics.

1　The first illustration shows the basic body shape with a basic cut and spread overlaid shape. This is gathered and stitched to the underlying body shape.
Draw in the neckline and armhole shape.
Divide the body into sections; one vertical line should be dropped from the bust dart point.
Cut up the sections and spread at the hem. The bust dart should half close.

2　The basic cut and spread 'A' line body shape (ref. 1) can be extended at the front neck to create gathers.
Over-yokes of many shapes and fabrics can be cut from the basic body block or the 'A' line shape.

3　Overlays of different lengths, fabrics and amounts of 'spread' can create infinite variety.
The illustration shows different shaped back and front overlays with extra spread. Notice that this allows the bust dart to close completely.

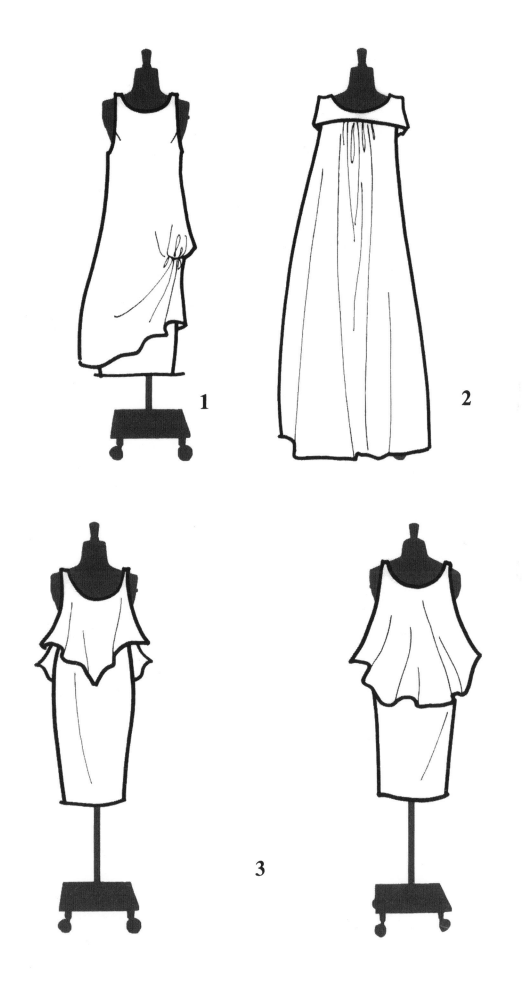

1

2

3

1

2

Simple wraps and ties 1

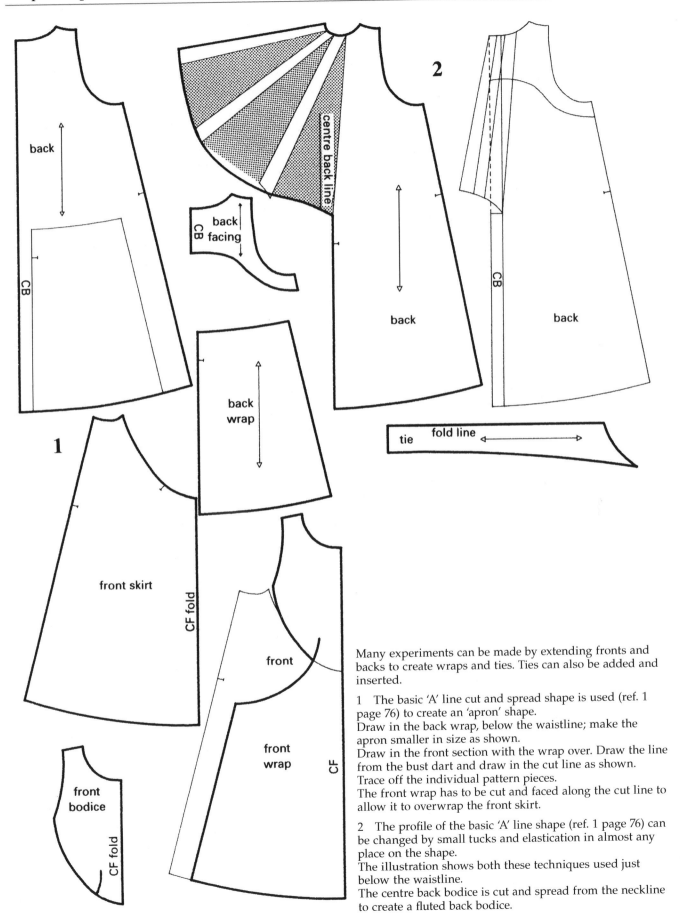

Many experiments can be made by extending fronts and backs to create wraps and ties. Ties can also be added and inserted.

1 The basic 'A' line cut and spread shape is used (ref. 1 page 76) to create an 'apron' shape.
Draw in the back wrap, below the waistline; make the apron smaller in size as shown.
Draw in the front section with the wrap over. Draw the line from the bust dart and draw in the cut line as shown.
Trace off the individual pattern pieces.
The front wrap has to be cut and faced along the cut line to allow it to overwrap the front skirt.

2 The profile of the basic 'A' line shape (ref. 1 page 76) can be changed by small tucks and elastication in almost any place on the shape.
The illustration shows both these techniques used just below the waistline.
The centre back bodice is cut and spread from the neckline to create a fluted back bodice.

Simple wraps and ties 2

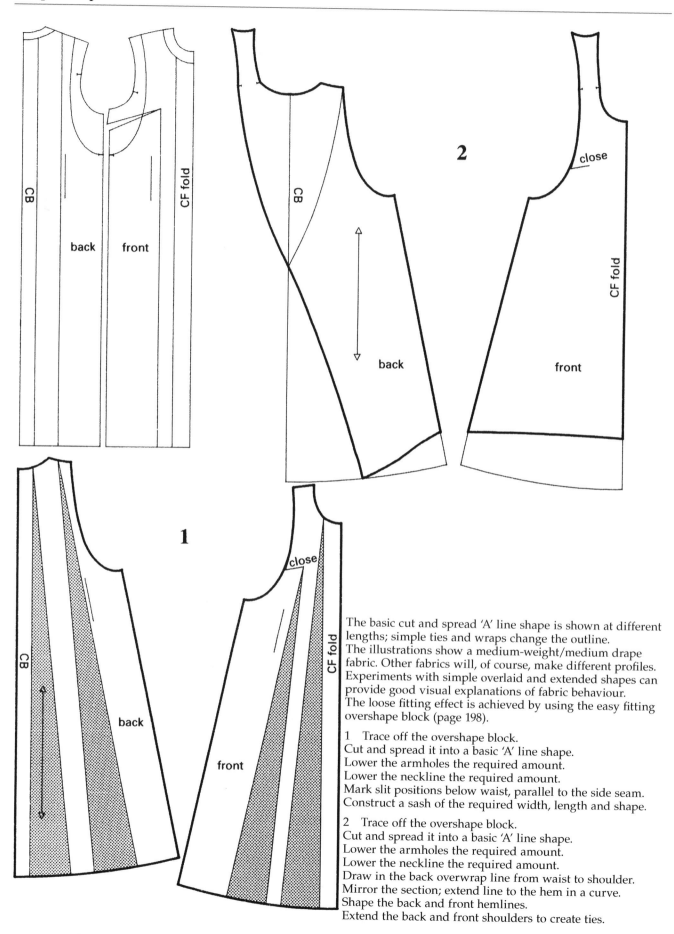

The basic cut and spread 'A' line shape is shown at different lengths; simple ties and wraps change the outline.

The illustrations show a medium-weight/medium drape fabric. Other fabrics will, of course, make different profiles. Experiments with simple overlaid and extended shapes can provide good visual explanations of fabric behaviour.

The loose fitting effect is achieved by using the easy fitting overshape block (page 198).

1   Trace off the overshape block.
Cut and spread it into a basic 'A' line shape.
Lower the armholes the required amount.
Lower the neckline the required amount.
Mark slit positions below waist, parallel to the side seam.
Construct a sash of the required width, length and shape.

2   Trace off the overshape block.
Cut and spread it into a basic 'A' line shape.
Lower the armholes the required amount.
Lower the neckline the required amount.
Draw in the back overwrap line from waist to shoulder.
Mirror the section; extend line to the hem in a curve.
Shape the back and front hemlines.
Extend the back and front shoulders to create ties.

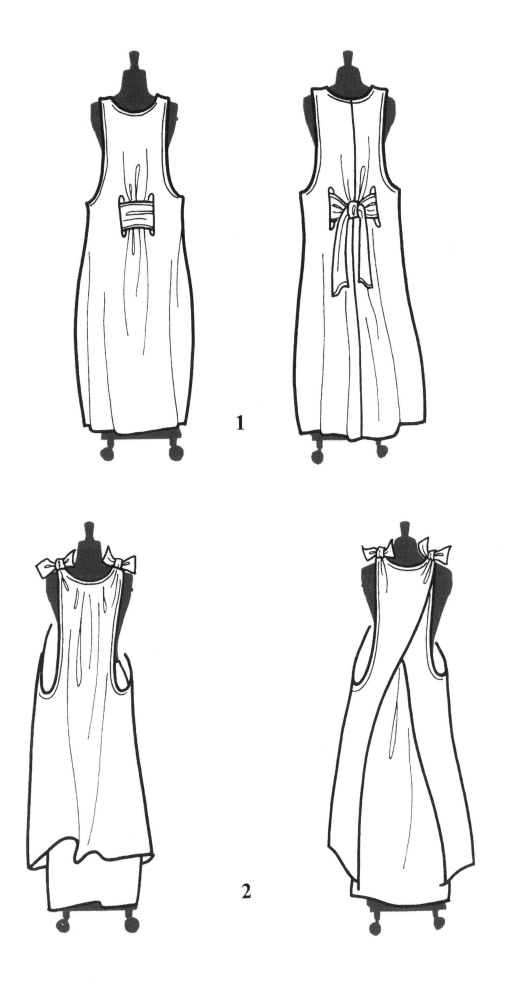

1

2

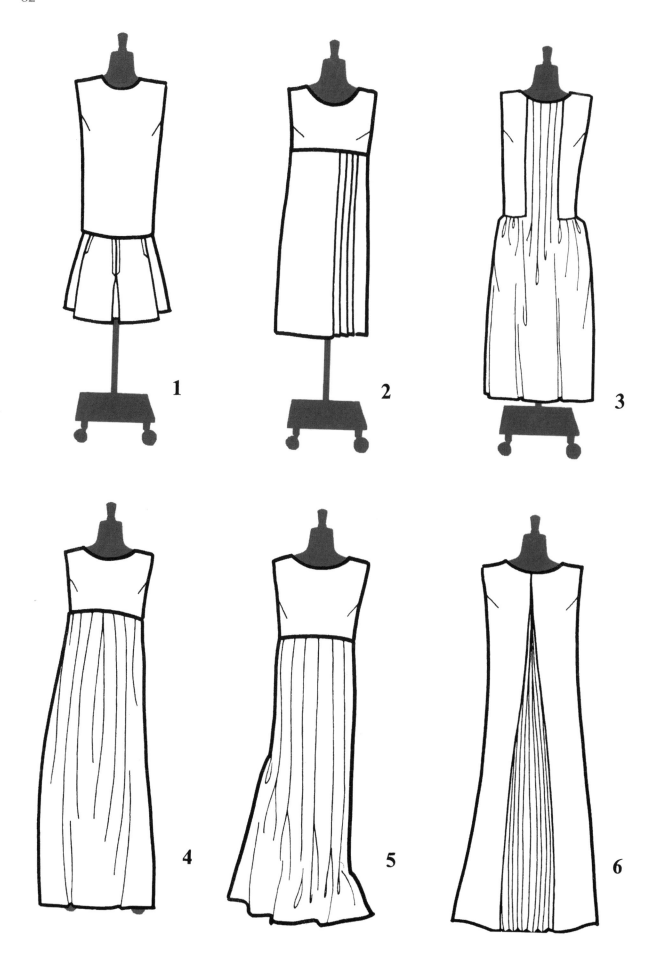

1

2

3

4

5

6

Pleats

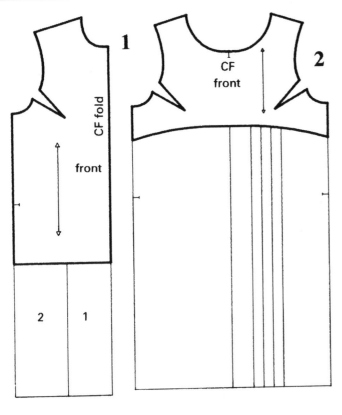

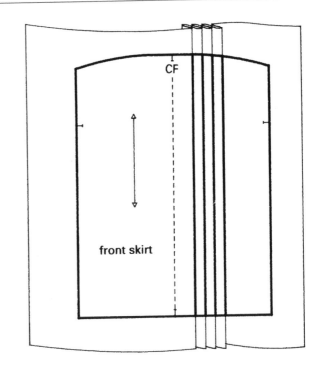

There are two basic ways of drafting pleats:
(1) Direct measurement of straight lengths of fabric;
(2) Integrating pleats into a garment shape.
NOTE For making waist shaping in classic pleated tailored skirts, see the skirt section of *Metric Pattern Cutting*.

1 Example of direct measurement **(1)**:
Draw a vertical line the length of the skirt.
Square out from the top and bottom.
Draw two vertical lines the width of the centre pleat.
Measure the width of skirt section 1.
Mark the width of the skirt section 1 and square down.
Draw two vertical lines the width of the side pleat.
Measure the width of skirt section 2.
Mark the width of skirt section 2 and square down.

2 Example of integrating pleats into a shaped pattern **(2)**:
Draw in the shaping required on the body block.
Mark pleat positions.
On a new piece of paper mark out pleats as described above.
Fold pleats carefully. Lay the pattern on top of the paper, matching pleat positions. Trace around the pattern. Cut out.

3 Example of combining techniques **(3)**:
Draw in the style lines and pleat lines on the block.
Trace off the side panel.
Extend the skirt the amount required for gathers.
Use technique 2 to complete the pleats on the front.

4 An illustration of drapeable fabric and unpressed pleats **(4)**.

5 An illustration of the change of outline achieved by stitching unpressed pleats at varying lengths **(5)**. Ballooning, horizontal stitching and twisting can give bizarre effects.

6 Inserting accordian pleats **(6)** gives interest and movement.

Tonal effects on shapes

It is important to take into account the visual effects of tonal density on shape. The illustrations show how a basic circular opaque fabric shape appears to change its width in black or white fabric or against a different background. This is a simple illustration of the effects of extreme tonal values and context, but students must be aware that the added complexities of translucence, texture, colour and patterning have to be taken into account when creating even the most simple basic shapes.

PART TWO: FABRIC AND FORM

5 Enveloping the body shape

Geometric shapes

If you think of a large envelope (without a flap), cut some holes in the top and the side, make it of a soft fabric and you have a covering for the body. Many beautiful flat garments can be seen in costume museums that are only small modifications of this shape. Simple shapes are often the most affinitive for complex decorative fabrics and embroidery. They also provide the base for most of the garments made from knitted fabric. However, the basic flat grid shapes can be developed into very complex and 3D shaped garments. This is not a body fitting look, although garments may fit closely to the body in places. The basic flat draft is useful for exploring new elements of shape that complement rather than being *driven* by the body shape.

Some of the shapes in this chapter are greatly influenced by historical examples; Tilke's book on historical costume is a good standard reference work. It shows geometric shapes ingeniously inserted or added to seam lines and it is prolific with simple ideas that could be developed into garment ranges.

If non-stretch fabrics are used and if any limbs are enveloped, the flat fabric envelope has to be large enough to allow for movement; this factor particularly affects trousers. Patterns developed from geometric shapes have to provide gussets or increased fabric in the most stressed areas of the garment. The envelope shape can be comfortable, if it is large enough, if the fabric will stretch enough, or if gussets allow for movement.

This chapter starts with flat envelope shapes and demonstrates the use of the basic techniques described in Chapter 4 to create different outlines. It introduces the use of gusseting to create a box-like 3D shape and more subtle underarm gusseting for arm movement. The chapter also shows how by using the basic grid shapes a move can be made towards the look of the body fitting blocks by hidden gusseting and discusses the classic garment shapes (the shaped kimono block and the shirt block) that straddle the divide between flat and 3D body shapes.

The basic grid

The basic grid shape, used for most of the garments shown in this chapter, is constructed wider than the body; it has no bust darts and the back and front are the same shape except for the neckline.

The basic grid: flat shapes

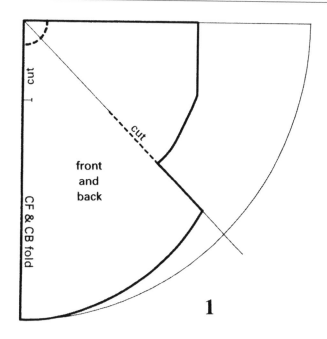

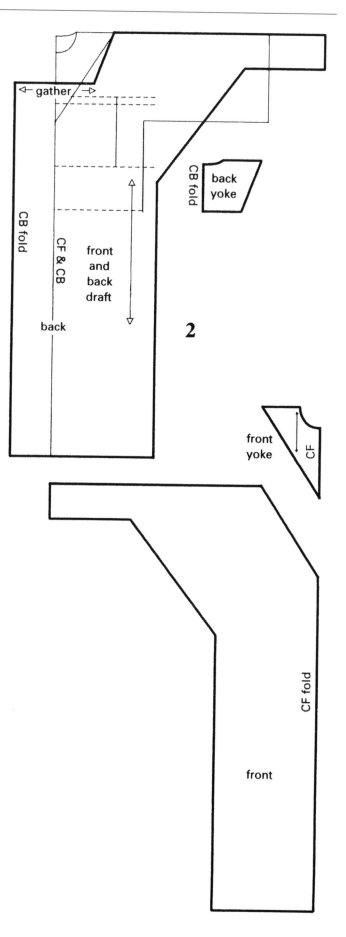

Basic geometric shapes, constructed independently or developed from the basic gridshapes (page 189), are used widely in their simplest form for loosely-woven fabrics, fabrics with high-shear or drape; the shapes are particularly used for knitted fabrics.

1 Circular shapes

The image shows the garment cut in one piece; however, this requires two-way fabric and an extravagant use of fabric.

Body Sections   construct a quarter circle of the required length.

Bisect the circle.

Draw in front neckline.

Draw in the hemline at the length required.

Draw in the sleeve length.

Draw in the sleeve hemline, shape it upwards towards the underarm to prevent 'drag'.

Mark the underarm slit (this can be widened and shaped).

2 Geometric shaping: the basic grid

The image demonstrates that rectangular shapes hang beautifully if the correct fabric is chosen. The shape is loose and held in position by the yoke and tight lower sleeves.

Body Sections   trace off the basic grid; widen the body sections at the side seam.

Lengthen the body the amount required.

Extend the sleeves and draw a rectangle at the base.

Join the sleeve rectangle to a point below the waist.

Draw in any style lines (e.g. yoke lines).

Trace off all pattern sections.

Extend the yoke line on the back to create gathers.

Fabrics used in the illustrations

			We	Th	Sh	Dr	St
1	Silk/cotton	woven	4	3	1	3	4
2	Silk/cotton/linen/ viscose	woven	2	1/2	1	2	5

1

2

The basic grid: simple 3D shapes

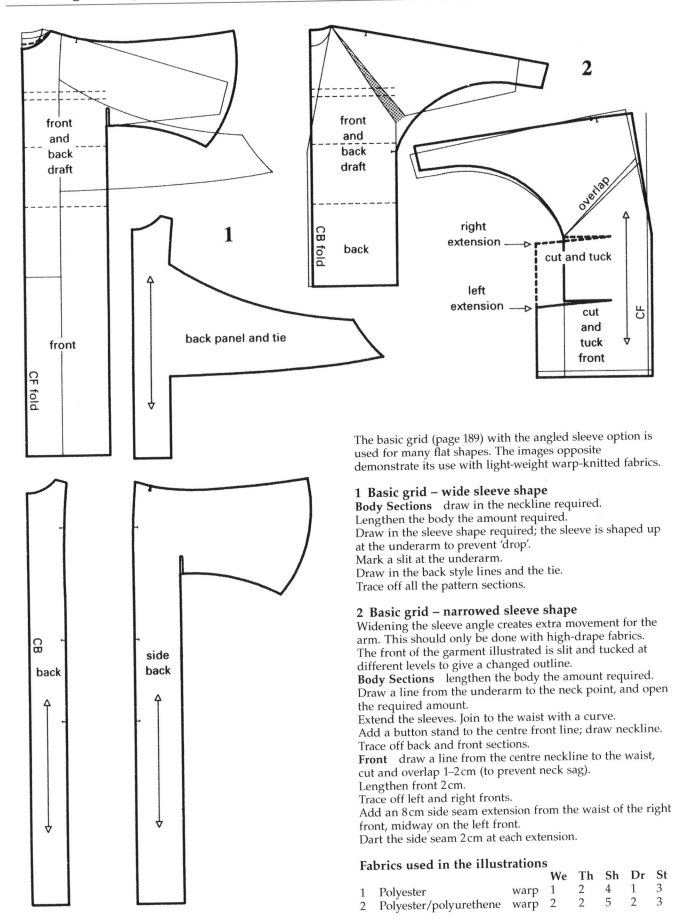

The basic grid (page 189) with the angled sleeve option is used for many flat shapes. The images opposite demonstrate its use with light-weight warp-knitted fabrics.

1 Basic grid – wide sleeve shape
Body Sections   draw in the neckline required.
Lengthen the body the amount required.
Draw in the sleeve shape required; the sleeve is shaped up at the underarm to prevent 'drop'.
Mark a slit at the underarm.
Draw in the back style lines and the tie.
Trace off all the pattern sections.

2 Basic grid – narrowed sleeve shape
Widening the sleeve angle creates extra movement for the arm. This should only be done with high-drape fabrics.
The front of the garment illustrated is slit and tucked at different levels to give a changed outline.
Body Sections   lengthen the body the amount required.
Draw a line from the underarm to the neck point, and open the required amount.
Extend the sleeves. Join to the waist with a curve.
Add a button stand to the centre front line; draw neckline.
Trace off back and front sections.
Front   draw a line from the centre neckline to the waist, cut and overlap 1–2 cm (to prevent neck sag).
Lengthen front 2 cm.
Trace off left and right fronts.
Add an 8 cm side seam extension from the waist of the right front, midway on the left front.
Dart the side seam 2 cm at each extension.

Fabrics used in the illustrations

			We	Th	Sh	Dr	St
1	Polyester	warp	1	2	4	1	3
2	Polyester/polyurethene	warp	2	2	5	2	3

The basic grid: complex 3D shapes

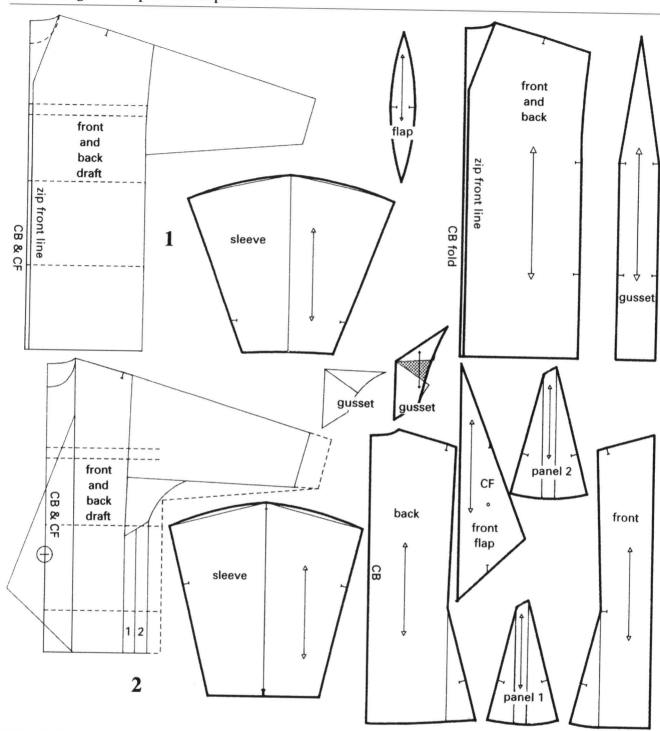

Whilst the box shape is useful for coarse knitted fabrics, these structured shapes work better in medium to heavy-weight fabrics with little drape or shear.

1 Basic grid – side seam gusset
A simple flat shape can be changed to a box shape.
Body Sections trace round block to length required.
Draw in the neckline.
Draw in armhole line and zip front line.
Trace off the pattern sections.
Sleeve draw a soft curve at the sleeve head.
Gusset construct a rectangle side seam length × approx. 10 cm; extend to a point, (meas. less than underarm seam).
Flap construct any shape of flap as required.

2 Basic grid – sectioned gusset
Increasing the style lines can create more complex shapes.
Body Sections trace round block to length required.
Draw in style lines and flap. Draw a shaped gusset section at the underarm.
Trace off the pattern sections.
Add flare to the skirt on the front, back and panel sections.
Gusset divide gusset through the centre: open approx. 4 cm.

Fabric used in the illustrations

			We	Th	Sh	Dr	St
1	Polyester	woven	4	3	3	3	5
2	Wool	woven	3	2	3	3	4

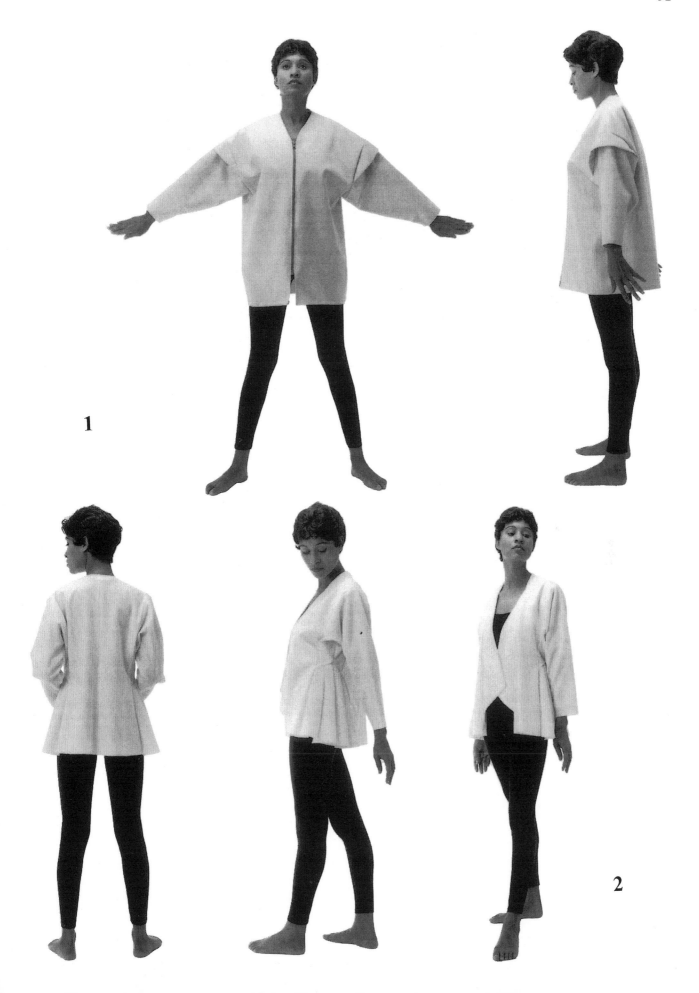

1

The basic grid: complex cut and spread

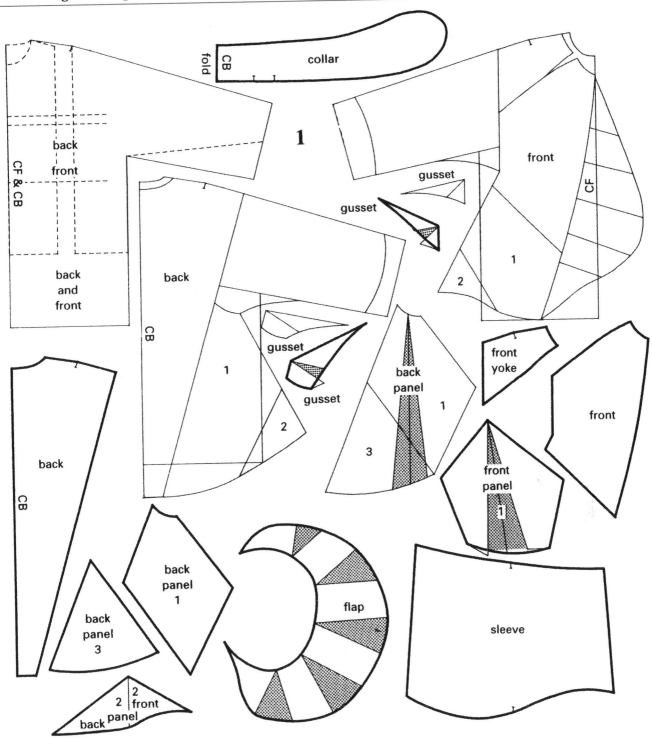

Designs influenced by folk costume can become complex shapes by using the principles of dividing the basic grid (page 189), gusseting and 'cut and spread' techniques. Lambskin is used for the garment and the shape of the skins determines some of the outer edges of the pattern sections.

1 Basic grid – complex shaping

Body Sections   trace off block to length required.
Widen body section of basic grid as shown (approx. 5 cm). Draw in style lines and flap. Draw in 1 cm neck dart. Draw in a shaped gusset section at the underarm.
Trace off the pattern sections. No grain lines are required.

Skirt Panels   join back and front panels 2 at the side seam. Cut and spread back and front skirt panels 1; divide back panel 1 to create back panel 3.
Sleeve   join sleeve and draw a slight curve at sleeve head.
Collar   construct a simple collar to the shape required.
Flap   cut and spread to shape of flap as required.
Gusset   divide gusset through centre: open approx. 4 cm.

Fabrics used in the illustrations

		We	Th	Sh	Dr	St
1	Lambskin with non-woven fleece	5	5	5	5	5

The basic grid: simple hidden 3D shaping

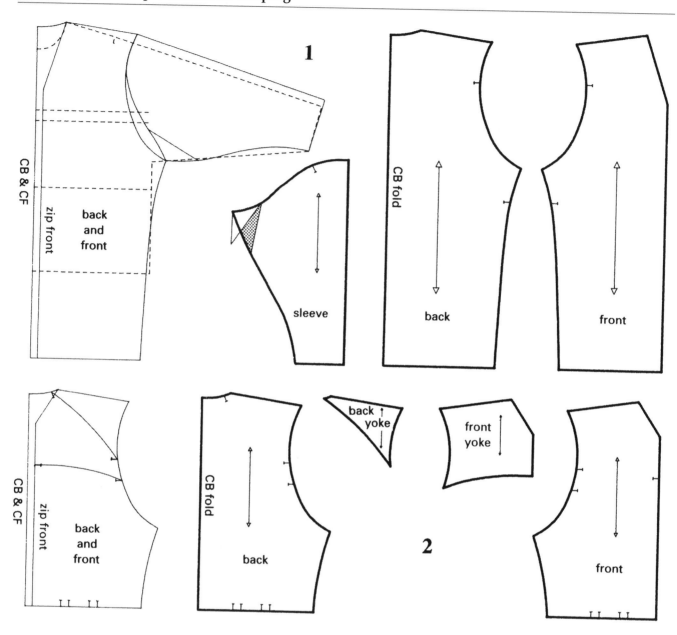

This simple shape is often known as the 'dolman sleeve' and provides the base for many casual jacket designs. It works best in fabrics with drape qualities. It is useful for thick fabrics (1) because some of the bulk is removed from the armhole area. Because of its simplicity it is often used for weatherwear with over panels; however stiff drape lines (2) will be a characteristic of these garments.

1 and 2 dolman sleeve: basic grid – angled sleeve option

Body Sections lengthen draft the amount required. Raise the shoulder and widen the body at the underarm; narrow slightly at the hemline. Draw curved side seam. Draw in front neckline and zip line.

Draw in a curved armhole line; draw in sleeve line making a shaped dart ¾ the length of the seam, approx. 2 cm wide. Draw a gusset line from the armhole (approx. ¼ of armhole length) to approx. 7 cm down the sleeve seam. Trace off the pattern sections.

Sleeve draw a soft curve at the sleeve head if necessary. Open the gusset approx. 4 cm: re-draw underarm seam.

The second example demonstrates a shortened version of the shape with a tucked waistline and shoulder over yokes.

Fabrics used in the illustrations

			We	Th	Sh	Dr	St
1	Hemp/cotton/wool	woven	3	4	1	4	4
2	Polyurethene film	non-woven	3	1	5	3	4

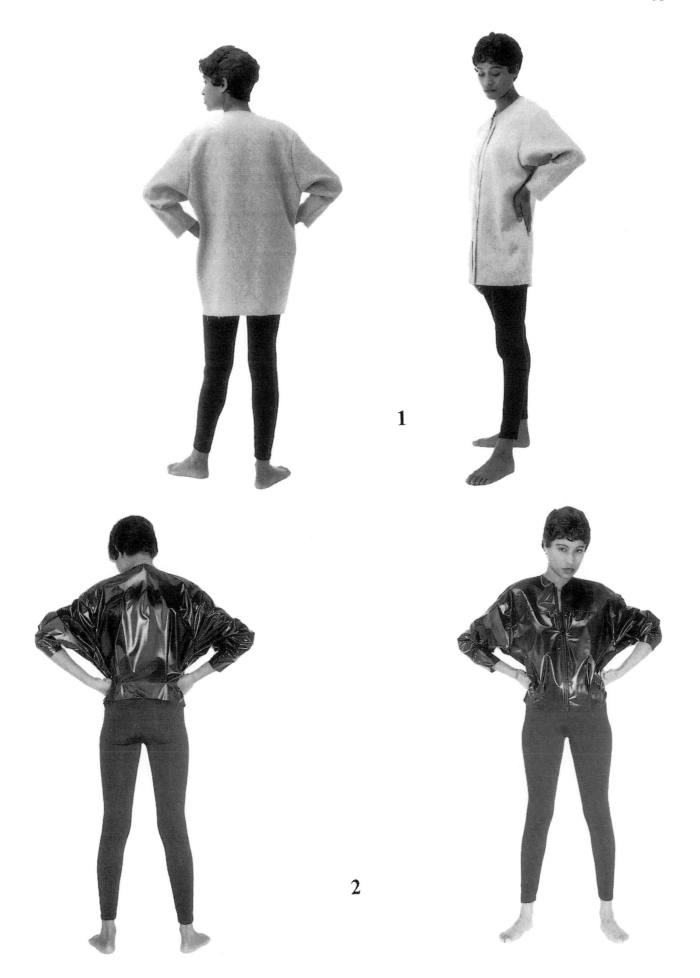

1

2

1

2

The shaped kimono block: more complex 3D shaping

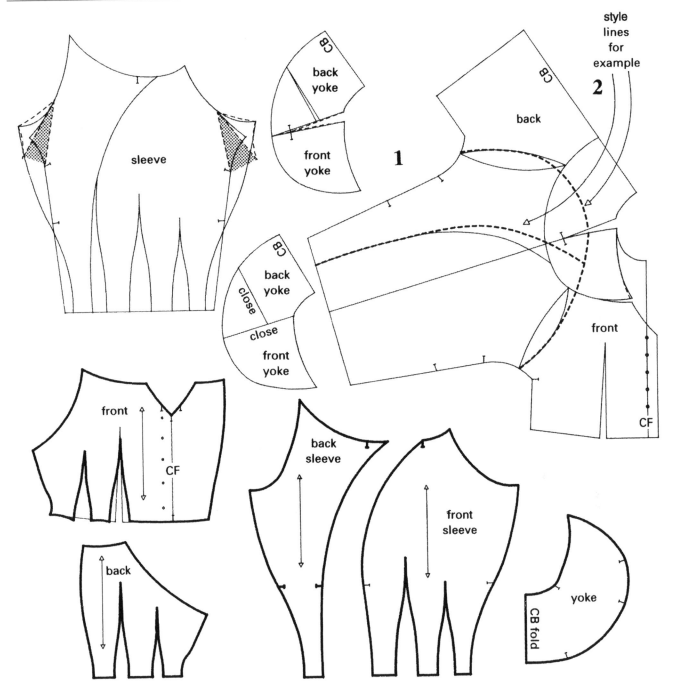

The shaped kimono sleeve block (page 190) has a bust dart (angled from the waist) and therefore includes some 3D body shaping. The block can be used for complex shapely garments. The centre sleeve lines of the draft can be joined to give a 'map' on which an infinite number of style lines can be drawn. This gives a lot of opportunity for complex styling. If the shape of the garment is the dominant feature or there are many oblique style lines then more structured fabrics should be used; but high-drape or high-shear fabrics can be used in vertical and horizontal styling.

1 & 2 Complex shaping

Body Sections   place the centre sleeve lines of the draft together, draw in the style lines required.
On the armhole line draw a shaped dart approx. 2 cm wide. Draw in button stand and neckline.

Draw a 1 cm dart at the front yoke line to prevent sag. Trace off the pattern sections.
Construct darts in the front and back sections.
Sleeve   draw a soft curve at the sleeve head if necessary. Open the gusset approx. 4 cm: re-draw underarm seam shaping in required amount. Add shaping to seam line. Construct darts in the front sleeve section. Trace off sleeves.
Yoke   construct a dart 0.5 cm in the back shoulder (ease allowance). Extend shoulder dart to the edge of the yoke. Close darts, re-trace the pattern.

The second example is a version in very thick knitted fabric. The yoke is not used and the sleeve line is re-drawn.

Fabrics used in the illustrations

			We	Th	Sh	Dr	St
1	Embossed polyester	woven	4	3	3	3	5
2	Wool/viscose pile	weft-knit	5	5	4	5	3

The 'flat' block: the shirt block

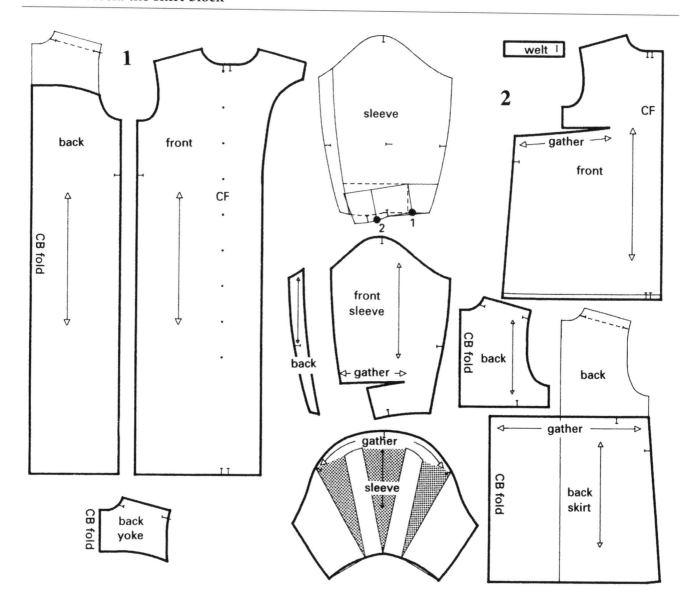

The shirt block (page 192) has no 3D body shaping (bust darting); however if you try to lay the garment flat you will find it will rise slightly under the arms, showing that a form of 'hidden gusseting' exists within the shape. The block in this book is an easy fitting women's shirt block that can be used for all types of garments from formal to casual wear, and in virtually all fabrics and all lengths. The shoulders can be joined to create a map (page 97).

1 Basic shirt styling

Body Sections   trace round the block. Extend the length. Draw in button stand. Add an extended facing. (Ref. *MPC* bodice section.) Draw in back yoke line (if required). Trace off the pattern sections.

Sleeve   Draw in the back style line; divide front lower section into three parts, mark points 1 and 2.
Cut out the lower front section from section 1 and swing forward approx. 2 cm. Cut off the line at 2.
Trace off back and front sleeves.

2 Adapted shirt styling

Body Sections   trace round the block.
Extend length: make front length 2 cm longer than back length.
Draw in button stand. Add a 6 cm extended facing. (Ref. *MPC* bodice section.) Draw in back yoke line and front gather line. Construct a 2 cm dart at front gather line.
Extend front skirt the required amount.
Trace off the pattern sections.
Extend back skirt the required amount.
Sleeve   trace round sleeve to required length.
Divide the middle section and cut and spread as shown.
Raise the sleeve head for extra fullness.
Trace round the pattern.
Trace off back and front sleeves.

Fabrics used in the illustrations

			We	Th	Sh	Dr	St
1	Wool	woven	3	3	3	3	4
2	Polyester (micro-fibre)	woven	2	2	2	1	5
3	Polyamide	woven	2	1	4	5	5

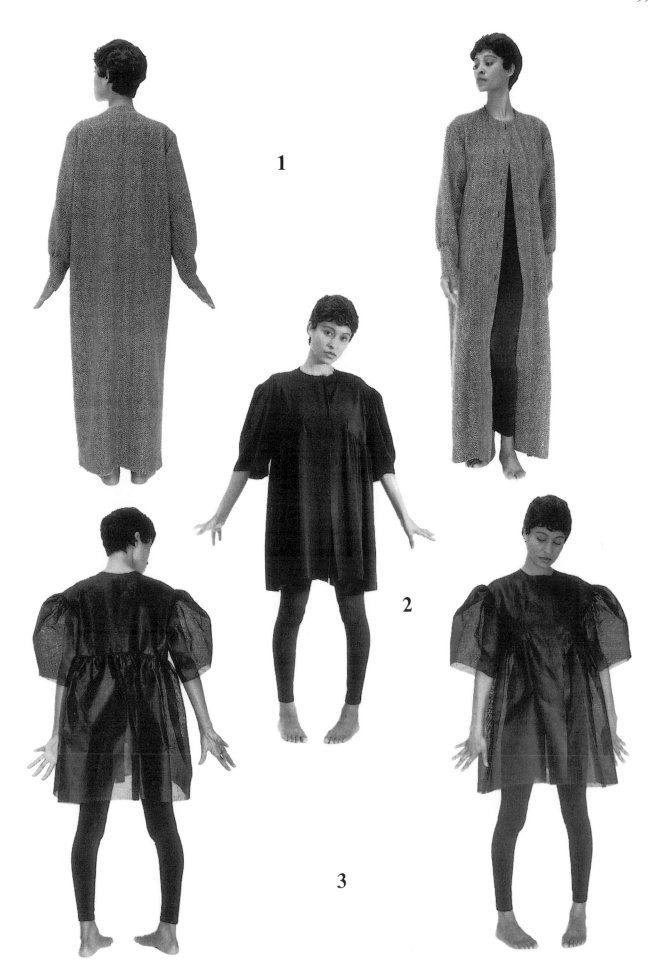

1

2

3

1

Simple flat geometric forms: trousers

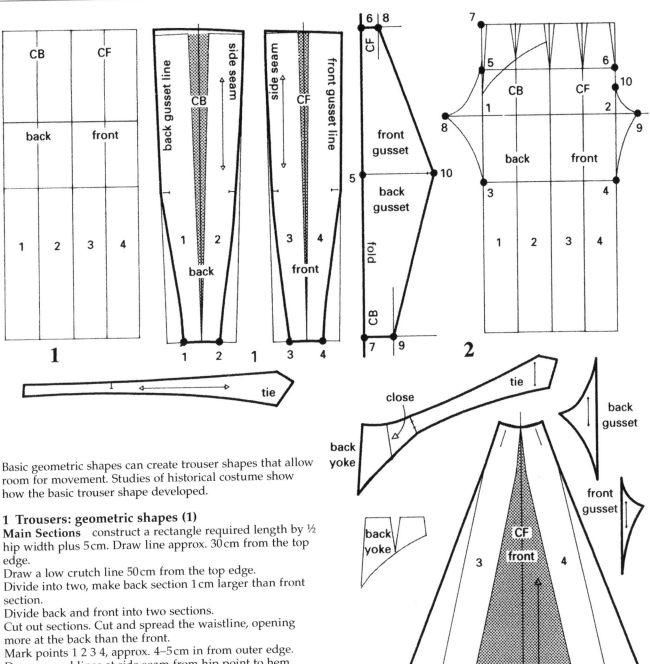

Basic geometric shapes can create trouser shapes that allow room for movement. Studies of historical costume show how the basic trouser shape developed.

1 Trousers: geometric shapes (1)

Main Sections construct a rectangle required length by ½ hip width plus 5 cm. Draw line approx. 30 cm from the top edge.

Draw a low crutch line 50 cm from the top edge.

Divide into two, make back section 1 cm larger than front section.

Divide back and front into two sections.

Cut out sections. Cut and spread the waistline, opening more at the back than the front.

Mark points 1 2 3 4, approx. 4–5 cm in from outer edge.

Draw curved lines at side seam from hip point to hem.

Draw curved lines at inside leg from crutch point to hem.

Gusset square up and across from point 5.

5–6 = 47 cm; 5–7 = 48 cm; 6–8 = 6 cm; 7–9 = 10 cm; 5–10 = 24 cm. Join all outer points of the shape.

Construct a tie the required length and shape.

2 Trousers: geometric shapes

(illustration **2** over page)

Main Sections construct a rectangle as above.

Construct darting on each vertical line to a total of 14 cm.

Draw in the back yoke line and a line midway between hipline and waistline.

Mark points 1 2 3 4 5 6 7 on horizontal lines.

1–8 = ½ width of back section; 2–9 = ½ 1–8 plus 1 cm.

10 is midway between 2 and 6; 5 is midway between 1 and 7.

Draw in gusset shapes. Cut out all sections.

Add approx. 10 cm flare to hemline of trouser sections.

Cut and spread the hemline the required amount.

Back Yoke close dart and add shaped tie to hipline.

Mark slit lines for the tie on the front sections.

Fabrics used in the illustrations

			We	Th	Sh	Dr	St
1	viscose flocked polyester	weft-knit	3	2	4	2	2
2	hemp/cotton/viscose (top illustration)	woven	3	2	4	2	2
3	polyester (micro-fibre) (bottom illustration)	woven	2	2	2	1	5

2

3

PART TWO: FABRIC AND FORM

6 Fitting the body shape: woven fabrics

Fitting the body

Fitting the body in woven fabrics which do not stretch over the body curves presents great challenges for pattern cutters. These skills have to be developed. Many couturiers are masters of 'cut'. Cutting fitted shapes in woven fabric for the mass market is very difficult: that is why there has been such a growth in fabrics with stretch characteristics either in the yarn (e.g. elastane) or the construction (e.g. fancy crepe weaves or knitted fabrics). The use of these fabrics has solved some problems but has created others. These will be discussed in the next chapter. This chapter

concentrates on the creation of patterns for garments made in woven fabrics with little stretch ability. It illustrates the types of blocks available for achieving different shapes and *types* of 'fit'.

'Fit' is a word that is used quite often in a very loose way and it can be ambiguous. The word 'fit' should be accompanied by qualifiers such as 'body fit' or 'close fit.' The meaning of the qualifier should also be made clear (e.g. 'close fit' = body fit with ease included for movement) or the shape should be illustrated.

Basic loose shapes: the easy fitting overshape block

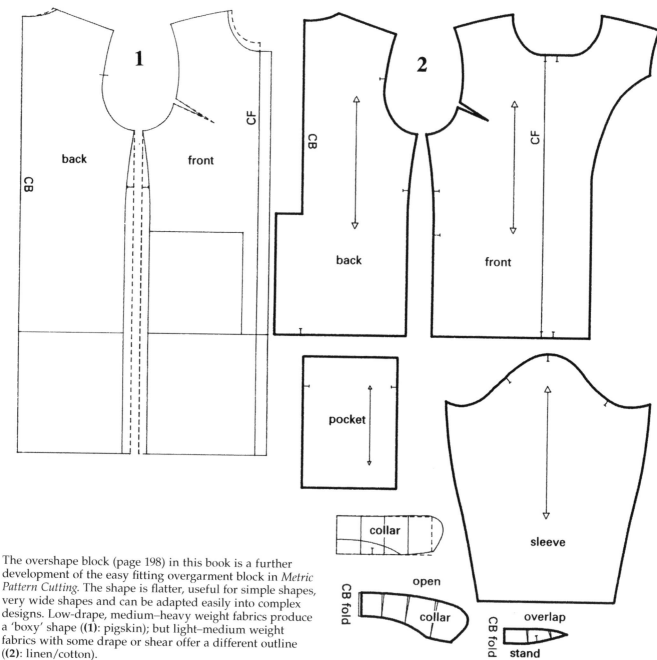

The overshape block (page 198) in this book is a further development of the easy fitting overgarment block in *Metric Pattern Cutting*. The shape is flatter, useful for simple shapes, very wide shapes and can be adapted easily into complex designs. Low-drape, medium–heavy weight fabrics produce a 'boxy' shape ((1): pigskin); but light–medium weight fabrics with some drape or shear offer a different outline ((2): linen/cotton).

1 & 2 Basic loose shapes

Body Sections trace round the block. Extend the length. Draw neckline, add button stand. Add extended facing. (Ref. *MPC* bodice section.)
Swing dart to armhole.
Shorten dart.
Shape in side seam 1.5 cm.
Draw in pocket line.
Trace off the pattern sections.
Add back vent (approx. 6 cm) if required.
Collar construct a shirt collar with back stand (Ref. *MPC*; collar section.)

Fabrics used in the illustrations

		We	Th	Sh	Dr	St
1 Pigskin	non-woven	3	3	4	4	4
2 Linen/cotton	woven	3	2	3	3	5

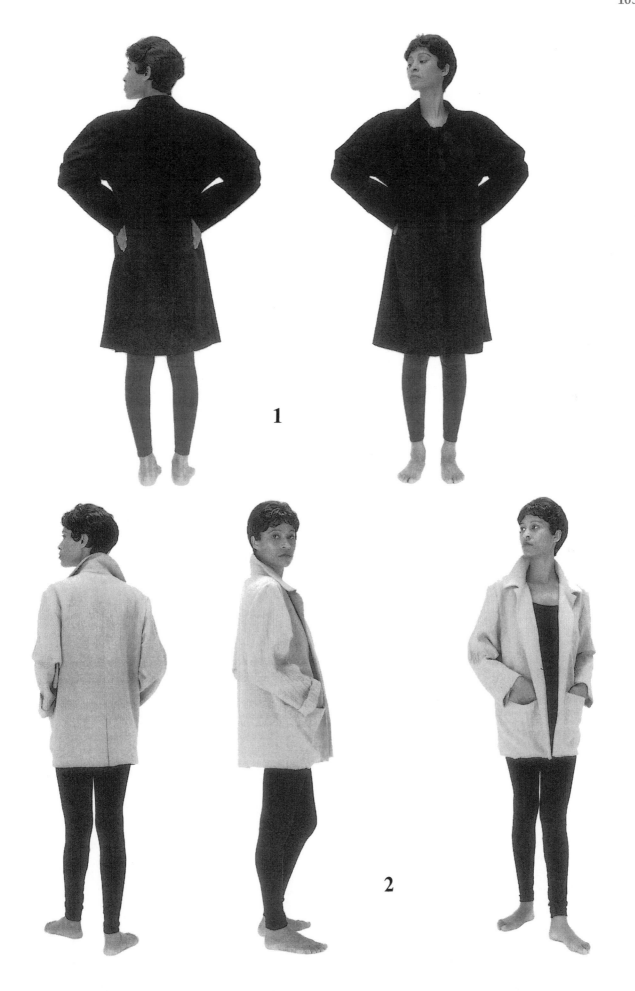

1

2

2

1

Extravagant shapes: the easy fitting overshape block

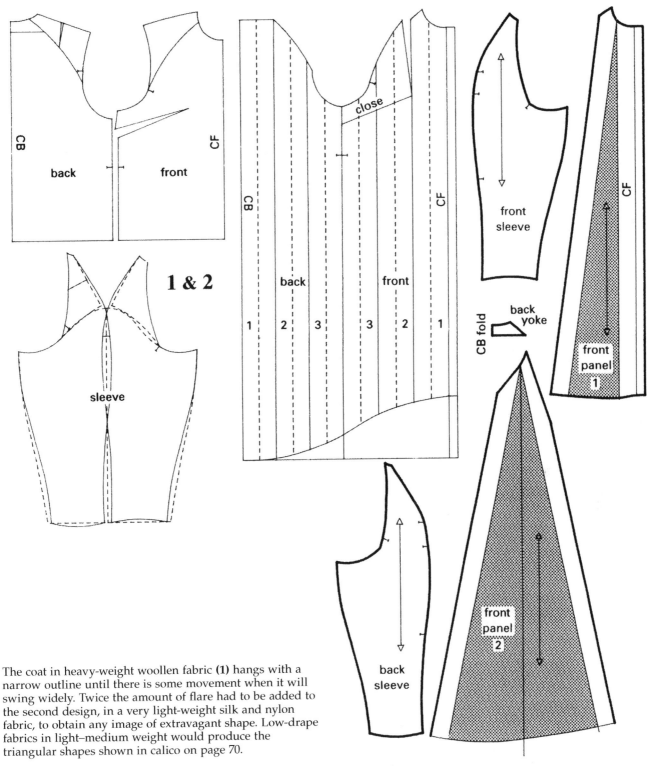

The coat in heavy-weight woollen fabric (1) hangs with a narrow outline until there is some movement when it will swing widely. Twice the amount of flare had to be added to the second design, in a very light-weight silk and nylon fabric, to obtain any image of extravagant shape. Low-drape fabrics in light–medium weight would produce the triangular shapes shown in calico on page 70.

1 & 2 Wide flared shapes

Body Sections   trace round the block. Extend the length.
Draw in raglan lines. Draw in back yoke line.
Draw back shoulder dart to replace ease allowance.
Trace off the pattern sections.
Front and Back   transfer the bust dart to the raglan line.
Place patterns together and draw in a shaped hemline.
Draw neckline, add button stand.
Divide patterns into sections as shown. Cut up sections.
Cut and spread all the sections the required amount.

Sleeve   add raglan sections to sleeve head, matching balance points. Leave some gap at the sleeve head for ease. Re-draw centre lines overlapping at the top sleeve, shaping in at the bottom. Shape in the underarm seam with a curve.
Scarf   fringed scarf lengths were inserted in the back yoke.

Fabrics used in the illustrations

			We	Th	Sh	Dr	St
1	Wool	woven	4	3	3	3	4
2	Silk/nylon	woven	1	1	3	3	5

Classic shaping: the easy fitting jacket block

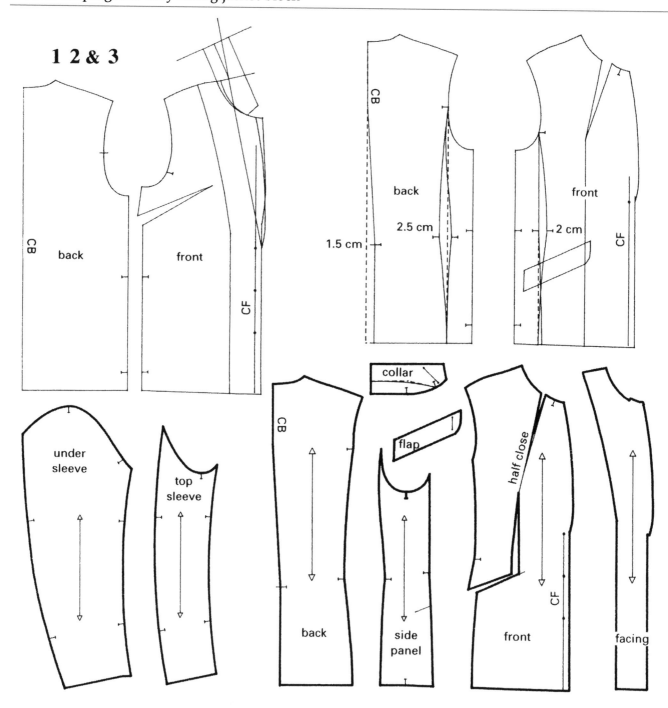

1 2 & 3

back

front

CB

CF

under
sleeve

top
sleeve

CB

back

2.5 cm

1.5 cm

front

2 cm

CF

collar

flap

CB

back

side
panel

half close

front

CF

facing

The easy fitting jacket block (page 199) is a basic shape. The half-width bust dart, the curved armhole shaping and the two piece sleeve bring it closer to the body shape. Semi-fitted waist shaping retains an easy fitting image. The jacket shoulder includes enough ease for a light thin shoulder pad; for extra padding see the adaptation (ref. 2 page 169).

Compare the shapes of a light–medium weight, medium-drape linen jacket (1) with a low-drape PVC coated jacket (3). A knitted wool jersey jacket (2) is shown for comparison; note that it appears to be a larger size and would need to be drafted with less ease to obtain the same outline. Compare the images with the jacket constructed with structured tailored interlinings (ref. 1 page 169).

1 2 & 3 Classic easy fitting waist shaping

Body Sections   trace round the block. Extend the length.

Construct a 'gents' collar. (Ref. *MPC* collar section.)
Swing bust dart to the neckline.
Draw in vertical lines from sleeve points and bust point.
Lower back waist approx 2 cm.
Shape panel lines as shown in diagram.
Trace off the pattern sections.
Cut along pocket line and the vertical line to bust point.
Half close the bust dart at the neck. Shorten dart.

Fabrics used in the illustrations

			We	Th	Sh	Dr	St
1	Linen/lurex	woven	3	1	3	4	5
2	Wool double jersey	weft-knit	3	3	4	3	3
3	Polyurethene coated cotton	woven	3	1	5	5	4

1

2

Easy different shaping: the easy fitting jacket block

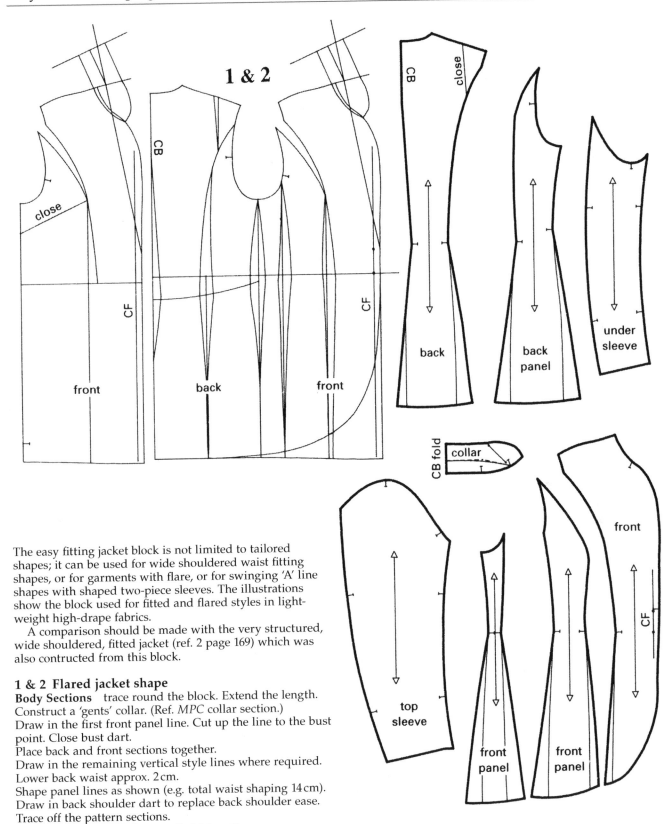

1 & 2

The easy fitting jacket block is not limited to tailored shapes; it can be used for wide shouldered waist fitting shapes, or for garments with flare, or for swinging 'A' line shapes with shaped two-piece sleeves. The illustrations show the block used for fitted and flared styles in light-weight high-drape fabrics.

A comparison should be made with the very structured, wide shouldered, fitted jacket (ref. 2 page 169) which was also contructed from this block.

1 & 2 Flared jacket shape

Body Sections   trace round the block. Extend the length.
Construct a 'gents' collar. (Ref. *MPC* collar section.)
Draw in the first front panel line. Cut up the line to the bust point. Close bust dart.
Place back and front sections together.
Draw in the remaining vertical style lines where required.
Lower back waist approx. 2 cm.
Shape panel lines as shown (e.g. total waist shaping 14 cm).
Draw in back shoulder dart to replace back shoulder ease.
Trace off the pattern sections.
Close back dart. Add flare to all skirt sections.

Fabrics used in the illustrations

			We	Th	Sh	Dr	St
1	Polyester/ polyurethene	warp-knit	2	1	5	2	4
2	Polyester	lace	2	2/4	4	1	3

Closing in on the body: the close fitting jacket block

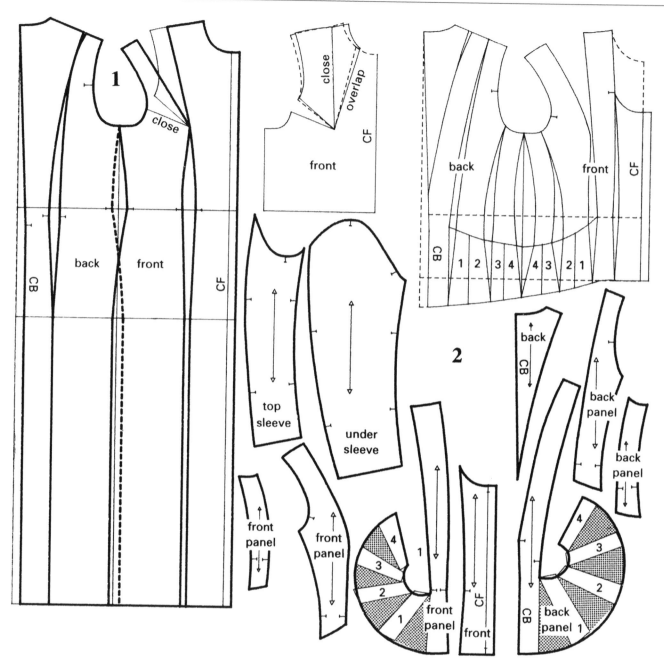

The close fitting jacket block (page 200) does fit close to the body with only basic ease for movement. The block is shown with semi-fitted waist shaping (1) to produce a long narrow line. Although there is a small amount of elastane in the cloth, the block is not modified and the elastane is seen simply as a 'comfort' factor. The weave of the fabric gives it a small amount of 'natural' stretch.

Using this block with high-shear, loosely woven fabrics would result in distortions, unless the fabric was supported (ref. 1 page 166). More ease would be required for thick fabrics.

1 Simple semi-fitting shape
Body Sections trace round the block. Extend the length. Reduce front neck curve (see above). Add button stand. Draw in style lines from shoulder to hemline. Lower back waist approx. 2cm.

Shape panel lines as shown in diagram (total waist shaping approx. 10cm).
Note that hip shaping is reduced at front and centre back and is added to the side seam.
Trace off the pattern sections.
Close bust dart to swing darting to panel line.

2 Fitted flared jacket
The diagram illustrates a different example of waist shaping; more style lines and close waist shaping (example 14cm), will give a sculptured look to designs, particularly when low-drape low-shear fabrics are used.

Fabrics used in the illustrations

			We	Th	Sh	Dr	St
1	Wool/polyester/ elastane	woven	3	3	4	4	3
2	Polyester	woven	3	3	5	5	4

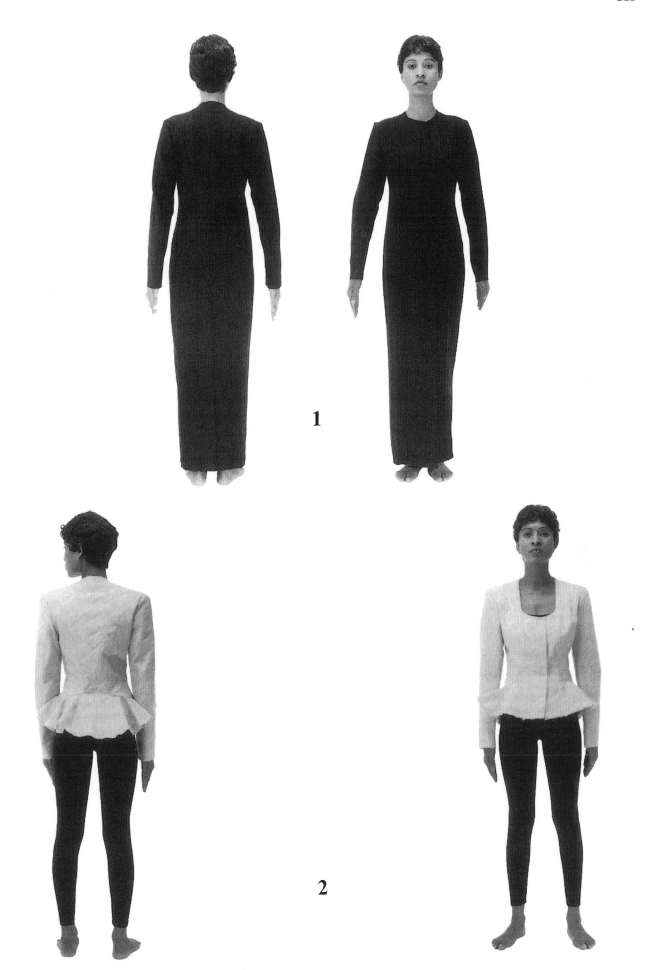

1

2

1

2

3

A closer fit: the close fitting bodice (dress) block

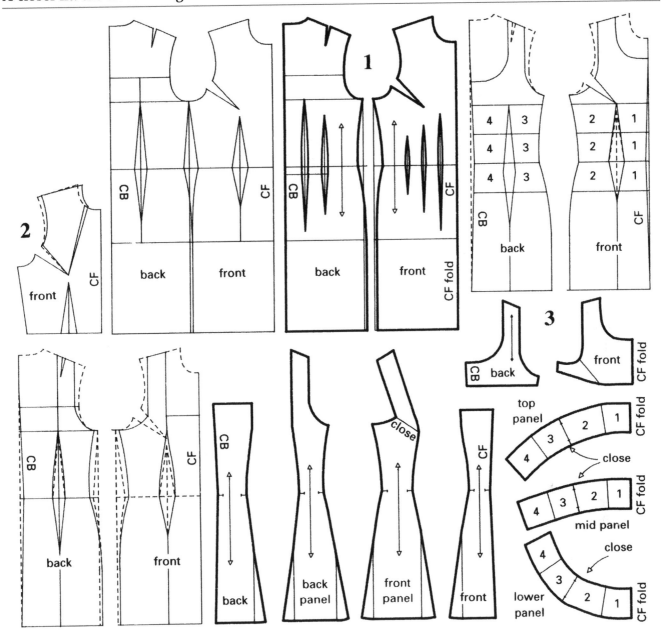

An easy fitting dress block is available in *Metric Pattern Cutting* for easy fitting styles. This section describes some techniques that can be applied to achieve better shapes and fit as you cut close to the body, using the close-fitting bodice block (page 202).

1 Basic waist shaping and equalising the side seam
Trace round the block. Extend the length.
Draw in bodice darts as shown (more shaping at the front).
Divide the hemline into two equal sections.
Square up to the hipline.
Draw in the hip shaping to the new side seam.
The darting can be distributed differently (1).

2 Low-necked and sleeveless dresses
Low-neck dresses will sag unless the neck is tightened.
Draw line from neck to bust point. Cut out the dart, cut up the line, overlap approx. 1 cm (depending on the depth of neck).
The side seam can be reduced for a closer fit if required.

Reduce by 1 cm at the underarm; 0.5 cm at the waist; join to the hip point.
Vertical seam lines and flare are added in (2).

3 Horizontal shaping
Darting can be transferred to horizontal lines (3).
Draw horizontal style lines on the block.
Make sure that the dart points touch or come close to one of the lines. Move dart points to the lines if necessary.
Trace off all the sections.
Construct horizontal panels closing the dart lines.

4 The design on page 116 has the same body pattern shaping used for ref. 2 page 113, but the dress block was used as a base. The garment, made up in nappa leather, shows the closeness of fit that can be achieved (4).

Fabric used in the illustrations

			We	Th	Sh	Dr	St
1	Nappa leather	non-woven	5	3	4	3	4

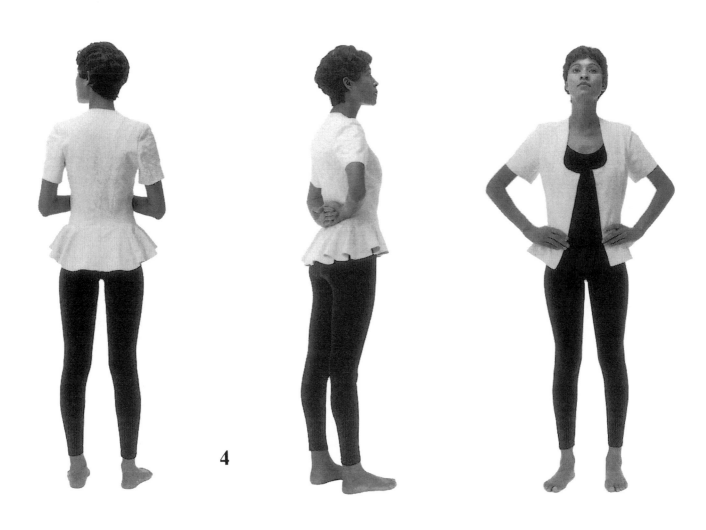

4

PART THREE: FABRIC, FORM AND FLAT PATTERN CUTTING

7 Exploiting fabric characteristics: crossway cutting, knitted and stretch fabrics

Crossway cutting

Crossway cutting can produce garments that fit in a sensual way around the figure and drape in soft fluid folds. It also gives bounce and life to folded frills and other decorative features. Crossway cutting is cutting directly across the material. This means that the vertical hang of the material is under strain at the crossway intersection of warp and weft. Cutting in this way takes full advantage of any shear characteristics; however very open weave high-shear fabrics can become uncontrollable. Cutting geometrically and cutting correctly on the true bias helps to retain some control. Crossway cutting was found mainly in expensive garments where the crossway fabric pieces were cut wider than the pattern shape, then left to hang for three days for the fabric to 'reach its initial limit' before the garment was cut out. This method was used for all the garments shown on the following pages. Crossway cut garments have become fashionable at High Street level, but quality control of crossway cut garments is difficult in mass production. Garments reach the stores having dropped and become too narrow for size; or garments cut off the true crossway grain distort in shape and wrinkle at the seams.

Knitted fabric

Knitted fabric has its own distinct characteristics. Some structured knitted fabric can be cut using the same principles as woven fabrics but exploiting the unique characteristics of high-drape and high-stretch inherent in most light–medium-weight knitted fabrics. Most knitted fabrics have a low-shear rating but loose tension or coarse gauge fabrics can distort when they are cut and seamed across the wales; or they can bow outwards when under

strain if they have a low recovery from stretch. Including elastane yarns in knitted fabrics increases their stability and their stretch-recovery ratings.

Geometric cutting of knitted fabrics is used widely for easy fitting garments; the measurements can be determined by fabric motifs and the stretch and drape characteristics will allow soft folds to be created where there is surplus fabric. Simple blocks with little or no 3D body shaping can be used for closer fitting garments: the natural stretch will accommodate the body shape. Close body fitting garments require calculations and considerations which are discussed on pages 134 and 137.

Attempts have been made to construct mathematical tables to draft or modify close fitting blocks in relation to stretch. This is possible in a very narrow style range and fabric range. I use a computer program in this situation. However, most design is not like that: many other considerations have to be applied and block shapes change quite dramatically in different groups. Blocks for different groups are offered and examples explained.

Woven/stretch fabric

The increasing use of elastane in woven fabrics has offered the opportunity to experiment with close body cutting. Woven/elastane fabric development has been concentrated in the production of stretch-swimwear, stretch-denim and stretch-suiting. Calculations for comparison body fit can be made in narrow product areas, but elastane is now appearing in fabric ranges of differing weights, thickness, structure and texture, and this requires a broader approach. It should also be noted that some woven fabrics without an elastane content can have quite high levels of stretch.

Crossway cutting: loose fitting

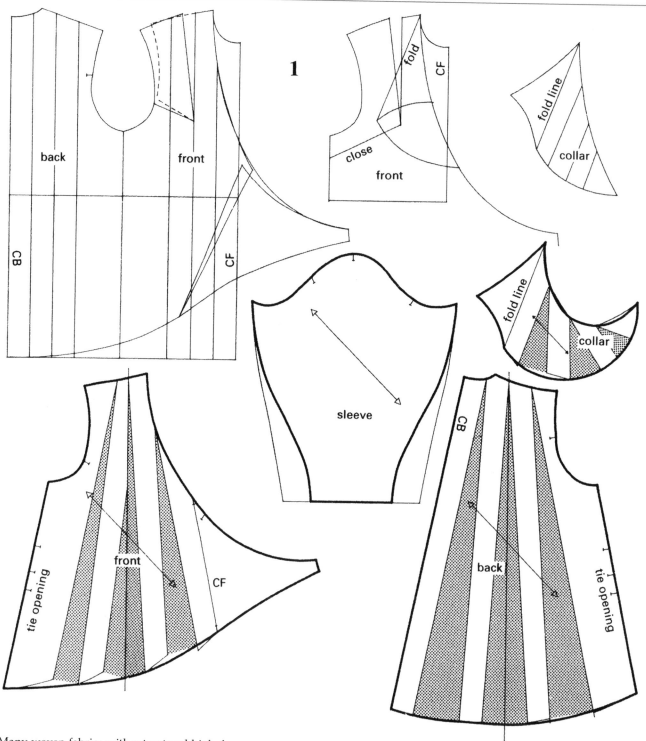

Many woven fabrics without natural high-drape characteristics can have their 'hang' improved by crossway cutting. When creating loose shapes (easy fitting overshape, page 198) a softer, narrower outline is obtained. The illustration in wool crepe illustrates how medium to high-drape fabrics have their characteristics enhanced; notice the amount of flare in the pattern and the narrow silhouette.

1 Wide flared shapes

Body Sections trace round front block. Extend the length. Draw neckline, extend it the full width of right front to below the waistline. Draw in folded collar as shown. Swing dart to the shoulder line (approx. ⅓ the length). Place back and front sections together.

Overlap the front neckline to prevent droop (approx. 4 cm). Divide patterns into sections, drop one line from the bust point as shown. Trace off the pattern sections. Cut up sections.
Cut and spread the required amount.
Sleeve shape in the underarm seams with curves.
Collar trace off collar; divide into sections. Cut up sections; cut and spread the sections the required amount.
Tie construct tie to width of right side seam tie opening.

Fabric used in the illustrations

			We	Th	Sh	Dr	St
1	Wool crepe	woven	3	2	3	2	4

1

1

Crossway cutting: classic shaping

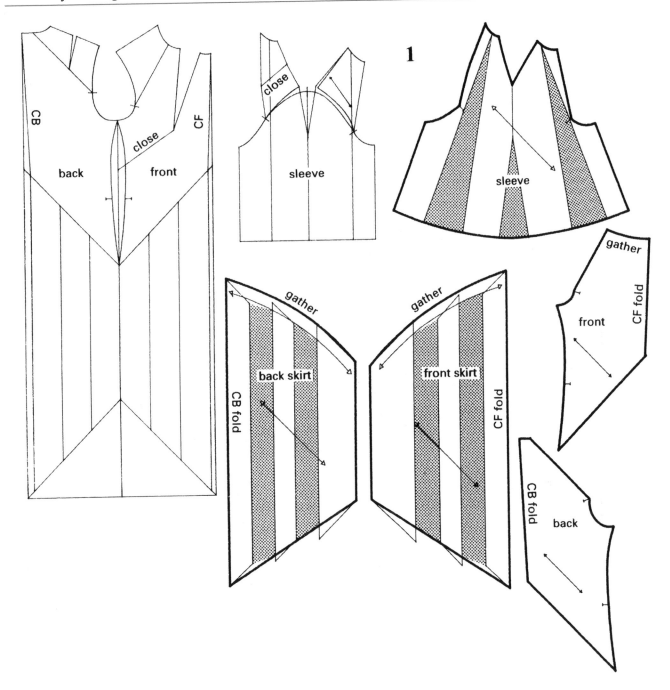

Seams across the grain of the fabric can buckle. One of the techniques of crossway cutting is to have seams drawn at a true 45 degree angle; this means that when the fabric is cut on the cross the main seamlines are on the straight grain. The dress is cut from the close fitting bodice block (page 202) to shape the body.

1 Total crossway cutting

Body Sections trace round the block. Extend the length.
Draw in raglan lines, skirt seam lines and hemlines at a 45 degree angle.
Swing the bust dart to the neckline.
Place back and front sections together.

Shape side seams to give a high waist.
Divide skirt patterns into sections as shown.
Trace off the pattern sections.
Skirt cut up sections. Cut and open the required amount.
Sleeve add raglan sections to sleeve head, matching balance points. Leave a gap at the sleeve head for ease.
Divide sleeve pattern into sections as shown.
Trace off pattern sections.
Cut up sections. Cut and spread the required amount.

Fabric used in the illustrations

			We	Th	Sh	Dr	St
1	Wool crepe	woven	3	2	3	2	4

Crossway cutting: mixing the grains

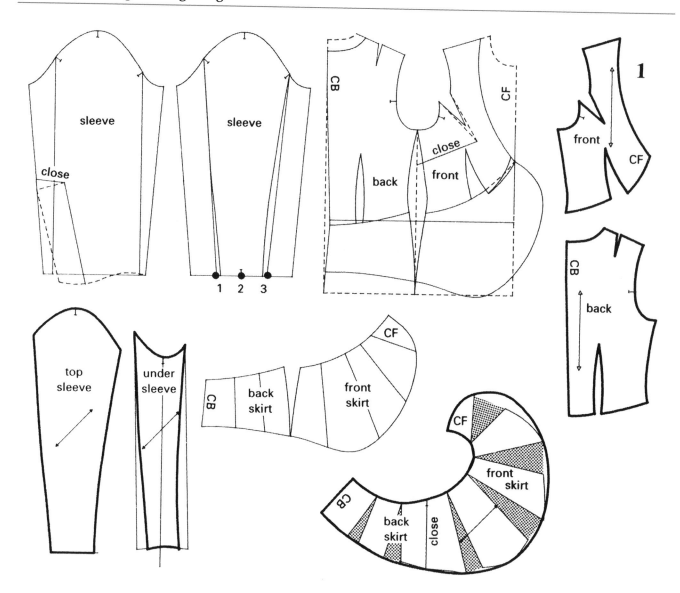

The design illustrated demonstrates how pattern sections cut on the crossway can be stabilised by some of the body sections being cut on the straight. Crossway cutting of tight fitting sleeves can ensure a close comfortable fit. Low-shear, high-drape fabrics ensure recovery from any strain. The skirt section is also cut on the crossway to maximise the drape characteristics. The design is cut from the close-fitting bodice block (page 202) to shape the body.

1 Straight/crossway design

Body Sections trace round the block to the length required.
Swing the bust dart to the armhole; shorten dart.
Draw in the neckline and waistline.
Lower the waist at the centre back approx. 2 cm.
Shape in the centre back seam approx. 1 cm.
Shape side seams to give a high waist; draw in waist darting.
Take a 1 cm shaping from the waist seam at the front neck edge to reduce neck 'sag'.

Trace off the pattern sections.
Skirt divide skirt patterns into sections as shown.
Place back and front sections together.
Cut and spread giving more spread at the front of the skirt.
Sleeve draw a line from the elbow dart to base of sleeve.
Cut up the line and close the dart.
Divide bottom line into four sections. Mark points 1, 2, 3.
Draw lines from the sleeve balance points to points 1 and 3.
Shape the lines as shown hollowing the line from 3 at the forearm and shaping the line from 1 from the elbow.
Trace off pattern sections.
Join the underarm seam and shape the outer lines of the undersleeve as shown hollowing more at the front seam.
The amount that is taken in will vary according to the amount of stretch in the fabric.

NOTE The peplum will be slightly gathered onto the bodice. If this is not required, overlap the sections of the peplum at the waist, the same measurement as the waist darts on the bodice.

1

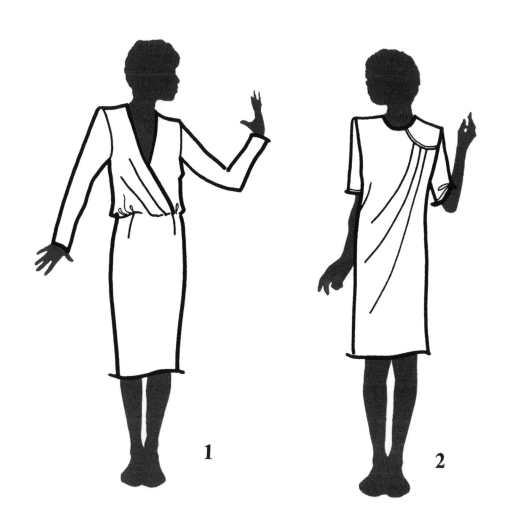

1
2

Crossway cutting: draped sections

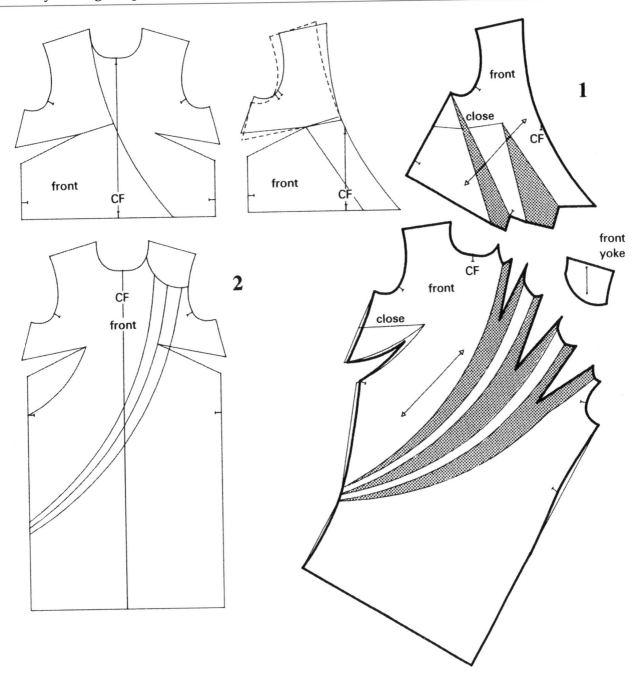

Just a draped section of a garment can be cut on the crossway. Because the rest of the garment is cut on the straight, there is more scope for experiments with less stable fabrics with higher shear qualities. Some knitted fabrics (where a crossway patterning feature is required) can be cut in this way. If deep draped folds are made some fabrics will require the bulk to be cut away as in (2). The designs can be cut from the close fitting bodice block (page 202). First stages of a draped pattern can be constructed by flat pattern cutting, the drape then refined on the dress stand. The pattern shape without the drape adaptation can be used as a mounting to hold the drape folds in place.

1 Front bodice draping

Body Sections   trace round a mirrored block to the length required. Draw in the neckline.

Draw a line from the front bust point to the neck edge, cut and overlap approx. 1.5 cm to reduce neck 'sag'.
Draw a line from bust point to the waistline.
Cut up the line, close the dart to create first drape fold.
Draw a line from armhole to the waistline. Cut and spread to create second drape fold.

2 Front bodice draping

Body Sections   trace round a mirrored block to the length required. Draw in the yoke line.
Draw in the dart line on the right side of the garment.
Draw in the drape folds from yoke to side seam.
Trace off the pattern sections. Swing the right dart.
Cut and spread the drape lines to create folds, closing the side dart to swing the shaping into the folds.
Shape the side seam slightly to give a smooth line.

Crossway cutting: body fitting

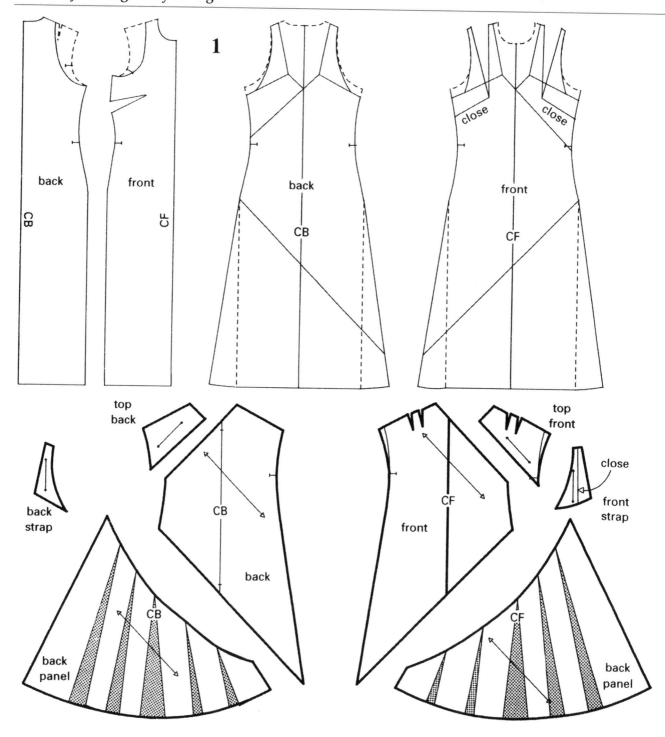

High-drape or medium–high-drape fabric cut on the crossway will cling to the body in a 'fluid' way. Cutting close to the body means the fabric should be prepared by hanging (see page 117) or unstable sizing will result. The technique of crossway cutting of seams at a true 45 degree angle was used, so that seam lines would be on the straight grain. The dress is cut from the close fitting bodice block (page 202). The design was constructed in sandwashed silk satin. Notice that, although the garment was cut in a simple semi-fitted shape, it clings to the body.

1 Total crossway cutting

Body Sections   trace round the block. Extend the length. Complete the sleeveless adaptation (page 115).

Mirror the blocks. Swing the bust dart to the shoulder.
Draw in the style lines and the neckline.
Trace off the pattern sections.
Close the dart on the front strap.
Add 2 cm to the side seam of the front and create an extra dart over the bust line.
Trace off the pattern sections.
Skirt   divide skirt patterns into sections as shown.
Cut up sections. Cut and spread the required amount.

Fabric used in the illustrations

		We	Th	Sh	Dr	St
1 Sandwashed silk	woven	2	1	3	1	4

1

1

2

Crossway cutting: body fitting

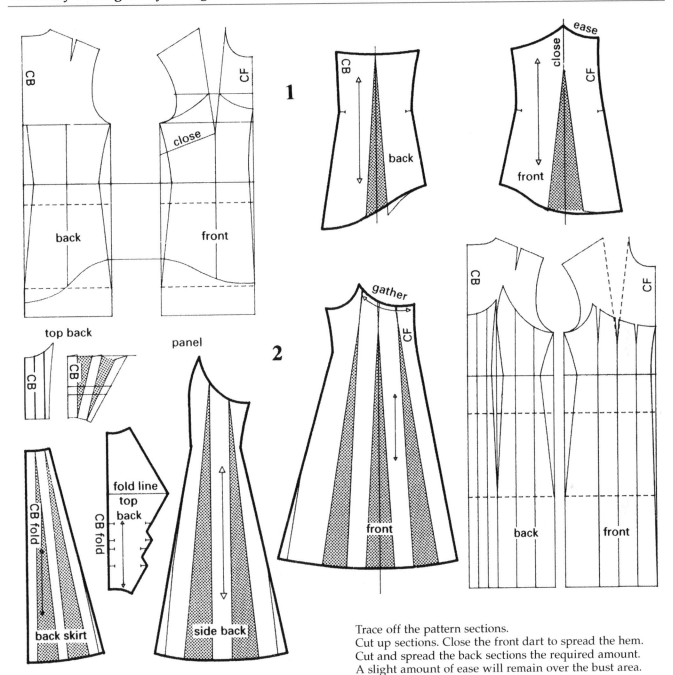

Cutting high-drape or medium–high-drape fabric on the crossway allows the fabric to cling to the body in a 'fluid' way. Cutting close to the body means the fabric should be prepared by hanging or very unstable sizing will result. Lingerie type garments are now worn as day-wear. The opposite page shows (1), a simple body shape in modal (viscose) and (2), a cowl back adaptation in black peachskin faille (micro-fibre). Although both the garments were cut with flare they drape around the body shape.
NOTE the skirt shape in (1) is described on page 146.

1 Simple body shape
Body Sections trace round the close fitting bodice block (page 202). Extend the length.
Complete the sleeveless adaptation (page 115).
Swing the bust dart to the neck point. Draw in the style lines for the top of the bodice and the hemline.
Draw vertical lines to divide the body sections as shown.

Trace off the pattern sections.
Cut up sections. Close the front dart to spread the hem.
Cut and spread the back sections the required amount.
A slight amount of ease will remain over the bust area.

2 Simple cowl back shape
Body Sections complete the first stages of adaptation as above but draw in a back panel line.
Draw vertical lines to divide the body sections as shown.
Divide bust dart into three small darts on the section lines.
Trace off the pattern sections. Cut across the back panel at the waistline.
Cut and spread the sections required, amount as shown.
Create a mirrored pattern piece for the top back (cowl) panel.
Pleat the top part of the panel, use the method (ref. 2 page 83).

Fabrics used in the illustrations

			We	Th	Sh	Dr	St
1	Modal	woven	2	1	2	2	4
2	Polyester (micro-fibre)	woven	2	2	2	1	5

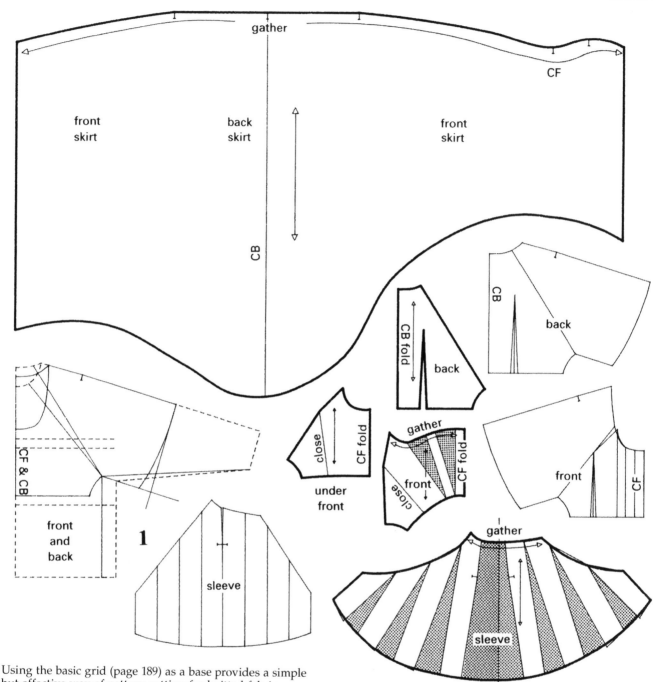

Using the basic grid (page 189) as a base provides a simple but effective way of pattern cutting for knitted fabrics. Many light to medium-weight knitted fabrics will drape beautifully when cut on the straight grain.

The illustration shows a dress in fine linen weft-knit fabric cut in a simple raglan shape. The bodice was cut by flat pattern cutting. The skirt draping was constructed by draping the actual fabric directly on the dress stand. This is usually the most successful method.

1 Simple draped style

Body Sections trace out the basic draft to length required. Draw in raglan lines, high waistline and side seam shaping. Draw in the neckline.
Draw in sleeve length, shape up at the underarm.
Trace off the pattern sections as front and back pieces.
Construct back and front waist darts in positions shown.
Take a 1.5 cm dart from the neckline to prevent sag.

Divide the front neck section into three parts as shown.
Cut off sleeve sections.
Cut and spread the front neck the amount required.
The original front pattern is retained for an under bodice.
Sleeve draw a vertical line. Place sleeve sections together at the line; a small shoulder dart will remain.
Divide sleeve pattern into sections as shown.
Trace off pattern sections.
Cut up sections. Cut and spread the required amount and make a gap at the centre shoulder for a gathering allowance.
Skirt a proportionate pattern is shown of the draped skirt section.

Fabric used in the illustration

		We	Th	Sh	Dr	St
1	Linen weft-knit	3	2/3	4	2	3

1

1

2

Knitted fabric: using blocks

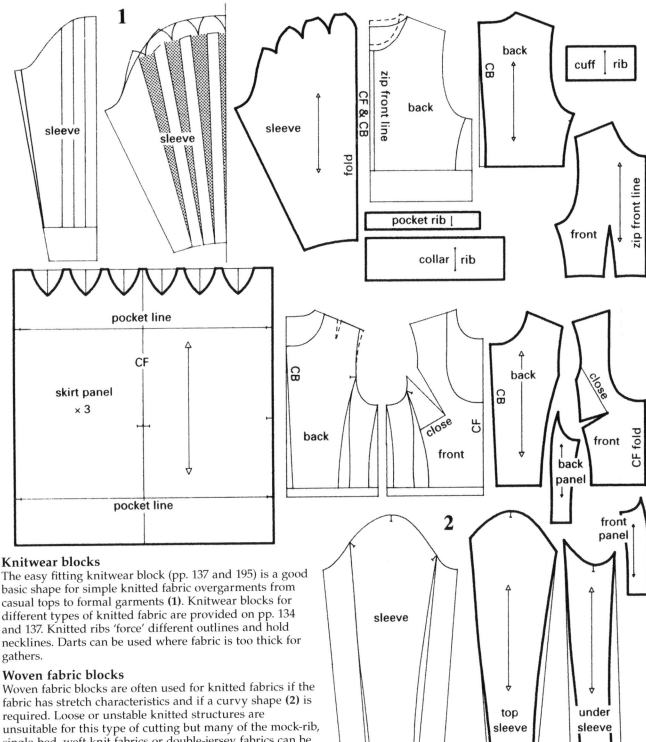

Knitwear blocks

The easy fitting knitwear block (pp. 137 and 195) is a good basic shape for simple knitted fabric overgarments from casual tops to formal garments (1). Knitwear blocks for different types of knitted fabric are provided on pp. 134 and 137. Knitted ribs 'force' different outlines and hold necklines. Darts can be used where fabric is too thick for gathers.

Woven fabric blocks

Woven fabric blocks are often used for knitted fabrics if the fabric has stretch characteristics and if a curvy shape (2) is required. Loose or unstable knitted structures are unsuitable for this type of cutting but many of the mock-rib, single-bed, weft-knit fabrics or double-jersey fabrics can be very successful cut in this way.

1 Styled overgarment

Body Sections   trace round body block. Mark in high waist line, shaped side seam line, neckline and front zip line.
Trace off the pattern sections as front and back pieces. Shape in back seam. Construct a front waist dart.
Sleeve   reduce the sleeve width; length by cuff depth. Divide sleeve into sections; cut and spread. Raise the sleeve head for extra fullness, draw in convex darts.
Skirt   the skirt panels and pockets are drafted as simple rectangles. The waist fullness is divided into concave darts.

2 Styled body fitting

The garment has a simple basic panel shaped boucle bodice, (ref. page 112), a rectangular mohair gathered skirt, and a shaped sleeve (ref. page 122).

Fabrics used in the illustrations

			We	Th	Sh	Dr	St
1	wool viscose	weft-knit	5	5	4	5	3
2	wool bouclé	weft-knit	5	3/4	4	4	2
	mohair	weft-knit	3	4	3	3	2

Knitted/stretch fabric: the close fitting blocks

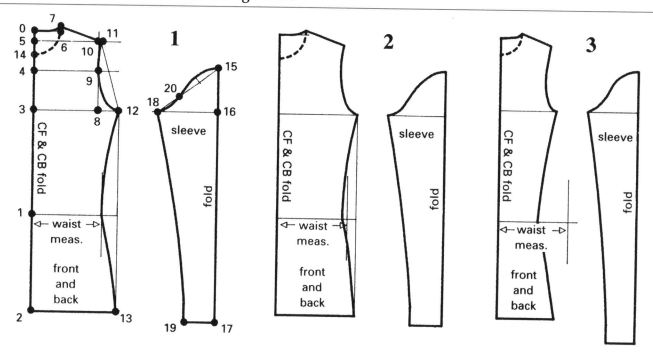

Pages 130–133 show knitted fabrics chosen as alternatives to woven fabrics and the block selection is made by simply assessing the five characteristics of the fabric. However, if knitted fabrics are to be exploited for their body-fitting potential, blocks with measurements that are less than the body measurements must be used. The % stretch must also be calculated to select the correct block. For details of how to do this see page 27. Other factors will also affect your judgement:

(1) The thickness of the fabric.
(2) The fabric should still look appealing (visual stretch) when it is stretched to fit the body.
(3) The fabric should still look acceptable (visual stretch) when under stress from body actions.
(4) The fabric should stretch to approximately twice its basic body-fitting 'visual stretch'.
(5) Fabric with horizontal stretch and bi-stretch will generally reduce in length when under tension. The vertical measurements may have to be adjusted for some fabrics.
(6) If the fabric does not recover well after stretching, more ease will be required in the block.

The range of close fitting body blocks provide a base from which close body-fitting designs can be constructed. But modifications may still be needed depending on the fabrics. This very often takes place after the first fitting when the appearance of the fabric on the body can be seen.

Blocks one and **two** are drafted for a visual stretch rating (see page 27) of between 3 and 5 (9.5–30%).

Block three is drafted for very high-stretch garment ratings 1–2 (over 50%). Working with this level of stretch in lingerie or swimwear ranges requires special skills and calculations.

Blocks for leggings and leotards can be found in *Metric Pattern Cutting*.

Measurements required to draft the block (example size 10) (refer to size chart page 188)

bust	82 cm	neck size	35.6 cm
nape to waist	39.5 cm	sleeve length	51.3 cm
armhole depth	20.5 cm	(jersey)	
back width	33 cm	wrist	15.5 cm

Body Sections square down and across from 0.
0–1 neck to waist plus 1 cm; square across.
0–2 finished length; square across.
0–3 armhole depth minus 2.5 cm (3 cm) (5 cm); square across.
0–4 half the measurement 0–3; square across.
0–5 one fifth the measurement 0–4; square across.
0–6 one sixth neck size (−0.5 cm) (−1.5 cm); square up.
6–7 1.3 cm; draw in neck curve.
3–8 half back width minus 2 cm (−2.5 cm) (−6 cm); square up to 9 and 10. 10–11 1 cm; join 7–11.
3–12 quarter bust minus 1.5 cm (−3 cm) (−8 cm); square down to 13 on hemline.
Draw in the armhole curve, from 11 through 9 to 12.
0–14 one sixth neck size minus 1 cm (−1 cm) (−1.5 cm); draw in front neck curve.
Shape in at the waist 3.5 cm (3 cm) (4 cm).
Sleeve square down from 15.
15–16 half the measurement 0–3 plus 1 cm.
15–17 jersey sleeve length plus 3 cm (3 cm) (6 cm); square across.
15–18 the measurement of the diagonal line from 11–12 on the body section plus 1 cm (0.5 cm) (no ease).
17–19 half wrist (−0.5 cm) (−1.5 cm); join 18–19 with a curve.
Divide 15–18 into three sections. Mark point 20.
Draw in sleeve head.
18–20 hollow the curve 0.6 cm. 20–15 raise the curve 2 cm.

Fabrics used in the illustrations and block choice

		We	Th	Sh	Dr	St
1	Cotton boucle (bi-str. 12.5%)	5	4	4	4	3
2	Cotton/elast. rib (bi-str. 15.5%)	4	4	5	4	2
both fabrics: thick + low recovery	**decision = block 1**					
3	Cotton rib (bi-str. 25%)	3	3	5	3	1
med thickness + low–med recov.	**decision = block 2 modified**					
4	Wool/elast. (bi-str. 19%)	2	2	5	3	2
thin–med + med–high-str. + high recov.	**decision = block 2**					
5	Polyam./elast. (25%)	2	2	5	2	1
thin–med + high-str. + high recov.	**decision = block 2**					
6	Polyam. (bi-str. 66%)	1	1	4	1	1
thin–med + very high-str. + high recov.	**decision = block 3**					

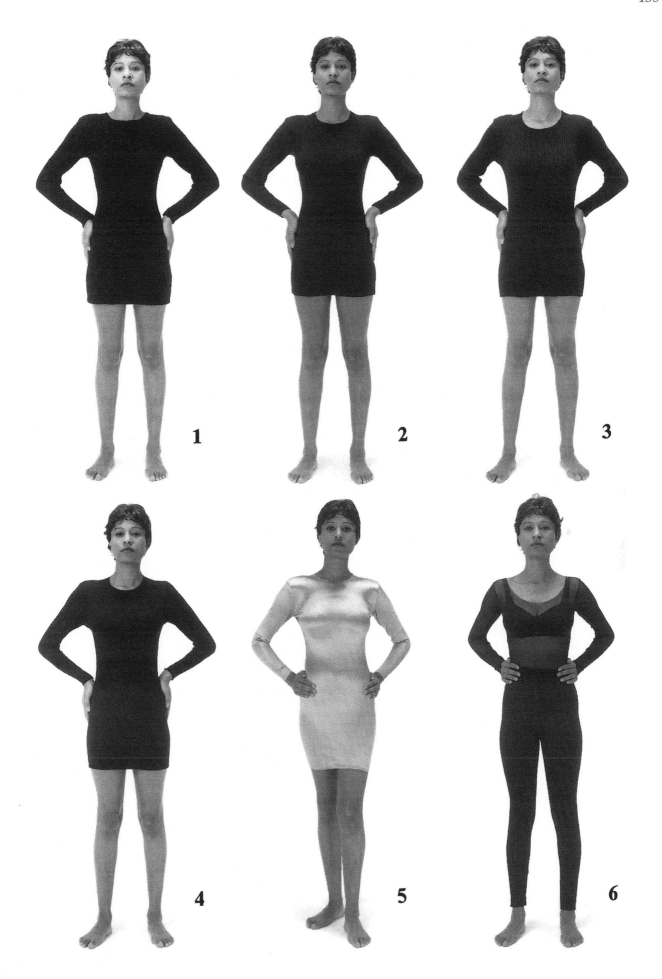

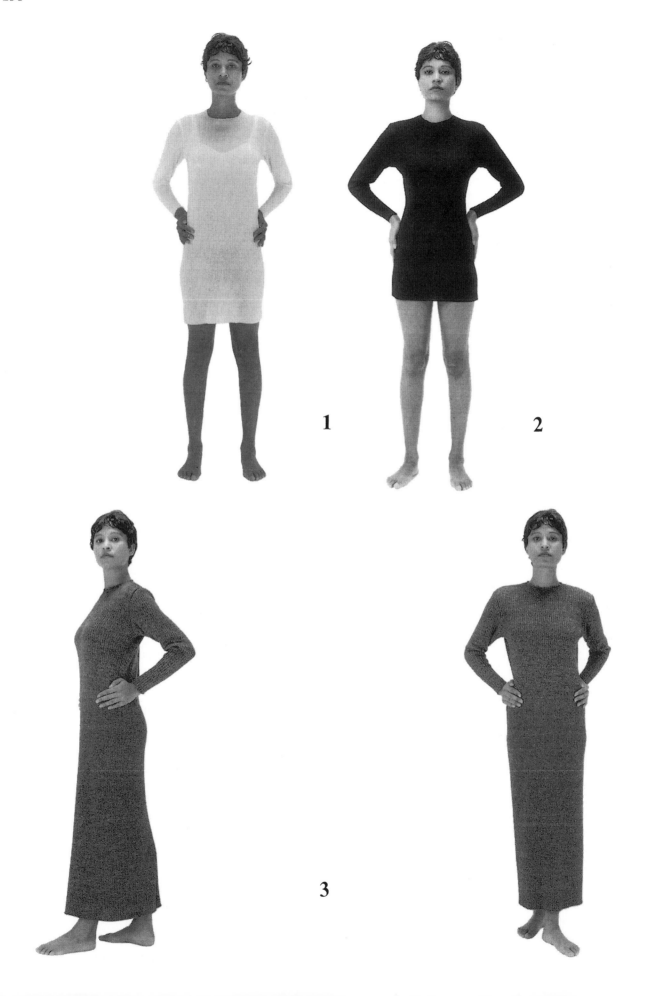

1

2

3

Knitted/stretch fabric: the basic and easy fitting blocks

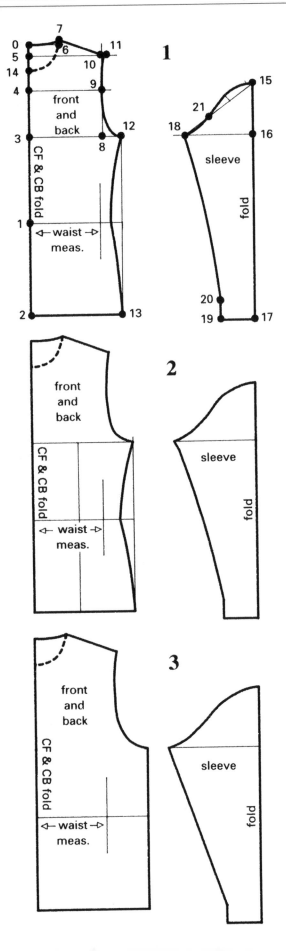

Thick fabrics or fabrics with medium-stretch require stretch blocks with more ease. As more easy fitting designs are required the criteria are less essential and the blocks can be used as shown on pages 130–133. If some body fitting is required the six criteria listed on page 134 still apply.

The three blocks are:
(1) A basic body fit with no ease allowance.
(2) A block with 2 cm ease allowance and the position for any waist darting required.
(3) An easy fitting block with 4 cm ease for the basic jersey shapes. Its use is shown on page 133.

Measurements required to draft the block (example size 10) (refer to size chart page 188)

bust	82 cm	neck size	35.6 cm
nape to waist	39.5 cm	sleeve length	51.3 cm
armhole depth	20.5 cm	(jersey)	
back width	33 cm	wrist	15.5 cm

Body Sections square down and across from 0.
0–1 neck to waist; square across.
0–2 finished length; square across.
0–3 armhole depth basic measurement (+1 cm) (+3 cm); square across.
0–4 half the measurement 0–3; square across.
0–5 one quarter the measurement 0–4; square across.
0–6 one fifth neck size; square up.
6–7 1 cm; draw in neck curve.
3–8 half back width basic measurement (+0.5 cm) (1.25 cm); square up to 9 and 10. 10–11 cm; join 7–11.
3–12 quarter bust basic measurement (+2 cm) (+4.5 cm); square down to 13 on hemline.
Draw in the armhole curve, from 11 through 9 to 12.
0–14 one sixth neck size minus 1.5 cm; draw in front neck curve.
Shape waist if required 2.5 cm (3.5 cm) (5 cm).
Added waist shaping can be achieved by waist darts.
Sleeve square down from 15.
15–16 half the measurement 0–3 plus 1 cm.
15–17 jersey sleeve length plus 2 cm; square across.
15–18 the measurement of the diagonal line from 11–12 on the body section plus 1.5 cm (2 cm) (2 cm).
17–19 half wrist (+0.5 cm) (+1 cm); square up 6 cm to 20.
Join 18–20 with a curve.
Divide 15–18 into three sections. Mark point 21.
Draw in sleeve head.
18–21 hollow the curve 0.6 cm. 21–15 raise the curve 2 cm.

Fabrics used in the illustrations and block choice

	We	Th	Sh	Dr	St
1 Silk jersey (low bi-str. 9.5%)	2	2	4	1	3
thin–med + med-str. + med recov.	**decision = block 1**				
2 Wool jersey (bi-str. 12.5%)	3	3	4	3	3
med–thick + med-str. + med recov.	**decision = block 1**				
3 Wool/polyam. rib (bi-str. 15.5%)	2	2	5	2	1
med–thick + med–high-str. +	**decision = block 2**				
low–med recov.					

Woven/stretch fabric: using blocks

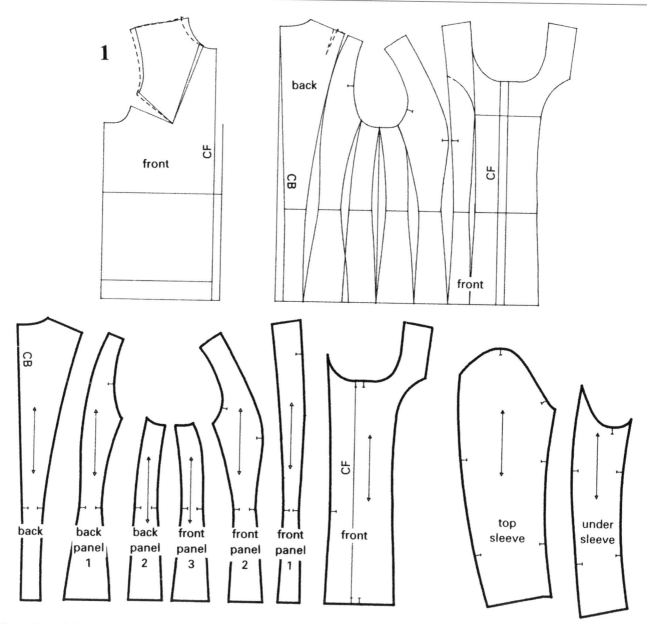

1

Woven/stretch fabrics that have a high degree of stretch can be treated as knitted stretch fabrics and the knitwear blocks can be used with the criteria described on page 134. **(2)**, **(3)** and **(4)** are garments in a diverse range of fabrics that were treated in this way. The recovery was the overriding factor. The cotton/elastane tee-shirt was put under more tension than the fabrics without the elastane content.

Fabrics in a narrow product range can have a set of criteria specially developed for them. Most worsted/elastane suitings have visual stretch characteristics that are low–medium with good recovery and stability. **(1)** shows a conventionally cut panelled garment with no alterations to the pattern. The elastane content is seen as comfort stretch.

A neater body fit can be achieved using the formula:

Reduce the pattern 5% in all horizontal measurements for every 10% visual stretch measurement.
Increase the vertical measure by 2% for every 5% where the fabric is under tension.

Ideally, this should be done at block construction or by computer to reduce the pattern evenly. If the pattern is

adjusted manually, by cutting and overlapping the pattern, the overlaps must take place proportionally in each section of the pattern controlled by the initial block construction (i.e. neck width, back width, bust).

Compare the fit of the close fitting jacket on the stand with **(1)** page 140. The fabric had 9.5% visual stretch; therefore the pattern had a 5% reduction horizontally and a 2% increase vertically.

Fabrics used in the illustrations and block choice

		We	Th	Sh	Dr	St
Close fitting jacket block (page 200)						
1	Wool/elast. (bi-str. 9.5%) high recov.	3	3	4	3	3
Knitwear block 1 (page 137) (basic body measurements)						
2	Cotton/elast. (bi-str. 9.5%) high recov.	4	3	5	4	3
3	Cotton crinkle (15.5%) low recov.		3	2	1	3	2
4	Wool boucle (bi-str. 15.5%) low recov.	3	1/3	2	2	2

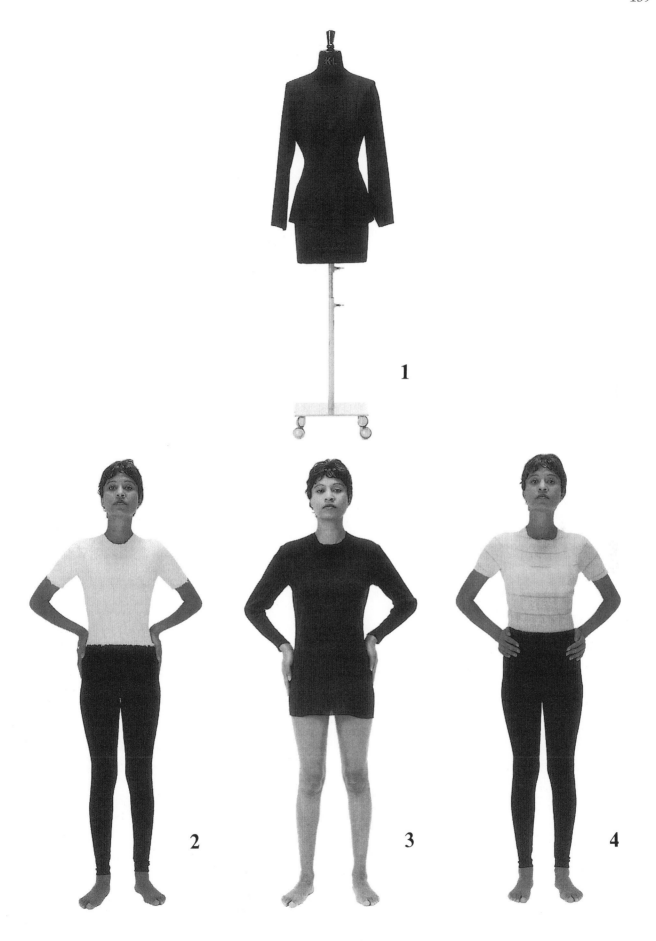

1

2

3

4

1

2

Woven fabric with elastane: comparisons of body fitting

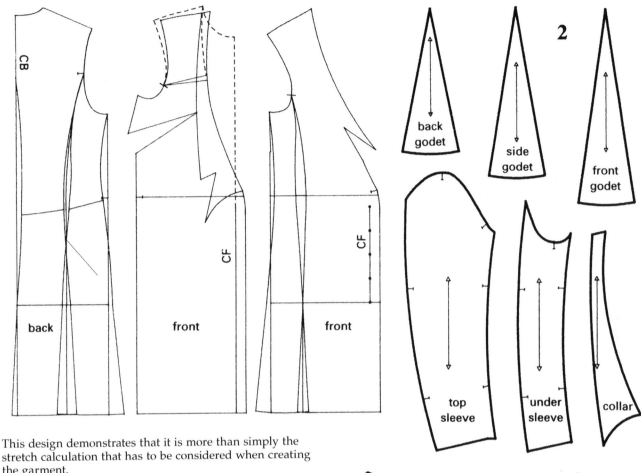

This design demonstrates that it is more than simply the stretch calculation that has to be considered when creating the garment.

The fabric in **(2)** has far higher basic visual and active stretch readings than **(1)**. Both are bi-stretch. Both have similar recovery ratings.

It would be expected that the pattern for the second garment would be reduced more than the first.

However, the design effect is the overriding consideration. Whilst a close body-hugging fit in **(1)** enhances the 'slick' quality of the fabric as it stretches over the body contours, the second design uses a thicker textured fabric which has a medium-shear characteristic. It is important that the unusual geometric ribbon-weave should not be distorted. The effect of this garment is ethnic, with contrasting back and front surfaces of the fabric used, seam godets and raw edge finishes.

The same amount of horizontal reductions and vertical additions were made for both garments, despite the difference in the stretch ratings. Note especially the contrasting fit of the garments. Note also that vertical additions only take place where the garment is under stress and will be stretched.

The procedures for cutting this simple design are not detailed. It is a simple coat with panel seams; the bust dart is transferred to the neck.

The diagrams are explicit and are only shown as an example of the principles discussed.

The close fitting jacket block (ref. page 200) was used for the examples.

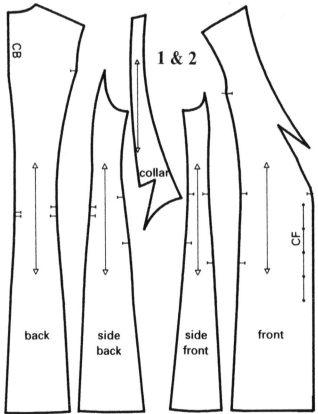

Fabrics used in the illustrations

			We	Th	Sh	Dr	St
1	Polyester/elastane	woven	3	2	5	4	3
2	Wool/polyamide/ elastane	woven	4	4	3	2	1

Comparisons of body fitting and fabrics

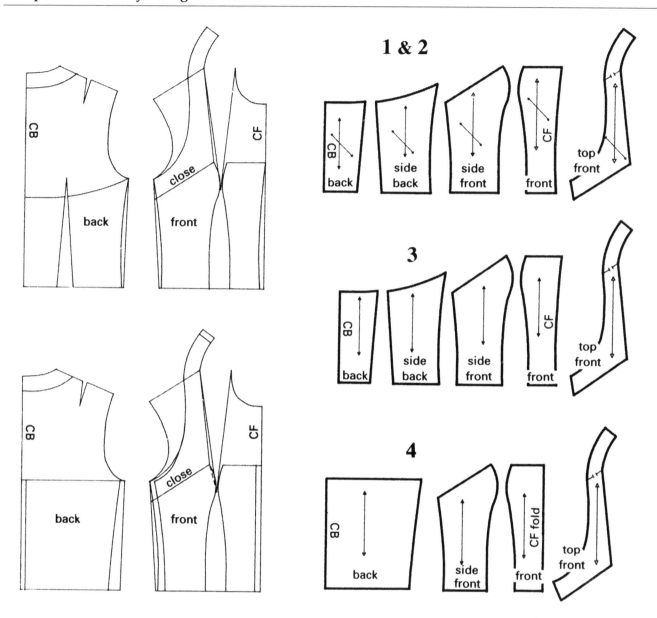

A simple halter neck close fitting garment pattern is reviewed in different fabrics and modifications.

These five examples show clearly that when designing body fitting garments the fabric will determine the pattern cutting procedures.

The procedures for cutting these simple designs are not detailed; the diagrams are explicit and are only shown as an example of the principles.

The close fitting body block (page 202) was used for the examples.

The front and back side seams were reduced by 1 cm before adaptation.

1 & 2 Adaptation in woven fabric
A standard adaptation of the design.
(1) is cut on the straight in a firm fabric.
(2) is cut on the crossway in a high–medium-drape fabric. Note how the tension on the strap makes it become narrower.

3 Adaptation in weft-knitted fabric with elastane
The adaptation is reduced on the horizontal close body measurements by 5 cm, the vertical measurements are increased by 1 cm to achieve a similar appearance to (1). **NOTE** that the back neck is seen as a horizontal measurement.

4 Adaptation in weft-knitted rib fabric
A seam has been eliminated from the back of this design which is cut straight and the back shaping increased on the side seam.

The horizontal measurement is reduced as above but no alteration to the vertical measurements is required.

Fabrics used in the illustrations

			We	Th	Sh	Dr	St
1	Silk	woven	4	2	3	4	5
2	Viscose	woven	3	1	4	3	4
3	Polyamide/elast.	weft-knit	2	2	5	2	2
4	Cotton/polyester	weft-knit	2	2	4	2	2

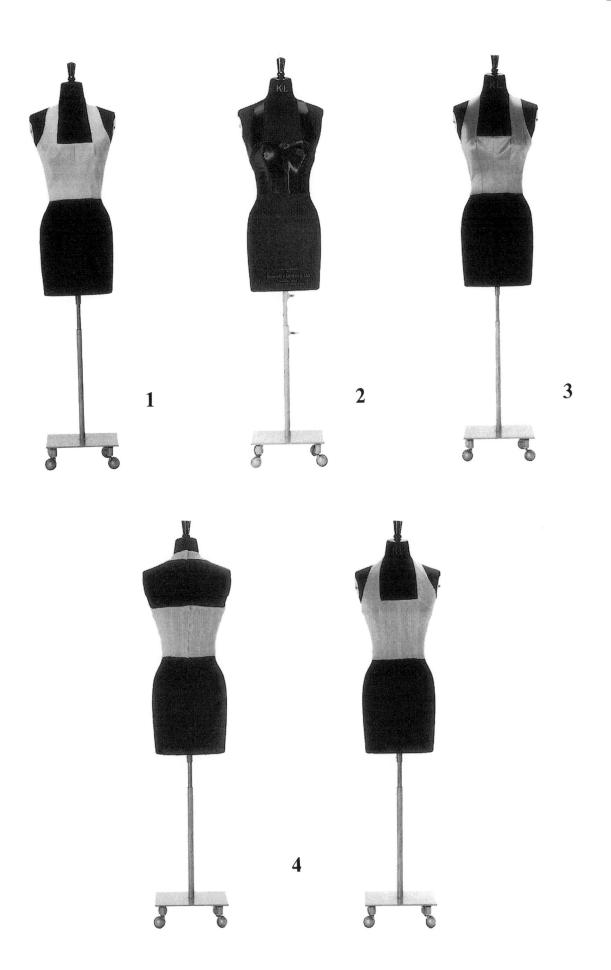

1

2

3

4

1

2

Comparisons of body fitting and fabrics

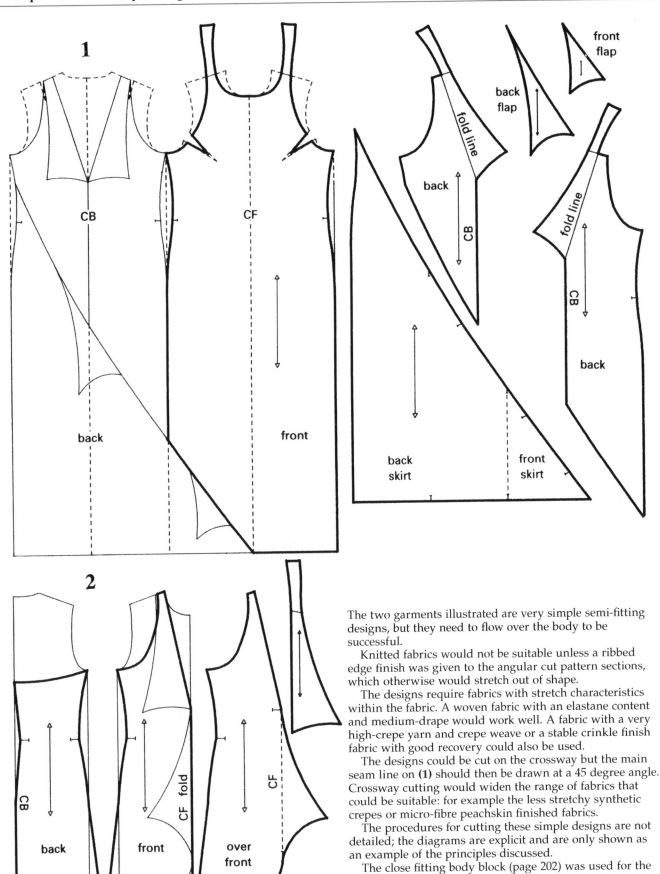

The two garments illustrated are very simple semi-fitting designs, but they need to flow over the body to be successful.

Knitted fabrics would not be suitable unless a ribbed edge finish was given to the angular cut pattern sections, which otherwise would stretch out of shape.

The designs require fabrics with stretch characteristics within the fabric. A woven fabric with an elastane content and medium-drape would work well. A fabric with a very high-crepe yarn and crepe weave or a stable crinkle finish fabric with good recovery could also be used.

The designs could be cut on the crossway but the main seam line on **(1)** should then be drawn at a 45 degree angle. Crossway cutting would widen the range of fabrics that could be suitable: for example the less stretchy synthetic crepes or micro-fibre peachskin finished fabrics.

The procedures for cutting these simple designs are not detailed; the diagrams are explicit and are only shown as an example of the principles discussed.

The close fitting body block (page 202) was used for the examples.

The front and back side seams were reduced by 1 cm before adaptation.

Comparisons of body fitting and fabrics

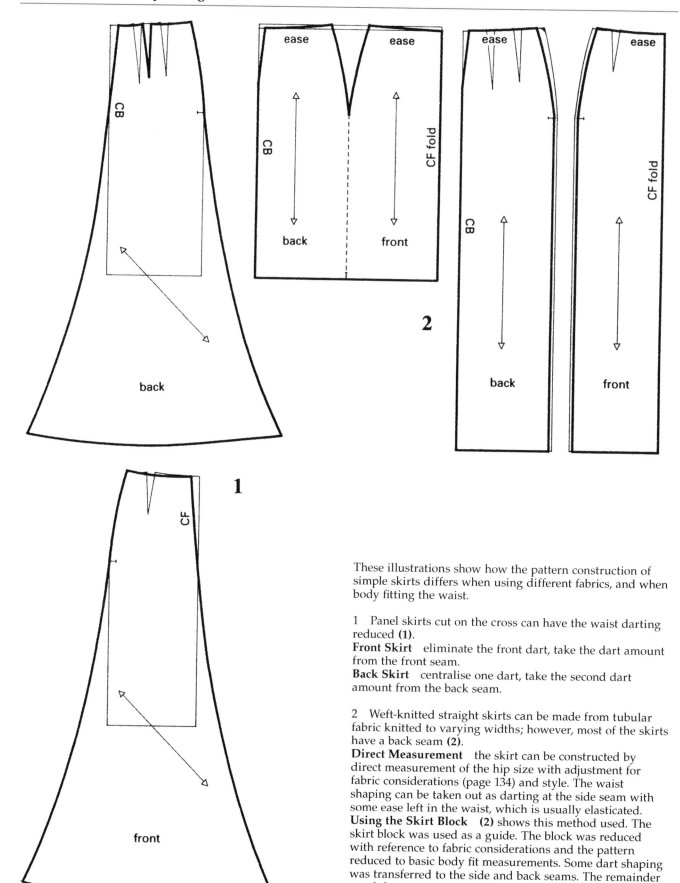

These illustrations show how the pattern construction of simple skirts differs when using different fabrics, and when body fitting the waist.

1   Panel skirts cut on the cross can have the waist darting reduced **(1)**.
Front Skirt   eliminate the front dart, take the dart amount from the front seam.
Back Skirt   centralise one dart, take the second dart amount from the back seam.

2   Weft-knitted straight skirts can be made from tubular fabric knitted to varying widths; however, most of the skirts have a back seam **(2)**.
Direct Measurement   the skirt can be constructed by direct measurement of the hip size with adjustment for fabric considerations (page 134) and style. The waist shaping can be taken out as darting at the side seam with some ease left in the waist, which is usually elasticated.
Using the Skirt Block   **(2)** shows this method used. The skirt block was used as a guide. The block was reduced with reference to fabric considerations and the pattern reduced to basic body fit measurements. Some dart shaping was transferred to the side and back seams. The remainder was left as ease and the waist elasticated.

3   (diagram page 148).

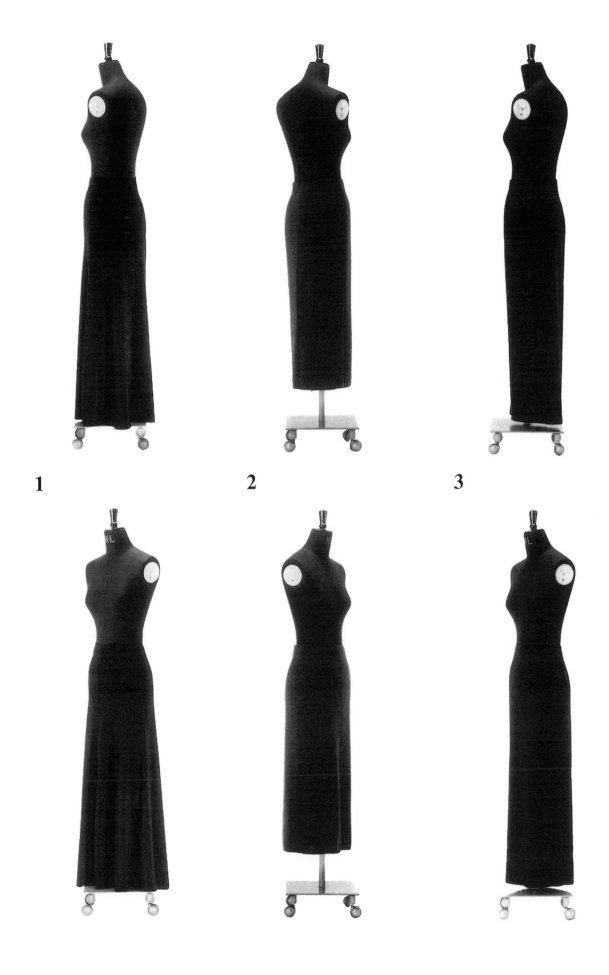

1

2

3

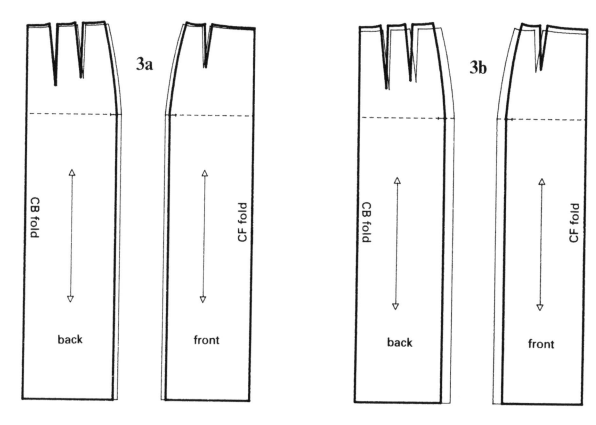

3a

CB fold

back

CF fold

front

3b

CB fold

back

CF fold

front

3   The diagrams show how the mathematical procedures of cutting woven/elastane fabrics with varying amounts of stretch can control and retain the complex shape of the pattern.

The diagrams show the changing shape as the percentage reduction is increased and the necessity of it being distributed evenly between all the block construction drafting points.

The garment **(3)** illustrated on page 147 had the horizontal measurements reduced by 5% and the vertical measurements of the areas under stress increased by 2% as shown in diagram 3a.

Diagram 3b shows horizontal measurements reduced by 10% and the vertical measurements of the areas under stress increased by 4%.

PART THREE: FABRIC, FORM AND FLAT PATTERN CUTTING

8 Combining fabrics

Framing fabrics

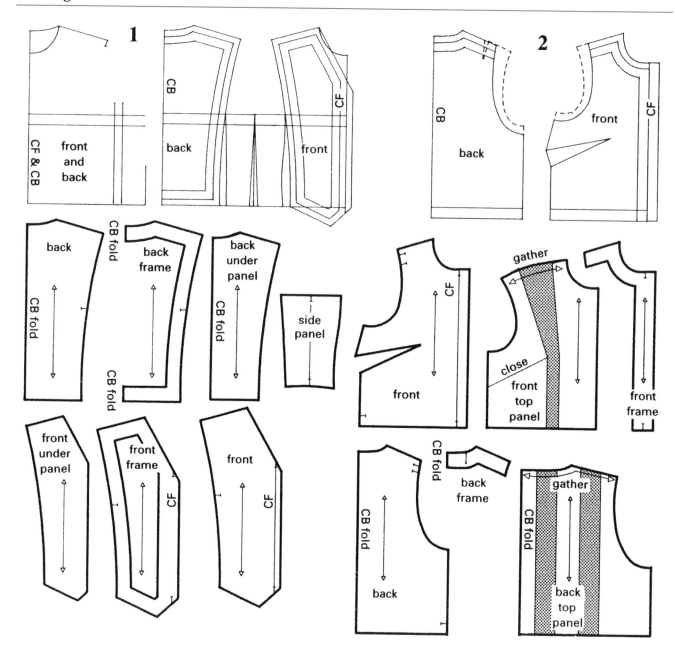

Some highly decorated fabrics are enhanced by framing; small sections or whole body sections can be framed. The fabric can be totally enclosed (1), or partially enclosed (2). Simple or more complex shaping can be used.

1 Total framing: simple shape

Construct a basic shape from the basic draft.
Draw in the frame lines. Add buttonstand.
Draw in the under-panel between the frame line and the main section.
Trace off the pattern sections.
Close side seam dart.

2 Partial framing: adding shape

Trace round block required.
Draw in the frame lines. Add buttonstand.
Draw in the under-panels between the frame line and the main section.
Trace off the pattern sections.
Cut and open the under-panels; close the bust dart.

Fabrics used in the illustrations

			We	Th	Sh	Dr	St
1	wool/nylon	woven	4	1/3	4	5	4
2	polyester	lace	3	1/3	4	3	4
	viscose	woven	3	3	3	2	4

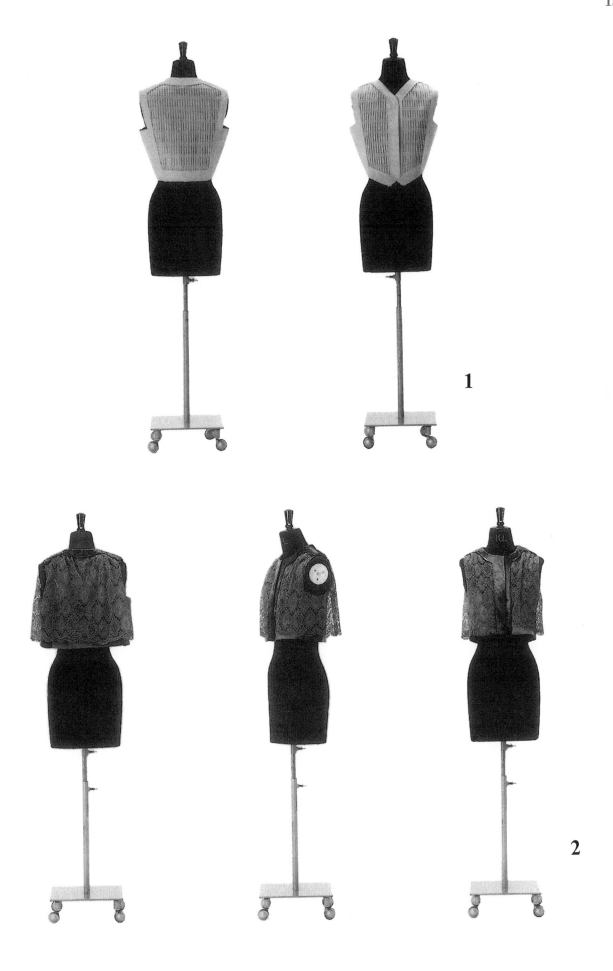

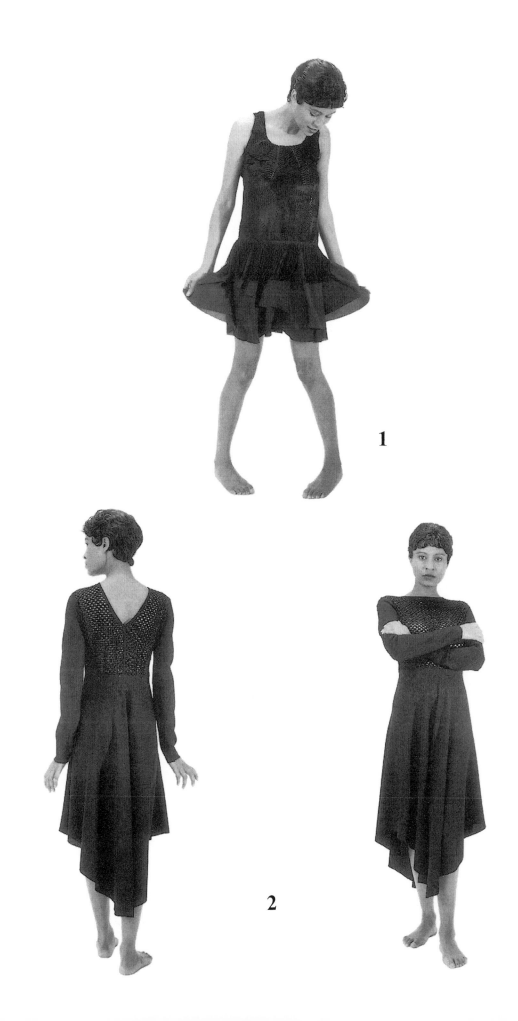

1

2

Sympathetic fabrics

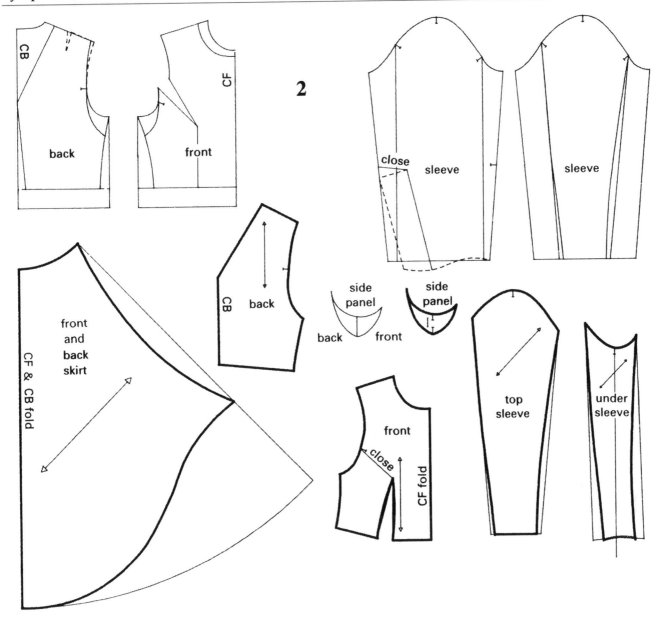

Different fabrics are often combined in the same garment. Few problems arise if these fabrics are 'sympathetic': that is, that they have a common or similar fibre source, and that their structure is compatible. The first illustration shows a dress made in antique devore silk velvet married to a skirt in fine silk crepe.

A stronger fabric can give a weaker one support. The fabrics used in the second illustration are acetate crepe with medium–high-drape and acetate/acrylic/polyester open ribbon-inserted warp-knit. The ribbon knit is surprisingly stable but requires an inset where there is strain (at the underarm). Although the crepe is cut on the crossway to accentuate the draping qualities in the skirt and to give a close fitting sleeve, the bodice (cut on the straight) is stable enough to support it.

1 'Combined' dress
The pattern for the design is on page 72.

2 'Combined' dress
Body Sections   trace round block.

Mark in the high waistline. Draw in the neckline.
Shape in at the centre back and side seams.
Transfer bust dart to the armhole.
Draw in the shape of the underarm panels.
Trace off the pattern sections.
Join the two panels at the underarm.
Sleeve   construct a close fitting shaped sleeve (page 122).
Skirt   construct a quarter circle panel (ref. page 67) to a measurement twice the high waist measurement; divide the panel in half. Draw in a skirt shape as required.

Fabrics used in the illustrations

			We	Th	Sh	Dr	St
1	Silk velvet (devore)	woven	3	1/3	4	3	4
	Silk crepe	woven	2	2	3	2	4
2	Acetate	woven	2	2	3	2	4
	Acetate/acrylic/ polyester	warp-knit	3	3/4	1	4	3

154

Sympathetic combination fabrics

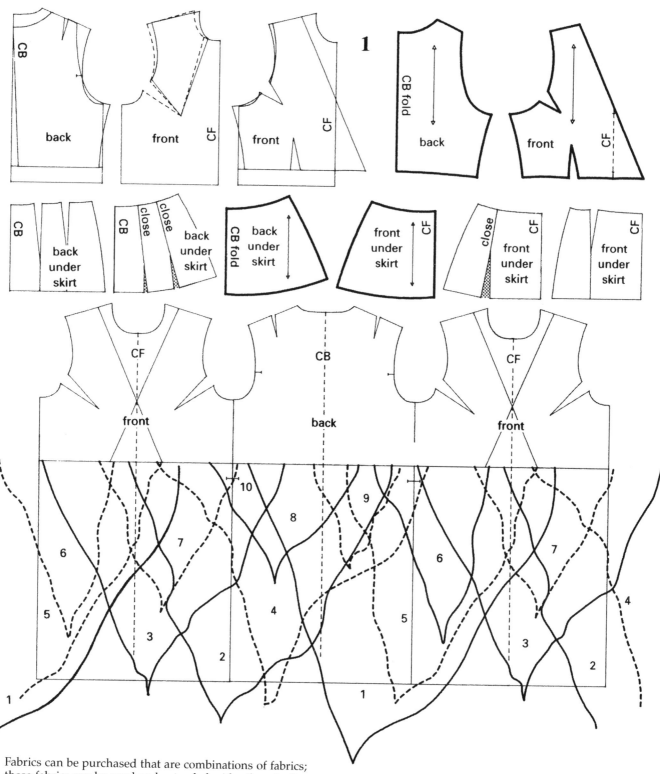

Fabrics can be purchased that are combinations of fabrics; these fabrics can be used and extended with other similar fabrics. The double-layered (wool flannel/cotton lawn) base fabric used for the bodice had the cotton lawn cut away in random shapes. The skirt design followed the theme. Shrunk calico and cotton lawn layers were used. The roughly cut random shapes were pre-washed to give the same effect as the main fabric.

A design can be taken to a first stage by flat pattern cutting methods to create a 'map'. The garment sections can then be taken onto the stand to refine the shape.

A simple wrap-front top was constructed. A skirt yoke was drafted to create a foundation for the skirt. The skirt sections were traced off; each section was widened to give gathered fullness at the waist. These pieces were modified as they were draped on the stand.

Fabrics used in the illustrations

			We	Th	Sh	Dr	St
1	Wool cotton	woven	4	4	2	5	4
	Cotton lawn	woven	2	1	3	3	4
	Cotton calico	woven	2	2	4	4	5

1

1

Sympathetic fabrics: knit/elastane/lace

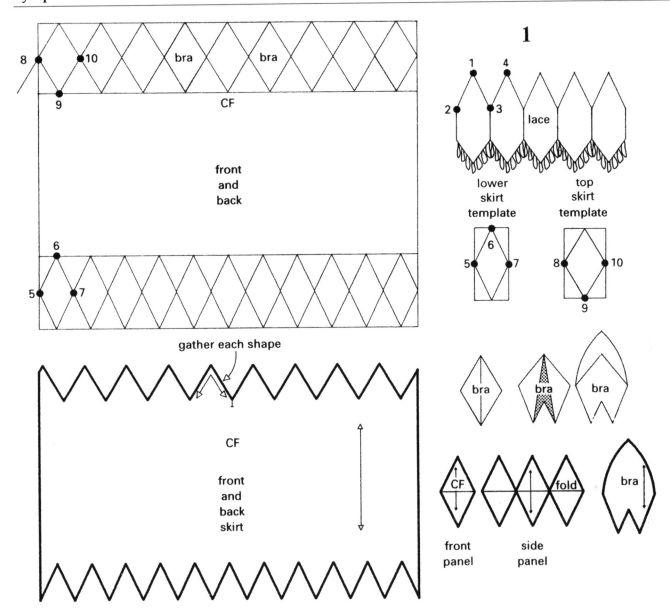

Many stretch warp-knit fabrics are used with lace in 'lingerie' type designs. However, here we see a design in wool/lycra single-jersey and cotton lace. Designs which are designed around a feature fabric (in this case the lace), or dominated by a fabric motif, are often mathematically constructed. Fabrics with elastane give a designer some flexibility around the body shape.

This type of design is usually constructed by direct measurement. This design took the motif around the body; this is often not mathematically possible and the motifs have to be inserted in pattern sections.

1 Simple body shape design
Create a rectangle the required length. Balance the width between the measurement of the hips and the lace repeat.

Calculate the number of motifs required to fit the hip measurement.
Mark out the motifs (11) along the base of the skirt.
A balance between the widest point of the garment and the lace repeat was made.
Calculate the measurement around the rib cage.
Calculate the number of motifs (9) required. Stretch the motif shape 120% to fit the rectangle.
Extend two diamond shapes into a bra shape as shown.
Cut folded diamond shapes to make a stable edge for the top of the garment.

Fabrics used in the illustrations

			We	Th	Sh	Dr	St
1	Wool/elastane	weft-knit	2	2	5	3	2
	Cotton lace	lace	4	3	1	4	4

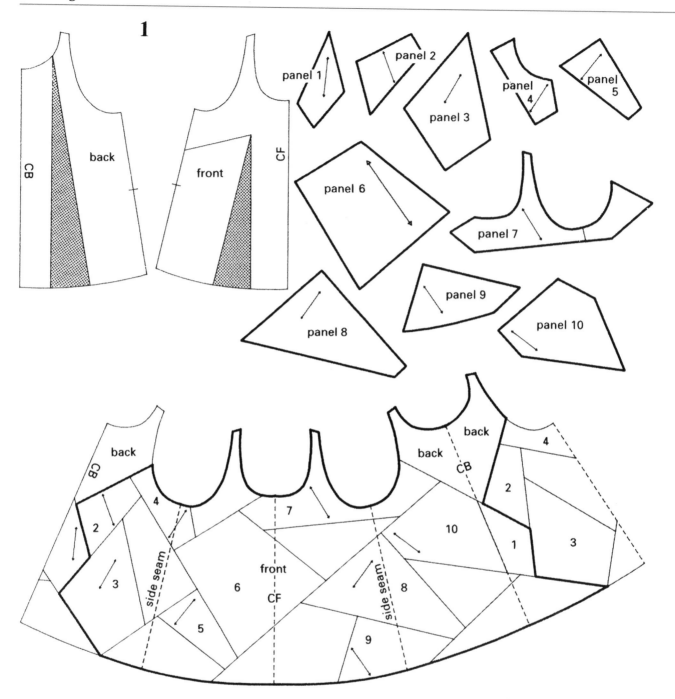

Unique fabrics can be created by many surface decoration methods: machine embroidery, appliqué decoupé, pulled thread and interwoven threads and ribbons and braids. These fabrics can give new dimensions to structure. The garment illustrated is constructed by appliqué of nylon/cotton stripe fabric onto a polyurethene coated net. Many of the heavier polyester or nylon warp-knit nets provide firm grounds for combinations of fabrics.

A basic simple shape was divided geometrically; note that the back seam is placed so that it integrates into the design.

The appliqué shapes are traced off the main pattern and cut on the grain required.

Fabrics used in the illustrations

			We	Th	Sh	Dr	St
1	cotton/nylon	woven	2	1/3	4	3	5
2	nylon/polyurethene	warp-knit	2	1	5	3	5

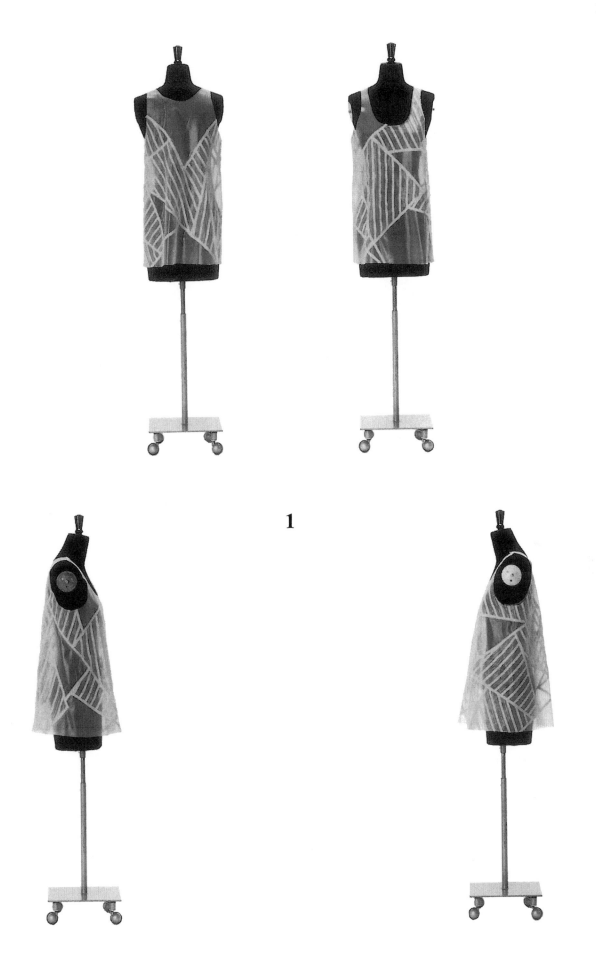

1

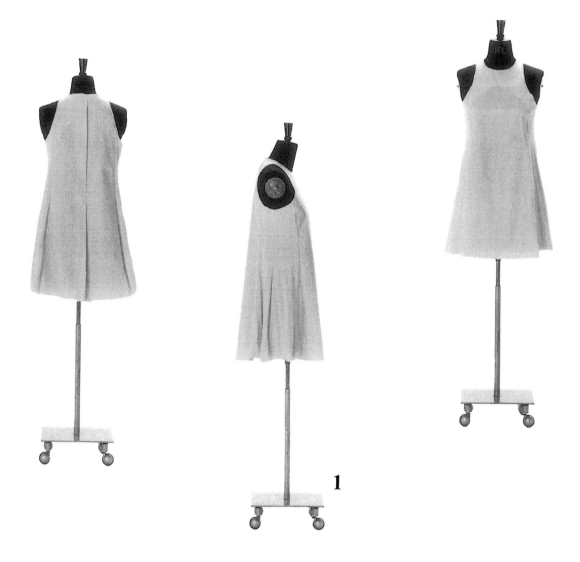

1

Contrasting fabrics: woven/knit

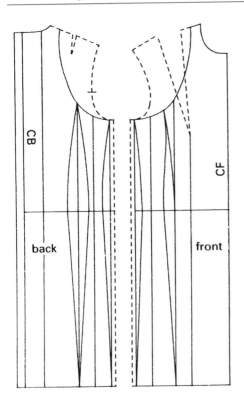

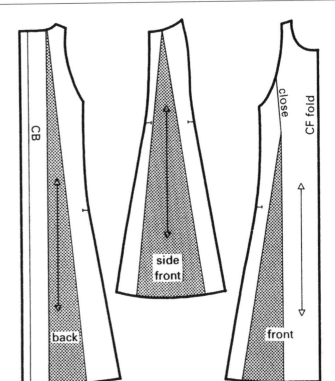

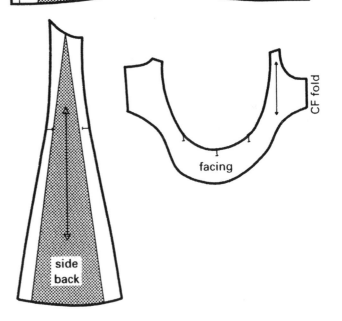

Knit and woven fabrics can be combined. They give added body movement and allow styles to be cut close to the body. The knitted fabric can be treated as woven fabric if it is of a similar or slightly heavier weight; it should be a close knit stable structure (e.g. fine rib).

The illustration shows a style where the pattern, cut from the close fitting bodice block (ref. page 202), is not reduced any more than is required for the standard sleeveless adaptation. However, a woven fabric facing stabilises the armhole area.

If knitted fabrics with high-stretch are used the side body would be reduced. An example of using this type of knitted fabric with woven fabric is shown on page 164.

1 Sleeveless adaptation
Body Sections   trace round the block to the required length.
Add buttonstand to the centre back line.
Swing the bust dart to the shoulder.
Remove 1 cm from the side seam.
Draw in the panel lines shaping dramatically with a slightly high waist.
Divide each panel into sections.
Drop one line from the bust point.
Trace off pattern sections, cut up lines and open the required amount, closing the bust dart on the front section.
Trace facings for the back and front sections. Join at the side seam.

Fabrics used in the illustrations

			We	Th	Sh	Dr	St
1	Cotton	woven	2	2	4	4	5
	Cotton	warp-knit	2	2	4	2	2

Contrasting fabrics: woven/elastane

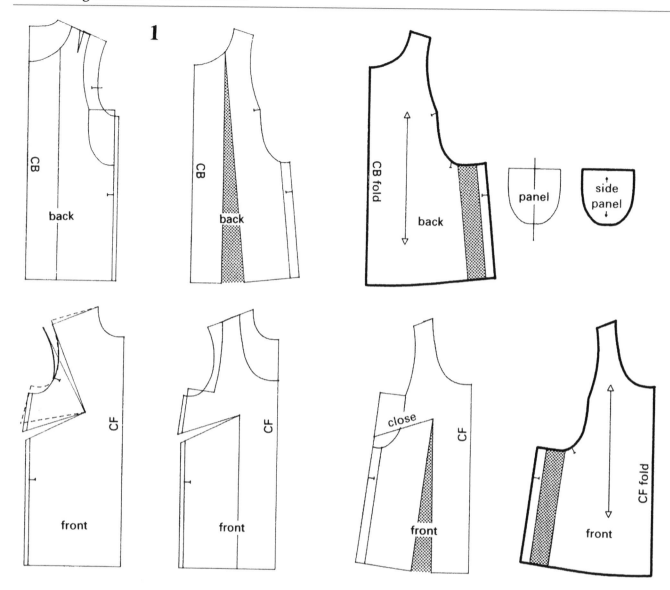

1

Standard woven fabrics and fabrics with elastane can be combined. The elastane fabrics give added body movement and allow styles to be cut close to the body.

The illustration shows a style where the pattern is cut from the close fitting bodice block (page 202). However a panel cut in fabric with elastane is inset to give a close but comfortable fit at the underarm. An examination of the panels used in corsets and underwear can provide ideas for inclusion in outerwear. The main areas of strain are the underarm and crutch areas.

Using elastane panels can allow new shapes to be produced. **(1)** shows how using an underarm panel with gathers creates different outlines to the garment from different views. The dart is reduced in this example; this should only be done when the fabric has some shear or stretch characteristics and extra fullness is introduced into the garment.

1 Sleeveless adaptation

Body Sections   trace round the block to the required length. To reduce the dart – draw a line from the bust point to the shoulder; cut up the line and swing the dart so that it is reduced by half.

Swing armhole line from notch back to shoulder point. Reduce the side seam by 1 cm.
Draw in neck and armhole shapes.
Front   drop a line from the bust point. Cut up the line; close the dart to flare the hem.
Draw in underarm panel. Trace off panel.
Draw line from the panel to hem parallel to the side seam. Cut up line and spread for gathers as shown.
Back   draw in underarm panel and parallel line as for front. Trace off panel.
Draw a line from centre back neck to hem.
Cut up line from the neck; cut and spread required amount.
Draw line from the panel to hem parallel to the side seam. Cut up the line and spread for gathers.
Side Panel   join back and front side panels at the side seam.
The diagrams for **(2)** are shown on page 164.

Fabrics used in the illustrations

			We	Th	Sh	Dr	St
1	Cotton	woven	5	4	3	4	3
	Cotton/elastane	woven	4	3	5	2	4

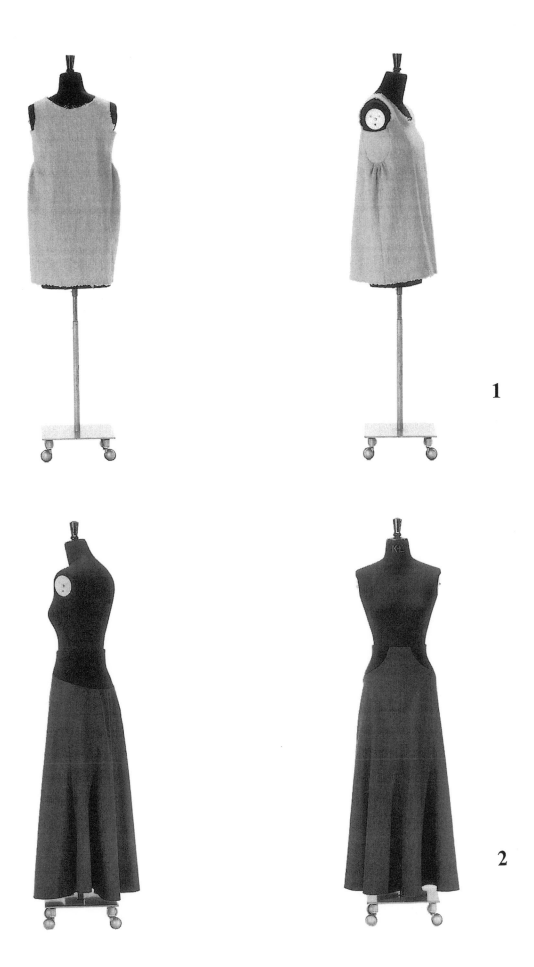

1

2

Contrasting fabrics: woven/elastane/knit

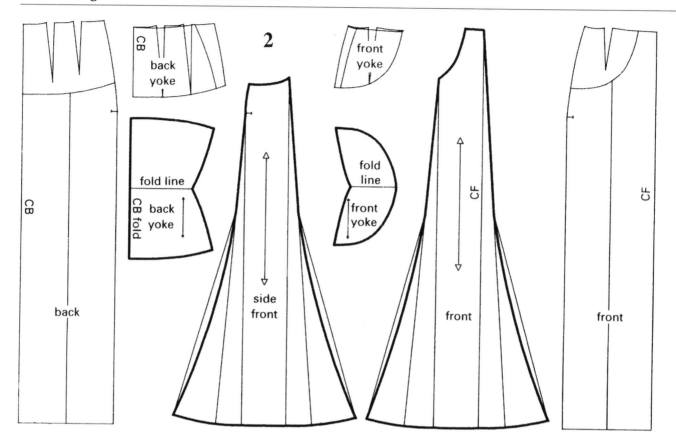

Knitted fabrics with elastane can give close body fit to areas and can be combined with standard woven fabrics. They give added body movement and allow styles to have areas cut close to the body where fitting is required, and yet the design can exploit the characteristics of woven fabrics. The illustration shows a cotton elastane rib fabric used with cotton denim, but softer effects could be obtained with silky knits/elastane and high-drape fabrics. Body panels or insets on dress styles can create a good body fit.

The illustration (2) on page 163 shows a simple flared skirt shape; the body fitting area is controlled by the stretch of the knit/elastane instead of darting. The proportion that the shape is reduced will depend on the stretch content of the fabric (see page 134).

2 Skirt adaptation

Body Sections   trace round the block to the required length.
Draw in yoke line.
Divide the skirt into panels as shown.
Trace off pattern sections; complete skirt as for the flare adaptation (page 70).
Yoke   ignore the darts on the yoke section; reduce the hip line, reduce the waist line.
Mirror the pattern along the top edge.

Fabrics used in the illustrations

			We	Th	Sh	Dr	St
2	Denim	woven	3	2	4	5	4
	Cotton/elastane	weft-knit	4	4	5	4	1

PART THREE: FABRIC, FORM AND FLAT PATTERN CUTTING

9 Subverting fabrics: adding extra structure

Structure

Most garments have some structure added to the fabric. It may only be a small amount of interlining to strengthen certain areas such as collars, cuffs and waistbands. A great deal of research has been focussed on providing fusible and non-fusible interlinings that are sympathetic to fabrics and will wear, launder or dry clean without distorting them. Because these interlinings are unseen, it does not mean that they are all inexpensive. The couturiers will use silk and cashmere to give delicate fabrics support yet retain a light and high-drape handle. The 'handle' of fabrics can be subtly or dramatically changed by the type of interlining: for example a fleecy domette will add softness and density to a limp fabric, a firm cotton base fabric will give structure.

Almost any fabric, woven, knitted or bonded, can be used to support another. However, most interlining and mounting fabrics have a close structure, are light in weight, and are black, grey, beige or white. These fabrics can be sew-in or fusible. The majority of interlinings today are non-woven. A garment may require substantial areas to have a different handle yet have the same surface appearance. Added structure may be required to create exaggerated or structured shapes that a fabric is unable to create alone. Shapes may be required for theatrical or performance garments which are not practical in the general sense. Standard techniques are often of little help and great ingenuity is required to build many of these constructions.

Interlining and mounting fabrics

Sew-in interlinings

Sew-in interlinings can be seen in ancient costumes. Techniques for using them became complex and demanding of skilled craftsmen. Conventional basic plain weave fabrics in natural fibres are still used as sew-in interfacings, particularly in couture and bespoke tailoring.

Non-woven and knitted interlinings are also used as sew-in interlinings; however, the amount of sew-in interlinings

used is continually decreasing. Fabrics must be pre-shrunk by launder or steaming.

Fusible interlinings

When fusible interlinings first became available in the 1950s and were used in garments, many strange things happened to the outer appearance. Fabrics shrank, bubbles appeared, 'board-like' sharp revers on jackets signalled their use.

Today most manufacturers use fusibles very successfully; the range is enormous in knitted, woven and bonded structures. They are used in all types of garments, from fine semi-transparent designs to heavy tailored or padded overgarments.

The fusible interlining consists of the base fabric and its coating (in scatter, paste or powder dot form) which heat-sets the interlining to the garment. Natural fibres are still used in many interlinings for tailoring, and graduated 'canvases' are available to give different thicknesses over the chest areas. However, man-made fibres dominate the fusible interlining market (mainly polyamide, polyester, viscose and polypropylene).

Problems with thermoplastic synthetic base fabrics (which can be damaged under the heat of ironing) are being addressed.

Warp-knitted fabrics are gaining popularity as a base fabric; although there can be problems of handling the fabric, they have a sympathetic handle, particularly when used on jersey fabrics.

Competition for knitted fusibles may come from the new developments in woven-stretch interlinings which are taking place. They are being developed to complement many of the new stretch and micro-fibre fabrics.

Non-woven interlinings

The fibres are bonded together by a variety of means: by entangling the fibres, stitch-bonding, or binding by chemical or heat processes. Many of the early problems of stiffness or disintegration of the lighter weights have been solved. Their greatest advantage is their stability in mass production.

Mounting: classic structure and flexible structure

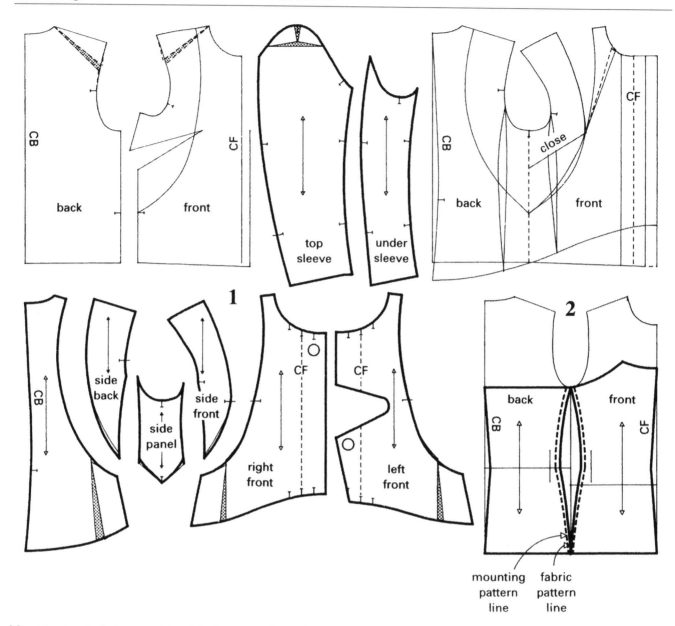

Mounting is a technique used (mainly in couture houses) to give particular strength or stability to high-shear or delicate fabrics. All the pattern pieces are cut out in both fabrics, basted together and made up as one. Mass production companies are more likely to use fabrics bonded together synthetically. The linen jacket (1) was developed from the close fitting jacket block. It was mounted on a fine strong black cotton. Compare the closer fit with the similar unmounted jacket on page 112. Mounted garments are most successful in designs with many seams. For mounting larger areas see page 174.

1 Simple jacket shape: classic mounting

Body Sections   trace round the block to the required length. Cut and open armhole line, raise shoulder the depth of shoulder pad. Cut across sleeve head and raise same amount.

Draw in front style line.

Swing bust dart to the shoulder. Overlap neck (ref. 2, page 89).

Draw in remaining style lines and side panel lines.

Lower back waist approx. 2 cm.

Shape panel lines as shown in diagram.

Construct a double-breasted front (Ref. *MPC* bodice section), draw in shaped hemline.

Trace off the pattern sections.

Draw in cut-away overlap as shown.

On the main sections, close waist darts and flare the hem.

2 Body fitting: mounting on stretch fabrics (flexible structure)

Body fitting garments (2) in fabrics with high-shear can be stabilised, but their 'movement' controlled by mounting on slightly smaller stretch fabrics, particularly knitted elastane.

The example used the close fitting dress block (sleeveless adaptation) (page 115) as a base.

Fabrics used in the illustrations

			We	Th	Sh	Dr	St
1	Linen	woven	3	2	3	4	4
	Mounting – cotton	woven	2	1	4	4	5
2	Cotton	lace	4	3	1	4	3
	Mounting – wool/elastane	weft-knit	2	2	5	3	2

1

2

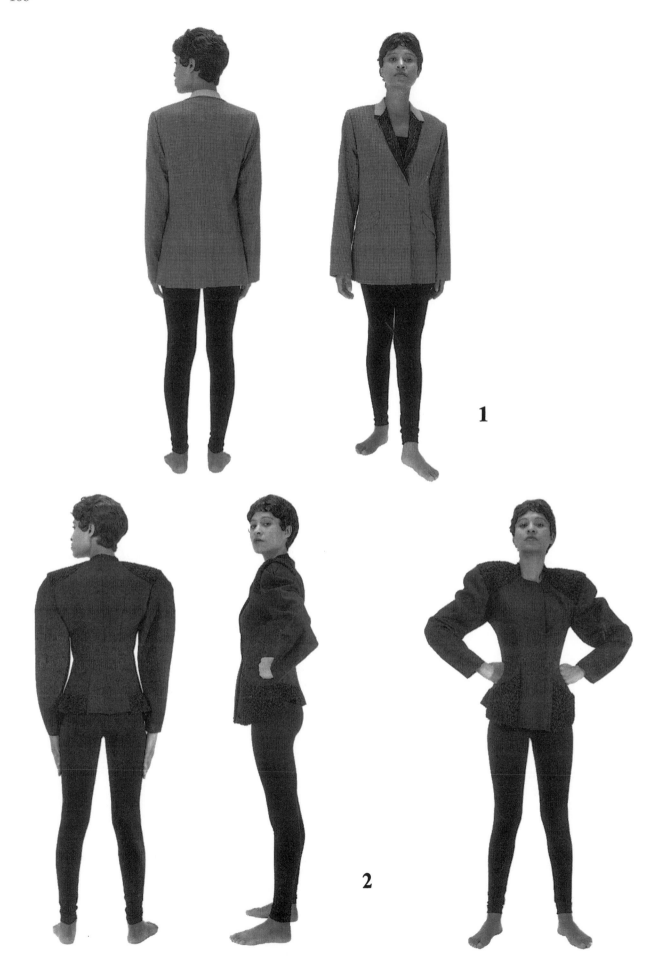

1

2

Interlinings: classic and exaggerated shape

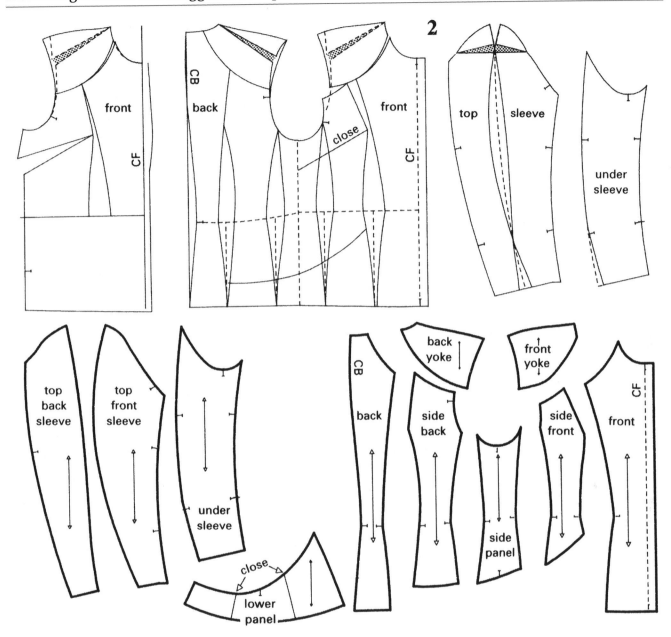

Interlinings are used in most shaped or tailored garments; they can be used to give light support (the fabric itself determining the shape), medium support, or used to exaggerate dramatic shapes.

1 Classic tailored structure – easy fitting jacket block

The basic easy fitting jacket shape with semi-fitted waist shaping is shown (1). The fabric is wool worsted and it has been interlined by traditional methods with non-fusible wool/hair canvas, chest canvas, felt and linen holland. Compare the jacket with the same pattern shown in different fabrics on page 108.

2 Exaggerated shape – easy fitting jacket block

The block is used with widened shoulders and very fitted waist. Firm, fusible interlining, large shoulder and hip padding is used to hold the shape. Synthetic fur (Astrakhan) emphasises the design.

Body Sections trace round the block to the required length. Add straight buttonstand.
Cut and open armhole line, raise shoulder the depth of shoulder pad. Cut across sleeve head and raise same amount.
Draw in yokes and front style line.
Swing bust dart to panel line, join side seams.
Draw in style lines and side panel lines.
Lower back waist approx. 2 cm.
Shape panel lines as shown in diagram.
Draw in 1 cm shaping at front neck in yoke line.
Trace off pattern sections.
Close panel seams on hip yoke.
Sleeve split the top sleeve, shaping outwards at top arm and shaping in at the wrist. Shape under sleeve slightly in at back wrist.

Fabrics used in the illustrations

			We	Th	Sh	Dr	St
1	Wool worsted	woven	3	3	3	3	4
2	Polyester suiting	woven	4	3	4	4	5

Padding: exaggerated shapes

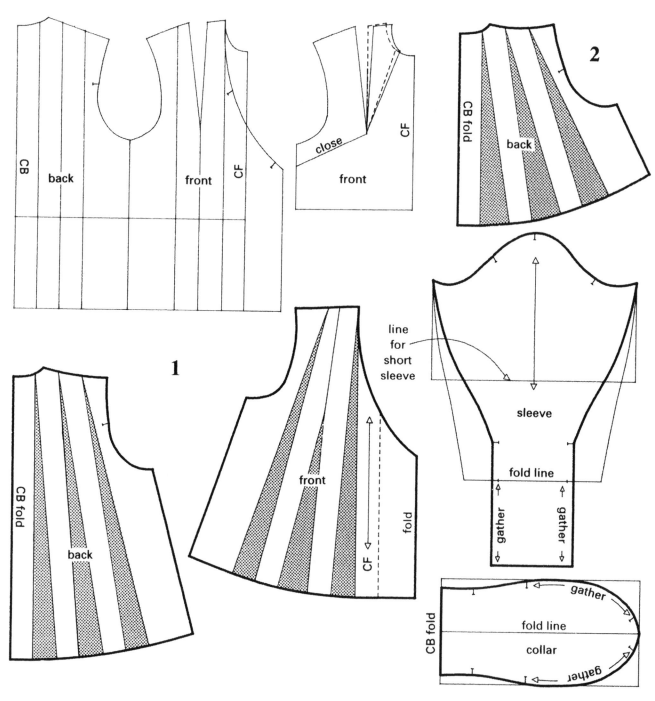

Interesting contrasts can be made by using very light-weight fabrics in transparent fullness and padding sections. Different stitching, gathering, braiding and appliqué techniques can create padded fabrics with surface interest.

(1) shows a simple 'A' line jacket in polyester chiffon. Contrast the shape with (2), the same pattern shape (totally padded) with more flare in the body sections and flare in the sleeves. The block used was the easy fitting over shape (page 198). Closer fitting shapes have to be cut with extra ease. The fabric should be padded before cutting out.

1 Wide overshape

Body Sections   trace round the block to the required length. Swing bust dart to the shoulder. Overlap neck (ref. 2, page 89).

Draw in a wide buttonstand, draw in a low neckline.
Divide block into sections, drop a line from the bust dart.
Trace off pattern sections.
Close bust dart and flare the hem.
The front and back are cut in double fabric.
Sleeve   shape in the sleeve as shown, extend the cuff section at least twice the length.
Collar   draft a straight rectangle the neck measurement; extend the amount of gather required. Draw in collar shape.

Fabrics used in the illustrations

		We	Th	Sh	Dr	St
1 Polyester	woven	1	1	2	2	4
2 Polyamide/elastane	woven	2	1/4	4	4	3

Mounting, boning and wiring: exaggerated shapes

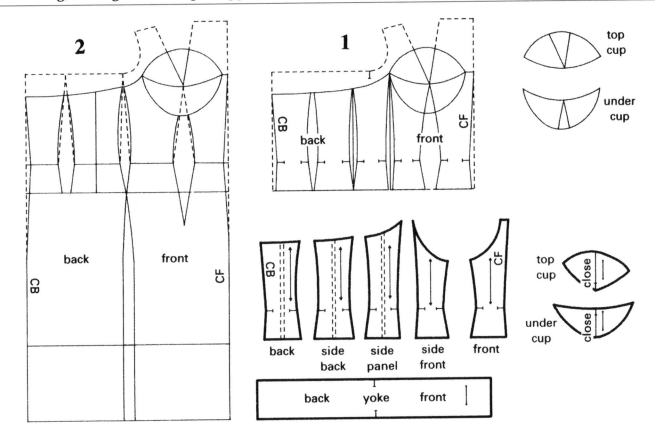

Permull (known as body stiffening) provides a good base for strapless designs or corset shapes. It will mould into shape with steaming, and boning will retain the structure where required. The fabric used for the cups was just interfaced with a fusible jersey fabric.

Structured body shapes can be difficult to achieve with fabrics of low-shear (PVC). **(1)** shows the tendency to buckle around complex shapes. **(2)** shows the same pattern made up by the same method in silk brocade and a silk-mix light-weight tweed. Many more seam lines are required for the PVC garment in the first illustration to achieve the same shape. Wiring can be used to control the shape around cups or to give distorted shaping to fullness in any area of the garment. Illustration **(2)** shows the hem twisted and buckled.

Skirts can be cut in any dramatic width or shape. The thickness of the fabric will determine the amount of fullness that can be gathered onto a tight bodice. The fabric used in the designs illustrated is a light-weight high–medium-drape fabric. **(1)** shows its unsupported hang.

Underskirts of paper nylon and layers of net achieved the exaggerated bell shape in **(2)**. Underskirts for this type of design should always hang from skirt yokes to lessen the bulk at the waist.

Close fitting boned bodices should be drafted from the lingerie block (page 203) which has a wide dart shaping.

1 & 2 Classic boned bodice

If a bust cup is required draw in the shape required.
Draw in panels and waist shaping.
Trace off body sections.
Close the darts in the upper and lower cups.
Suggested positions for boning are shown.

Fabric used in the illustrations

			We	Th	Sh	Dr	St
1	Polyester/ polyurethene	weft-knit	4	2	5	5	4
2	Silk/linen/viscose	woven	2	2	1	2	4
	Silk/lurex	woven	3	2	4	5	4

Combining techniques

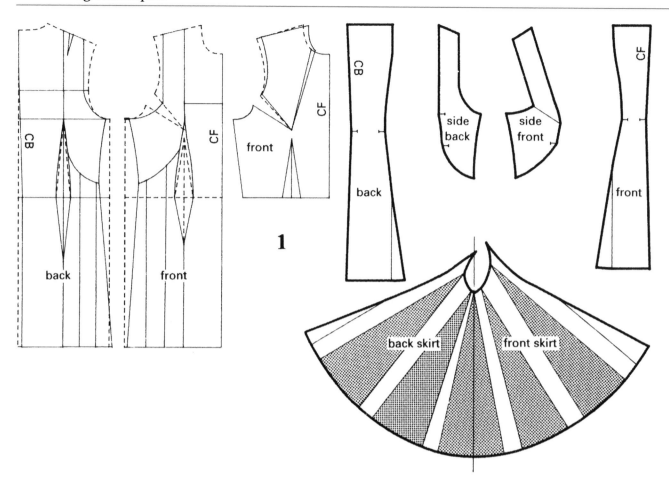

1

(1) and (2) show adaptations of the design constructed on page 115. (1) shows the skirt padded, stitched and wired to give 3D shaping. (2) shows the use of mounting and wiring with a fluid high-drape woven or knitted fabric to give acute contrasts in shape.

1 Padded skirt shape (1)
Begin the construction as the design on page 115.
Draw in the style line for the skirt.
Trace off pattern sections.
Divide the skirt into sections.
Cut off the skirt sections: cut and spread generously.

2 Diagram on page 176.

1

2

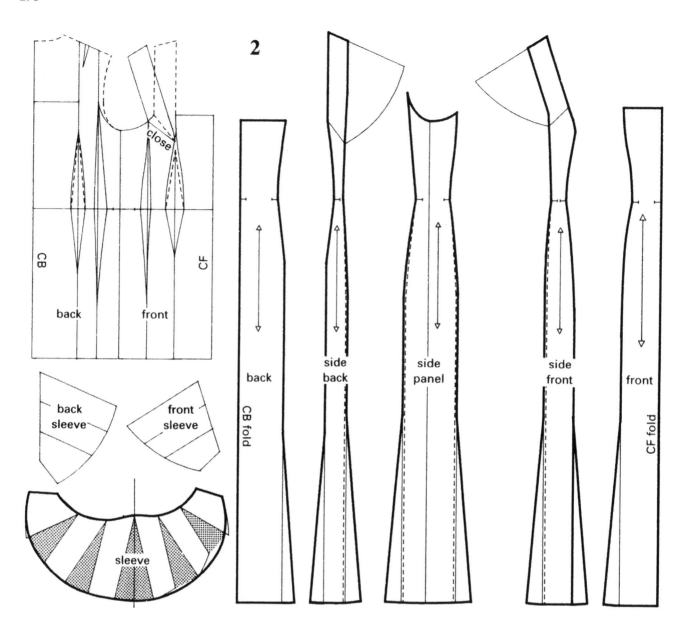

2 Structured sleeve shape (2)

2 Structured sleeve shape (2)

The design uses the sleeveless adaptation (page 115). It then illustrates the method of eliminating the side seam of a sleeveless dress.

Place the side seams together; the overlap at the hip must be distributed evenly onto the side panel seams as shown. Cut out pattern sections and add the hip allowance. Add flare to the lower skirt.

Draw in the style lines for the sleeve.
Draw in the sleeve shape required.
Sleeve divide the sleeve into sections: cut and spread the required amount.

NOTE Designs constructed in low-stretch fabrics would require a back seam to create a zip opening.

PART FOUR: MODEL FIGURES AND GARMENT BLOCKS

10 Model figures

NOTES The elongation or distortion of figure drawings is recognised as an essential part of stylistic image generation in the early stages of fashion design. They are an integral part of developing moods, ideas, stories and personal attitudes during the design process. This type of fashion image is also an essential part of fashion illustration and promotion. However, the design has to be developed into a technical design drawing with accurate information for pattern cutting. It also has to be proportionate to the human figure.

The following pages offer images of the garment stand and figure poses of the model used in the book illustrations. They can be photocopied up to A3 size. Detail paper can be placed over the figures, students can then produce accurate style development drawings that will be proportionate to the actual pattern shapes.

The images are labelled A, B, C etc. to enable students to match some front and back and side views.

178

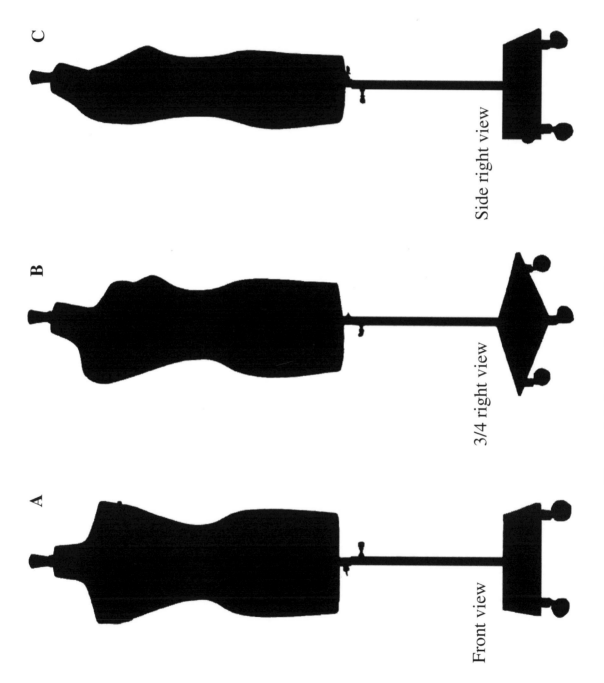

A

Front view

B

3/4 right view

C

Side right view

The model stands – front and right views

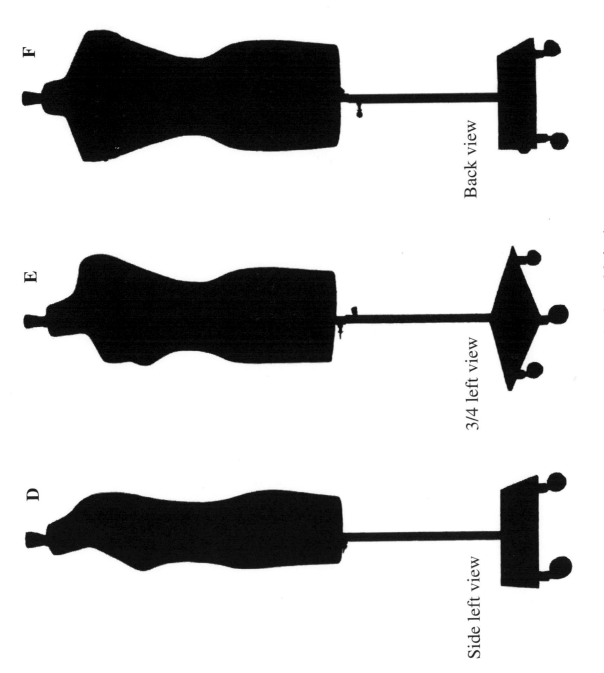

F

E

D

Back view

3/4 left view

Side left view

The model stands – back and left views

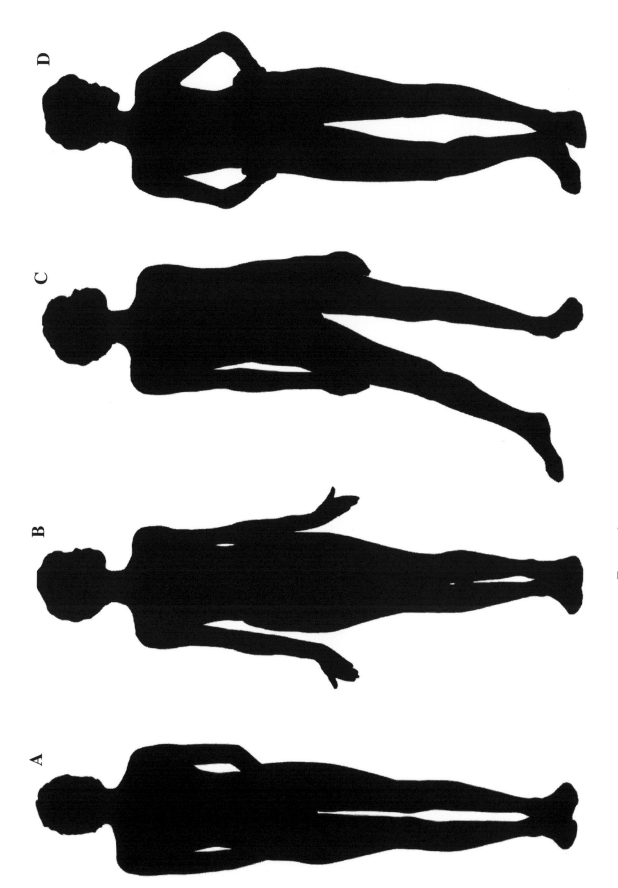

Front views – model poses A B C D

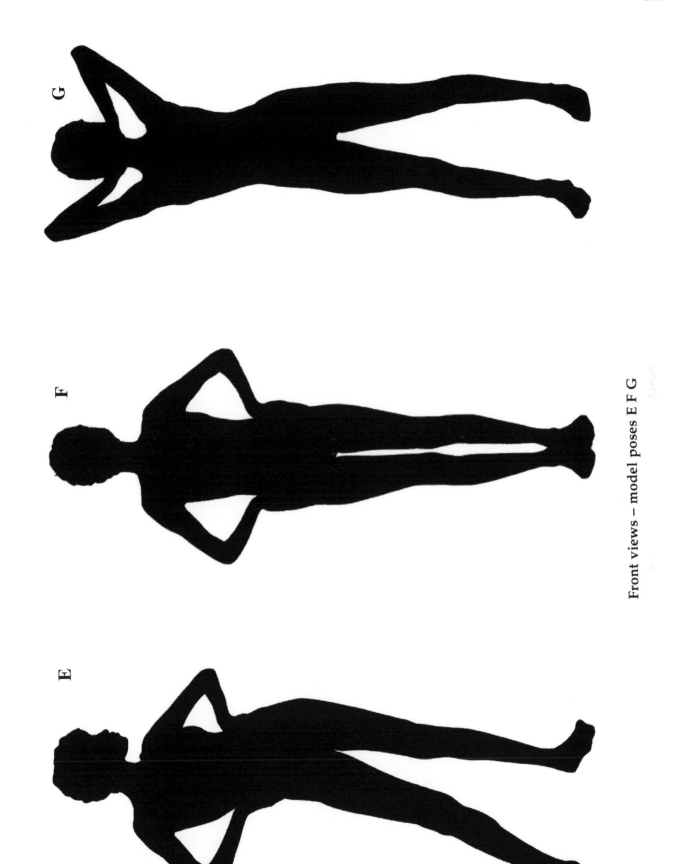

E

F

G

Front views – model poses E F G

A　B　C　D

Back views – model poses A B C D

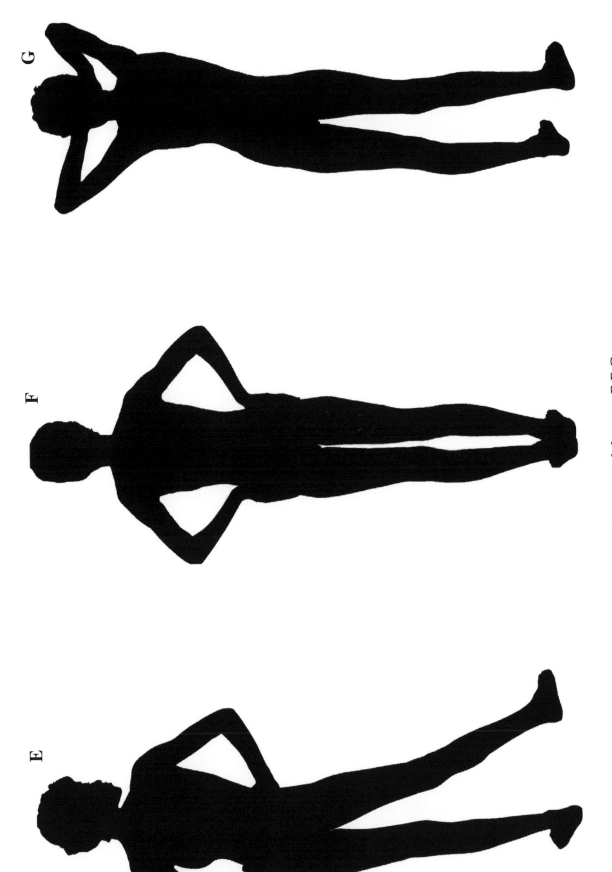

E   F   G

Back views – model poses E F G

Side views – model poses A E F

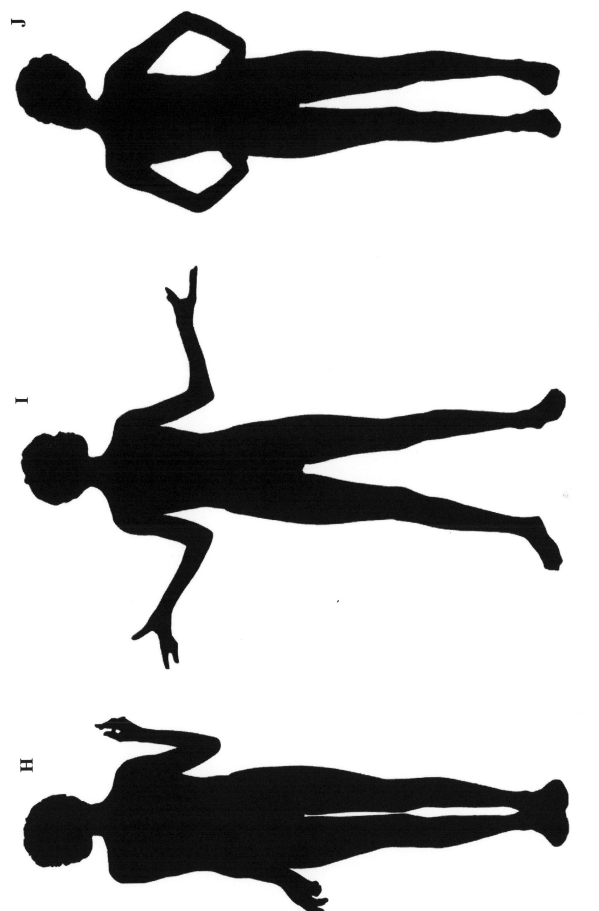

J

I

H

Additional front views – model poses H I J

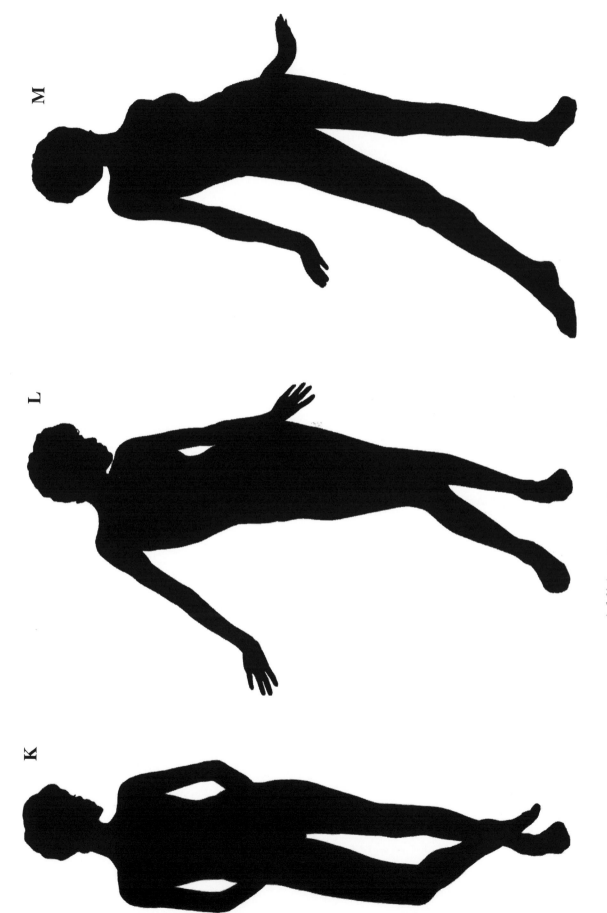

K L M

Additional front views – model poses K L M

PART FOUR: MODEL FIGURES AND GARMENT BLOCKS

11 The one-fifth scale garment blocks

Basic blocks

Block patterns are foundation patterns constructed to fit the body measurements of an average figure of one of the size groups (10, 12, 14, etc.), see the chart below. The blocks include the basic amount of ease (or reduction for stretch jersey fabric blocks) for the function of the garment. Underwear requires less ease than over-garments.

The basic blocks with full instructions are available in the books: *Metric Pattern Cutting*, *Metric Pattern Cutting for Menswear* and *Metric Pattern Cutting for Children's Wear and*

Babywear. These books are available for clothing and fashion students who need to understand the relationship between body measurements and the type of block construction that is used in industry today.

The designer completes a pattern in a sample size, usually size 10 or 12. The design is made up into a sample garment. When the design is accepted, the garment is graded into the remaining sizes required by the buyer.

Basic size chart of women's standard body measurements used to create the ¹/₅ blocks

WOMEN OF MEDIUM HEIGHT 160 cm–170 cm (5ft 2½in–5ft 6½in)							
SIZE	10	12	14	16	18	20	22
BUST	82	87	92	97	102	107	112
WAIST	62	67	72	77	82	87	92
HIPS	87	92	97	102	107	112	117
BACK WIDTH	33	34.2	35.4	36.6	37.8	39	40.2
CHEST	30.5	32	33.5	35	36.5	38	39.5
SHOULDER	11.9	12.2	12.5	12.8	13.1	13.4	13.7
NECK SIZE	35.6	36.8	38	39.2	40.4	41.6	42.8
DART	6.4	7	7.6	8.2	8.8	9.4	10
TOP ARM	26.4	28	29.6	31.2	32.8	34.4	36
WRIST	15.5	16	16.5	17	17.5	18	18.5
ANKLE	23.4	24	24.6	25.2	25.8	26.4	27
HIGH ANKLE	20.4	21	21.6	22.2	22.8	23.4	24
NAPE TO WAIST	39.5	40	40.5	41	41.5	42	42.5
FRONT SHOULDER TO WAIST	39.5	40	40.5	41.3	42.1	42.9	43.7
ARMHOLE DEPTH	20.5	21	21.5	22	22.5	23	23.5
WAIST TO KNEE	58	58.5	59	59.5	60	60.5	61
WAIST TO HIP	20.3	20.6	20.9	21.2	21.5	21.8	22.1
WAIST TO FLOOR	103	104	105	106	107	108	109
BODY RISE	27.3	28	28.7	29.4	30.1	30.8	31.5
SLEEVE LENGTH	57.3	58	58.7	59.4	60.1	60.8	61.5
SLEEVE LENGTH (JERSEY)	51.3	52	52.7	53.4	54.1	54.8	55.2

The one-fifth scale blocks and shapes available in this book

The blocks available in this book are for a different purpose. Students can see them simply as basic shapes; they are starting points to explore basic cutting methods and to experiment with fabric qualities. They are offered for experimental projects in a wide range of courses. They could be useful for printed textile and embroidery students who wish to apply their work to garment shapes. The range of blocks includes shapes based on a simple grid, to blocks that fit closely to the body contours. They provide the opportunity to use shape and fabric quality to generate an infinite variety of new experimental garment forms.

Reproducing the one-fifth scale blocks in full size

On the following pages size 10 and size 12 blocks and shapes are placed on grids of 5-cm squares. The blocks are one-fifth scale. They can be reproduced full scale manually, by photocopying or by computer aided design (CAD) in the following ways.

Copying out the blocks onto pattern paper

Draw a vertical line. Square out from the top point. Mark point 0. Divide each line into 5-cm intervals. From these points create a grid of 5-cm squares. Crucial points of the pattern can be found by measuring from the nearest square corner in vertical and horizontal directions. A one-fifth scale square will convert the block page measurements to full scale measurements.

Using an A3 or A4 photocopier

This method is complicated. Before attempting this method always check that the block will be the correct size by first measuring the copied squares on the grid, which should be 5 cm exactly. The block pages should be separated into individual pattern pieces. Magnify the block pieces by 200%, then by 200% again, and then by 125%. The separate sections can then be taped together.

Using CAD and A1 or A0 printers

Many colleges now have print shops that have A1 or A0 printers. The block pages can be scanned in at 600 dpi and saved as a TIF file. The printers can print out the blocks in full size at 120 dpi. The lines will be coarse but the blocks are still very useable.

Using CAD and A3 or A4 printers

This process is more complicated. However, tutors or students who have access to the CAD program *Adobe Photoshop* and A3 or A4 printers may be able to use them to reproduce the blocks in full size. Full instructions are given in Appendix Six.

Seam allowances

There are no seam allowances included in the blocks. These should be added after the pattern has been constructed. A standard seam allowance is 1–1.5 cm. Enclosed seams (i.e. collars and facings) can be reduced to 0.5 cm.

The basic grid

Very easy fitting garments can be cut from simple basic shapes; this is particularly so if you are working with knitted garment shapes, jersey fabrics, loosely woven fabrics or fabrics with stretch characteristics. The fabric will stretch over complex areas of the body (i.e. the bust), or areas which have extreme movement (i.e. the elbow). The basic grid registers important control points of the body (i.e. shoulder point, armhole depth position) to use as a reference when taking extreme design decisions. It is important to understand that the basic grid is based on body measurements and requires a substantial amount of extra ease on the body measurements points to allow the body to move. Working from a flat grid only

gives you a 2D envelope shape'; if a closer fitting shape is required, gusseted pieces have to be inserted for body movement.

The simple kimono

A simple one-piece (back and front from one pattern) kimono shape constructed from the basic grid is very useful for knitted shapes and dramatic overgarments. The sleeve angle can be varied, but if it becomes too acute the underarm movement will become restricted. A more complex kimono shape with some front bust darting can be found on page 190.

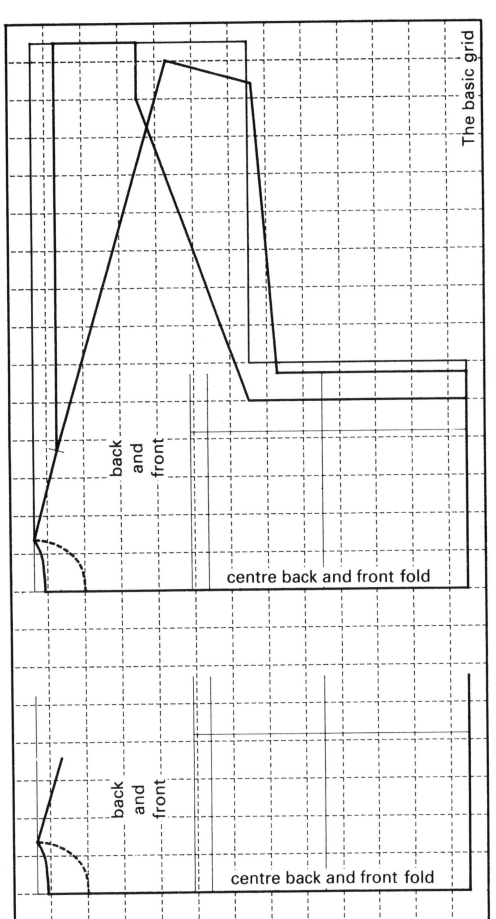

back and front

centre back and front fold

back and front

centre back and front fold

The basic grid

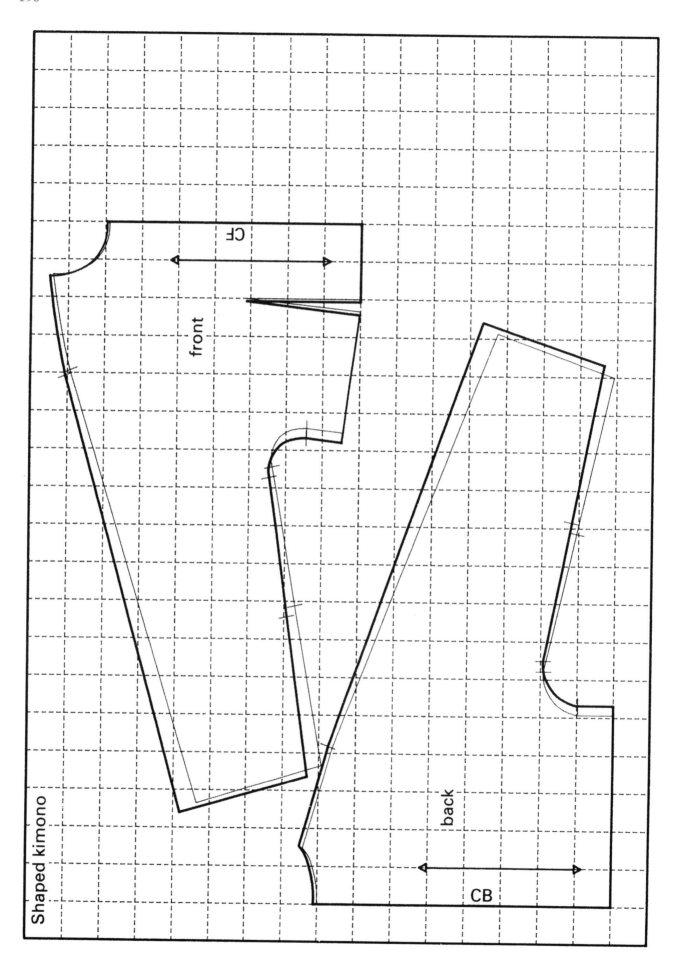

Shaped kimono

front

CF

back

CB

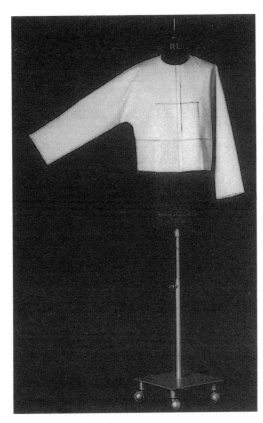

Shaped kimono

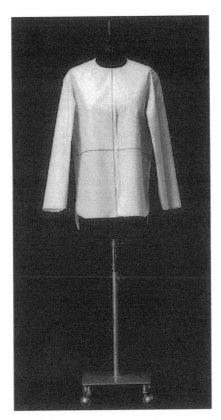

Shirt block

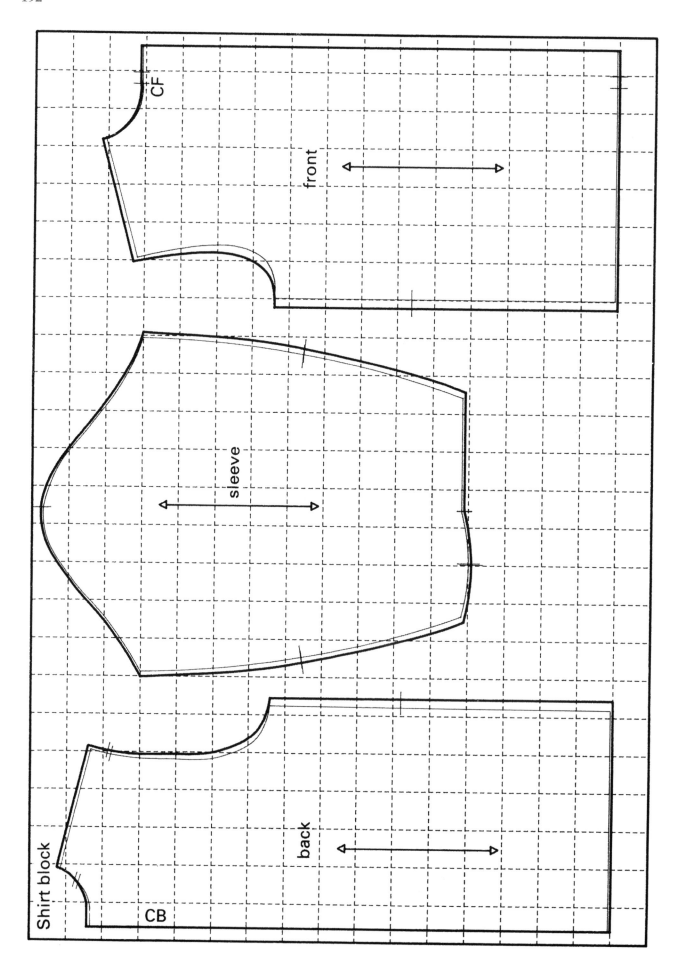

Shirt block

CB

CF

front

sleeve

back

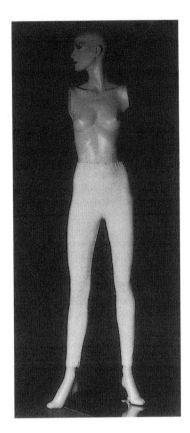

Knitted fabric leggings

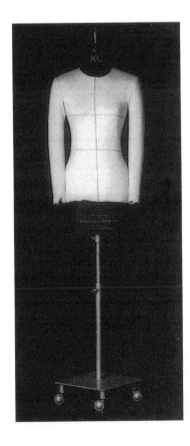

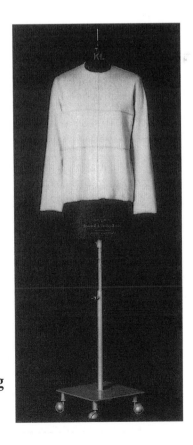

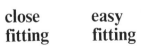

Knitted fabric body shapes

close fitting

easy fitting

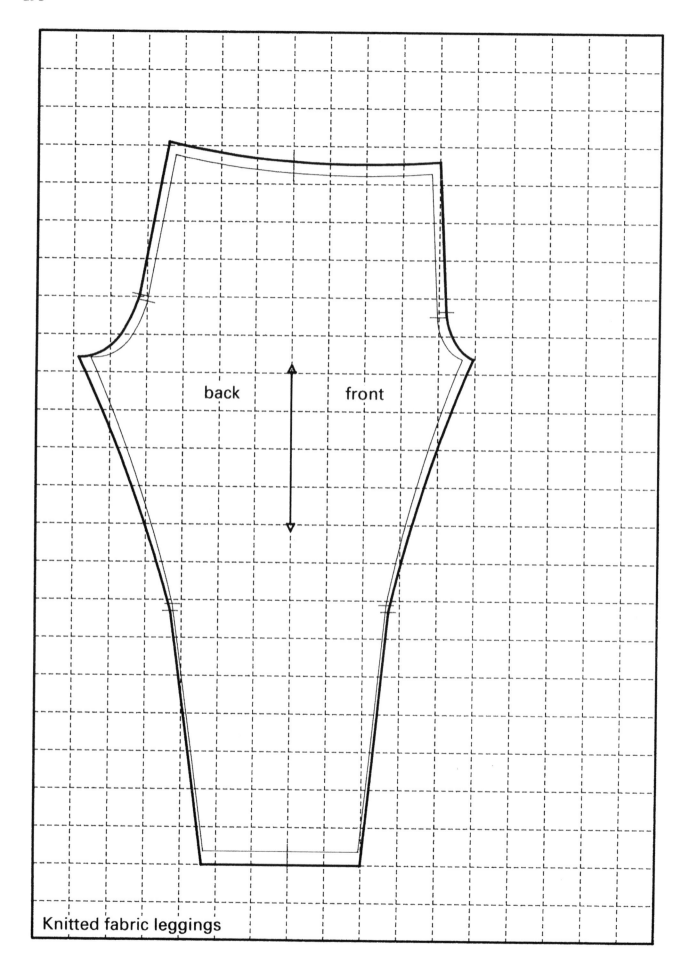

back   front

Knitted fabric leggings

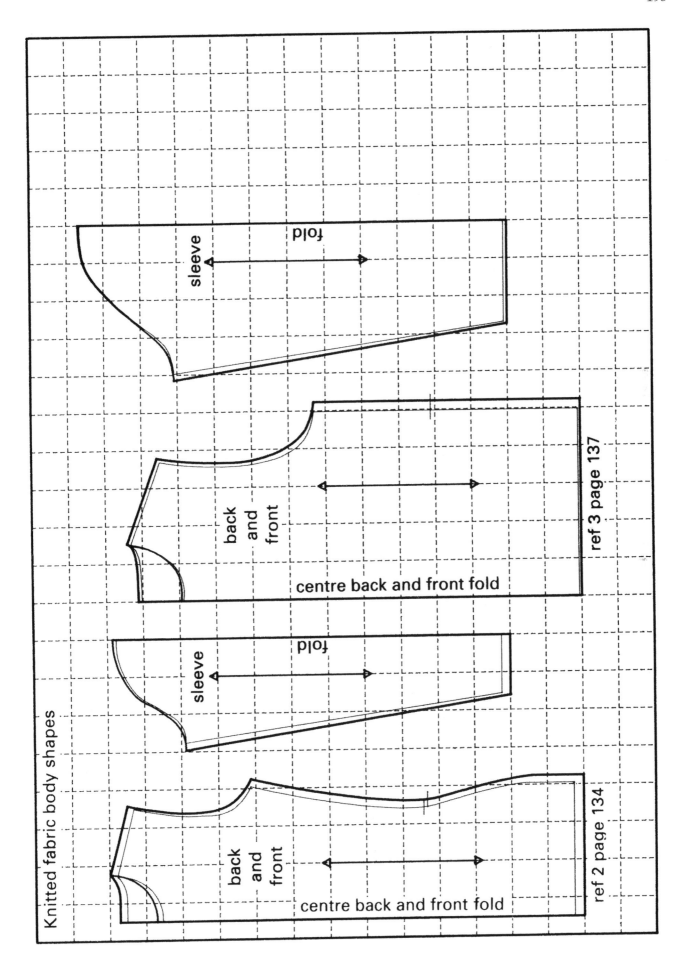

Knitted fabric body shapes

sleeve

fold

back and front

centre back and front fold

ref 3 page 137

sleeve

fold

back and front

centre back and front fold

ref 2 page 134

The bust and shoulder darts

Darts

The bust dart creates the shaping for the bust area, the shoulder dart for the prominence of the shoulder blades. The dart position can be moved to different places; temporarily if it gets in the way of drawing a style line, permanently if it is required in a new position, or it can be integrated into a seam. Some blocks do not include bust darts; these are usually used in certain styles which are loose fitting or where jersey or stretch fabrics are used. Many blocks and styles eliminate the back shoulder dart by transferring it to a seam or by substituting ease in the back shoulder length.

Moving the bust dart position

Trace round the front bodice block. Draw a line from the centre shoulder to the bust point. Cut up the line, close the original dart and secure with tape. The bust dart is now in the centre shoulder. Transfer the dart to other positions using the same method.

Eliminating the back shoulder dart

Mark point 1 at the neck point. Mark point 2 0.5 cm in from the armhole edge along the shoulder line. Draw a line from 1–2. Draw in a new armhole line from 2 to armhole notch; 0.5 cm ease will remain in the shoulder line.

Integrating the dart into a seam

Trace round the required bodice block. If the dart interferes with the style line, transfer it to a new position. Draw in the style line; the style line should be within a 5-cm circle around the bust point or back dart point if the conventional shaping needs to be retained. Move the dart point to the style line. Cut up the style line. Close the dart; the dart will become integrated into the style line.

Transferring the bust dart position

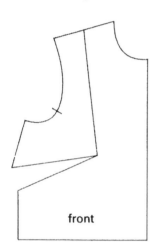
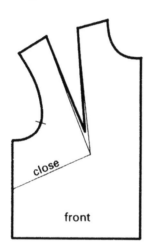
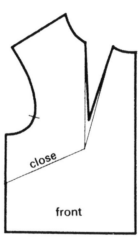

Eliminating the back dart

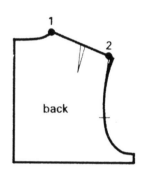

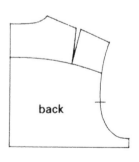

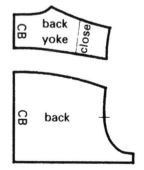

Transferring the bust dart and shoulder dart to a style line

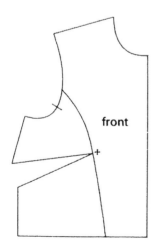

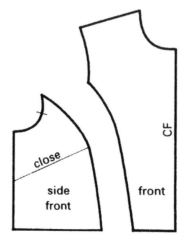

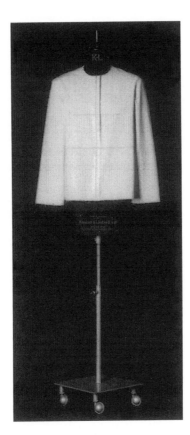

**Easy fitting
over shape**

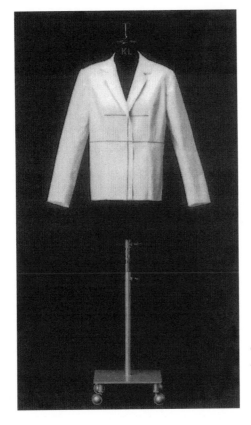

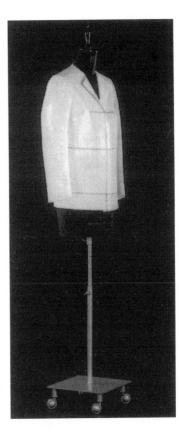

Jacket blocks

**easy
fitting**

**close
fitting**

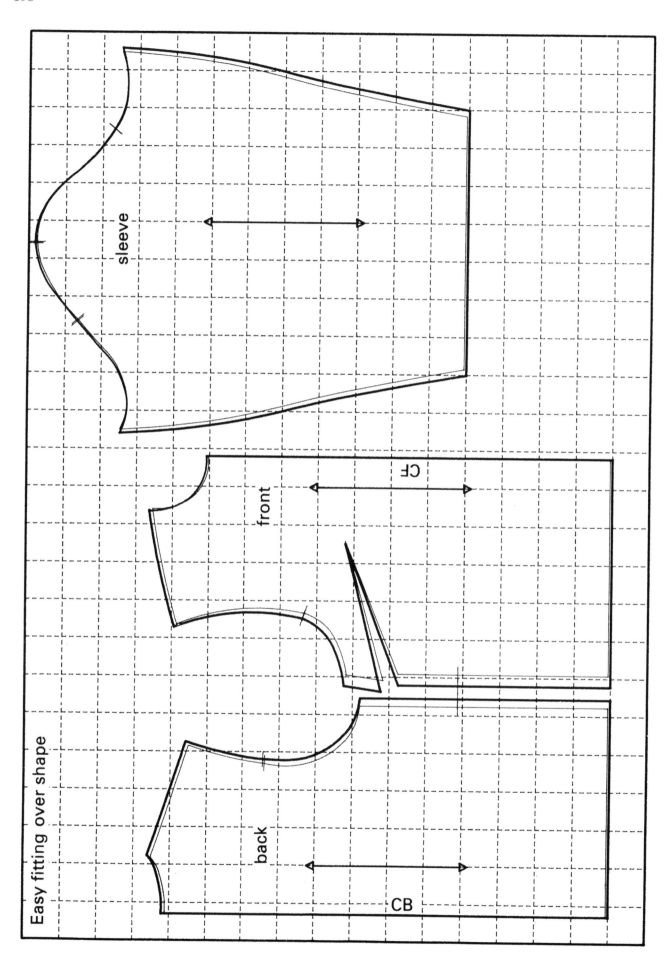

Easy fitting over shape

sleeve

front

CF

back

CB

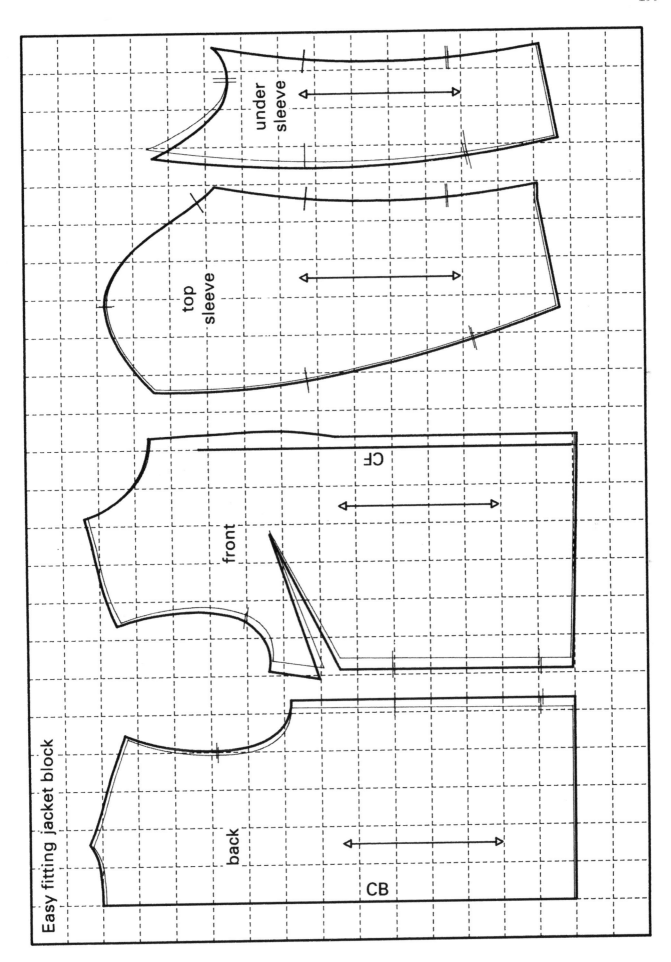

Easy fitting jacket block

under sleeve

top sleeve

front

CF

back

CB

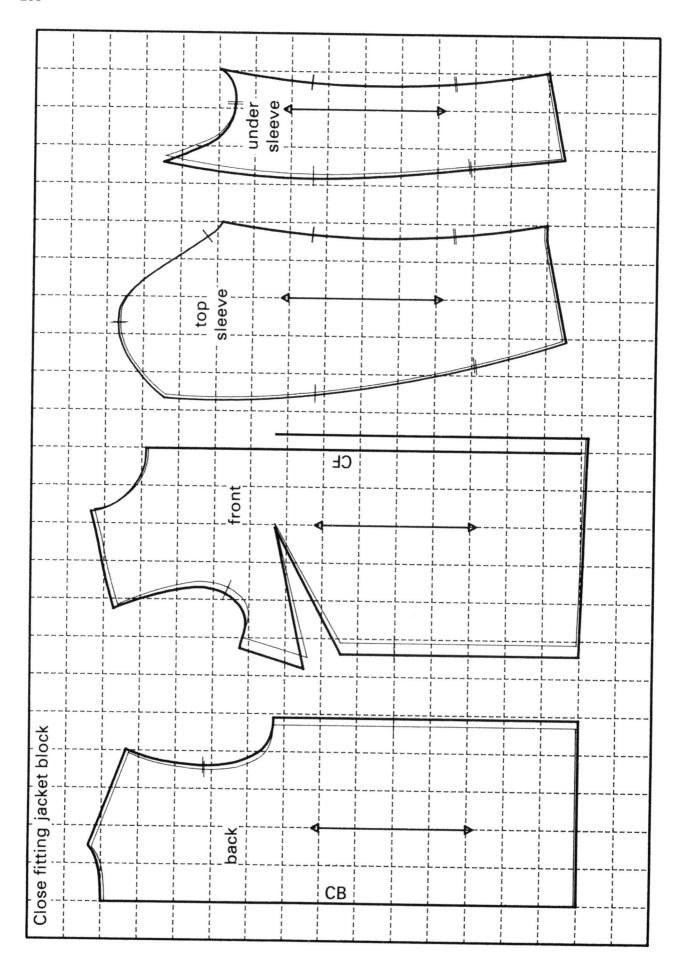

Close fitting jacket block

under sleeve

top sleeve

front

CF

back

CB

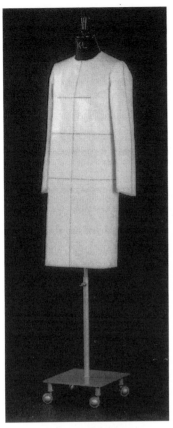

**Close fitting
dress block**

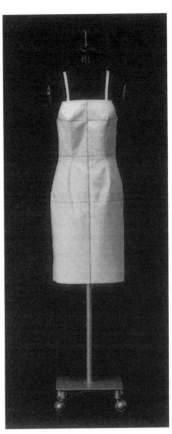

Lingerie block

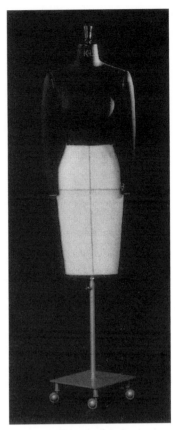

Skirt block

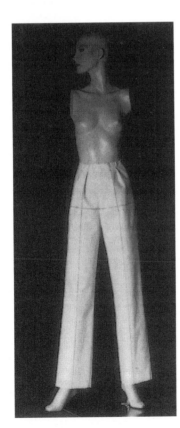

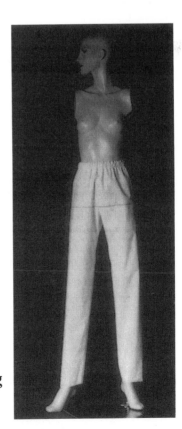

Trouser blocks

**easy
fitting**

**very
easy
fitting**

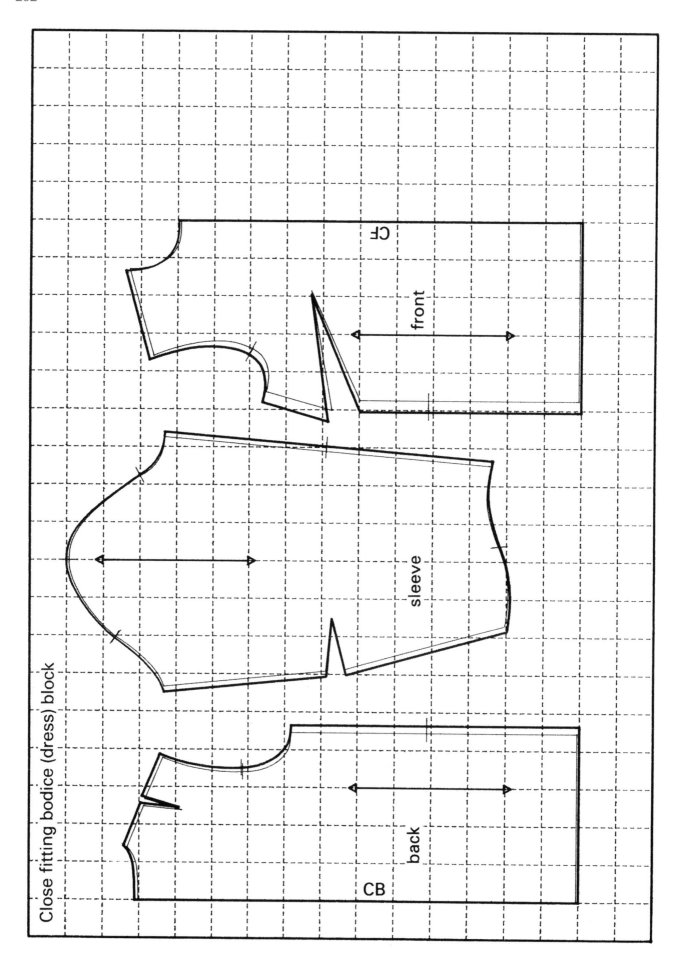

Close fitting bodice (dress) block

CF

front

sleeve

CB

back

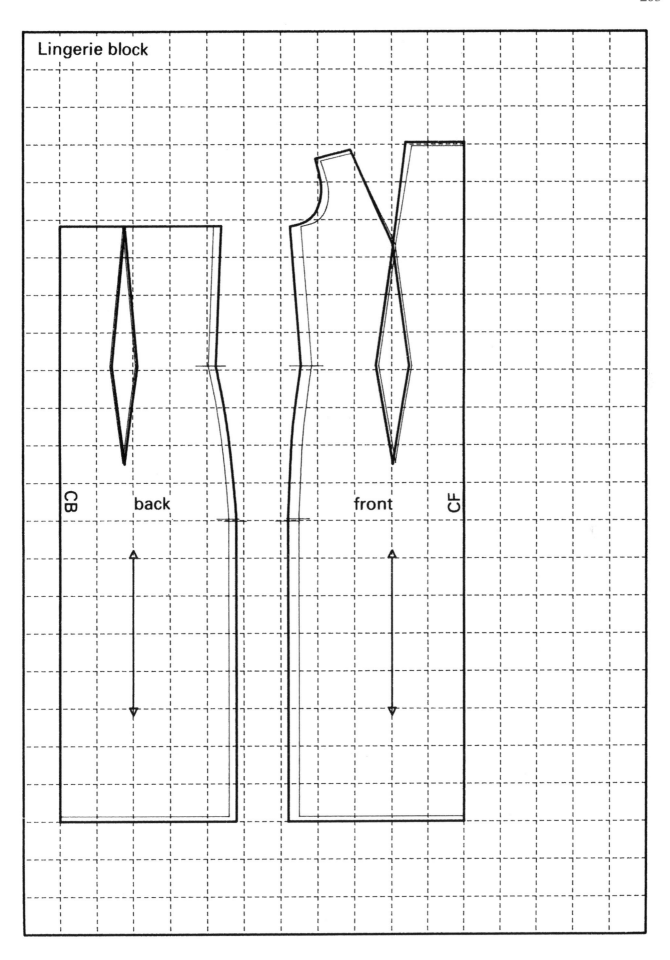

Lingerie block

CB   back   front   CF

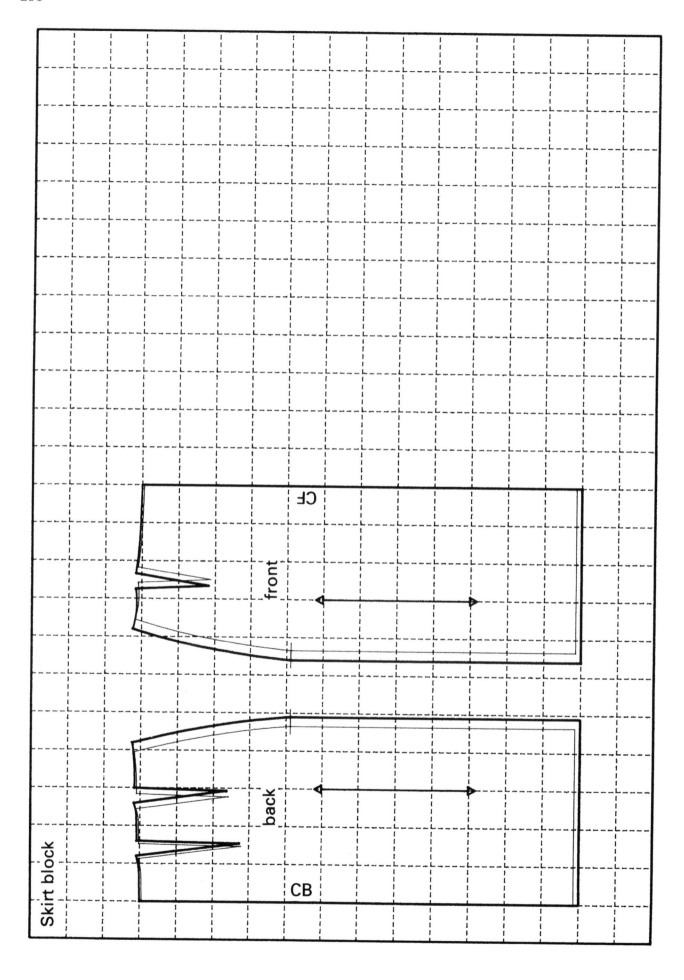

204

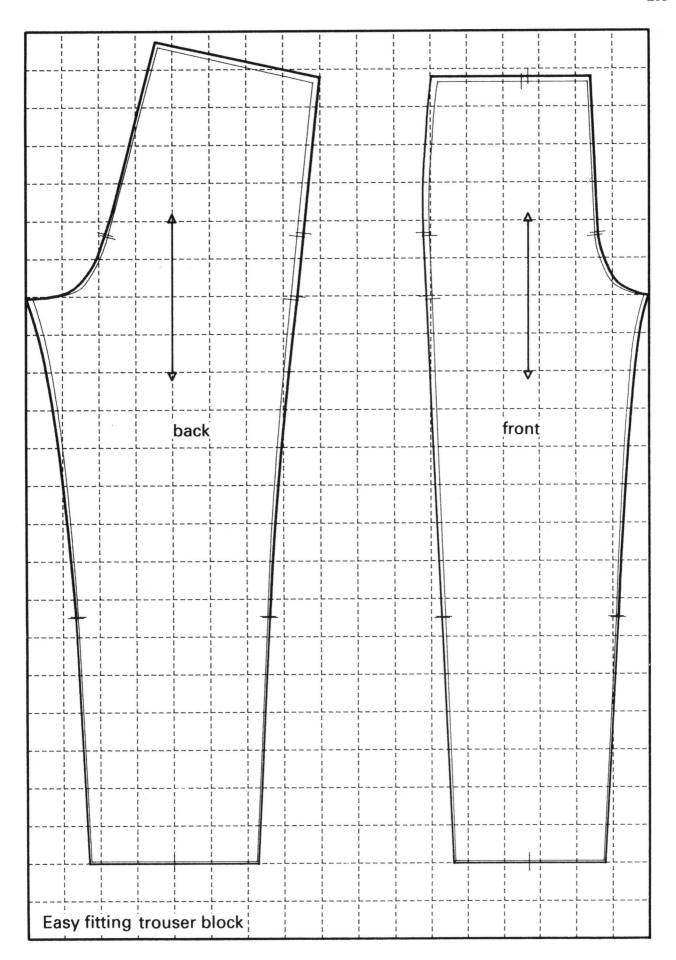

back

front

Easy fitting trouser block

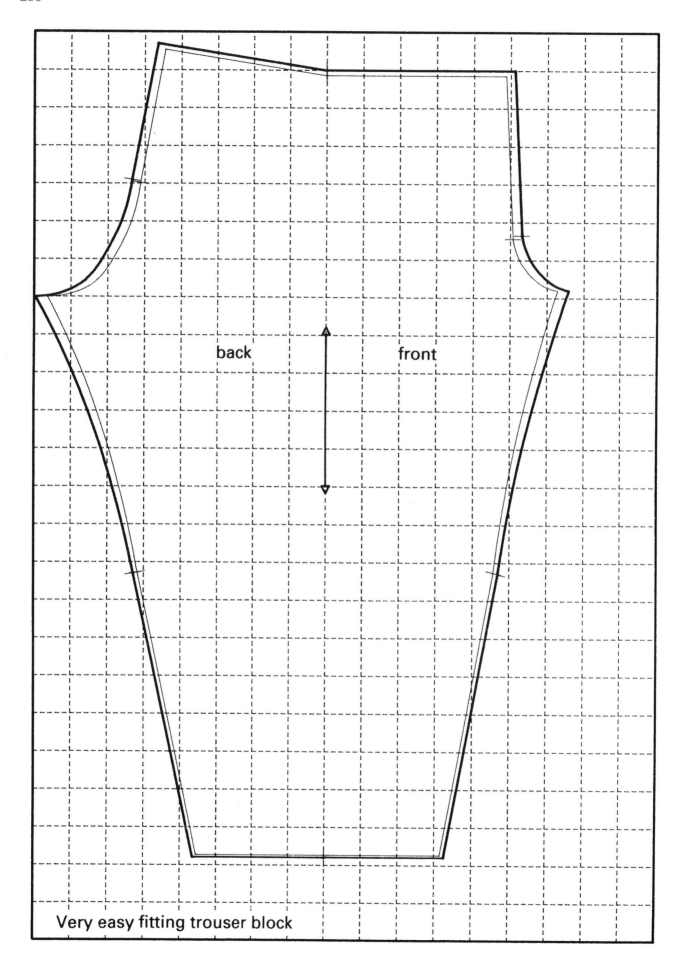

back

front

Very easy fitting trouser block

APPENDICES

Appendix one: major fabric names categorised approximately for pattern cutting

This glossary appears to be a historical list of mainly traditional fabric names but it also includes new terms that are becoming standard names to recognize at trade fairs or on fabric swatch samples. Fabric names originate from many sources. The principal source of a fabric name is the name of a weave or knitted structure. However, this name is often used liberally and may incorporate a group of fabrics; for example woven and knitted fabrics or fabrics in natural and man-made fibres. Other names have historical significance or geographical attachments where a particular fabric trade has flourished. Some fabrics now require a close inspection to decide their structure. Although many new fabric names appear, particularly in the area of man-made fibres, many are trade names that focus on the fibre source, or simply rather exotic range names given for a fashion fabric, which may disappear after a season or not even be produced if the buyers do not respond to the sample swatch.

Excellent fabric glossaries can be found in most textile books that give full descriptions of these fabrics. The purpose of this glossary is to give a guide to their weight. This is very approximate, because fabrics in man-made fibres bearing traditional names (for example gabardine woven in modal) can be much lighter than the medium weight one expects in gabardine fabrics.

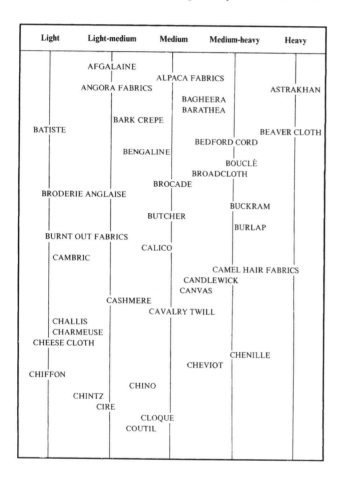

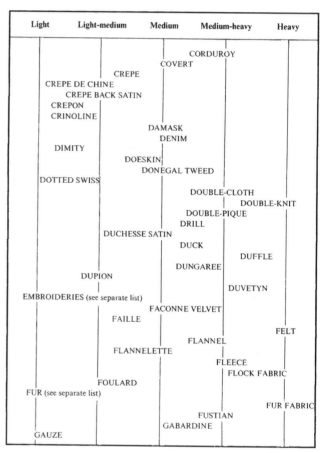

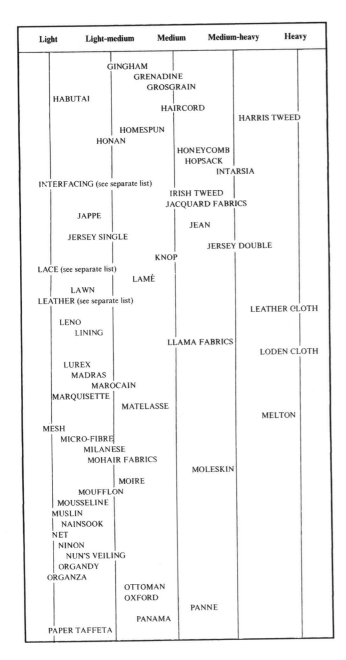

Light	Light-medium	Medium	Medium-heavy	Heavy
	GINGHAM			
		GRENADINE		
		GROSGRAIN		
HABUTAI				
		HAIRCORD		
			HARRIS TWEED	
	HOMESPUN			
	HONAN			
		HONEYCOMB		
		HOPSACK		
			INTARSIA	
INTERFACING (see separate list)				
		IRISH TWEED		
		JACQUARD FABRICS		
	JAPPE			
		JEAN		
	JERSEY SINGLE			
		JERSEY DOUBLE		
		KNOP		
LACE (see separate list)				
	LAMÉ			
LAWN				
LEATHER (see separate list)				
			LEATHER CLOTH	
	LENO			
	LINING			
		LLAMA FABRICS		
			LODEN CLOTH	
	LUREX			
	MADRAS			
	MAROCAIN			
MARQUISETTE				
	MATELASSE			
			MELTON	
MESH				
	MICRO-FIBRE			
	MILANESE			
	MOHAIR FABRICS			
	MOIRE			
		MOLESKIN		
	MOUFFLON			
MOUSSELINE				
MUSLIN				
	NAINSOOK			
NET				
NINON				
	NUN'S VEILING			
ORGANDY				
ORGANZA				
	OTTOMAN			
	OXFORD			
			PANNE	
		PANAMA		
PAPER TAFFETA				

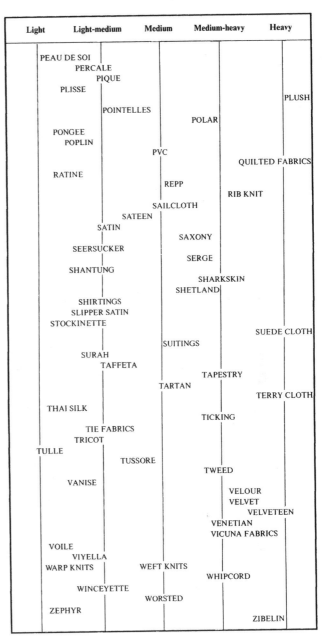

Light	Light-medium	Medium	Medium-heavy	Heavy
PEAU DE SOI				
	PERCALE			
	PIQUE			
PLISSE				
				PLUSH
	POINTELLES			
			POLAR	
PONGEE				
POPLIN				
		PVC		
				QUILTED FABRICS
RATINE				
		REPP		
			RIB KNIT	
		SAILCLOTH		
		SATEEN		
	SATIN			
			SAXONY	
	SEERSUCKER			
			SERGE	
	SHANTUNG			
			SHARKSKIN	
			SHETLAND	
	SHIRTINGS			
	SLIPPER SATIN			
	STOCKINETTE			
				SUEDE CLOTH
		SUITINGS		
	SURAH			
	TAFFETA			
			TAPESTRY	
		TARTAN		
				TERRY CLOTH
THAI SILK				
			TICKING	
	TIE FABRICS			
	TRICOT			
TULLE				
		TUSSORE		
			TWEED	
	VANISE			
			VELOUR	
			VELVET	
				VELVETEEN
			VENETIAN	
			VICUNA FABRICS	
VOILE				
	VIYELLA			
WARP KNITS		WEFT KNITS		
			WHIPCORD	
	WINCEYETTE			
		WORSTED		
ZEPHYR				
				ZIBELIN

Lace fabrics

The range of lace fabrics available is enormous; many of the names refer to the places where the lace techniques were created. Only a small selection of popular laces and lace type fabrics are listed in the characteristic of weight. Their placing is only a guide; they will vary with the density of the design, the yarns used and other decorative features. A large amount of fabric that is sold under the heading 'lace' is warp-knitted, for example raschel lace. Macramé and crochet are not technically lace but are listed with this group.

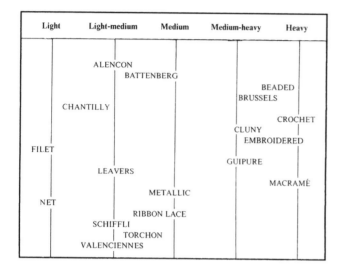

Types of leather

Terms used to describe the most popular types of leather used in garment production are listed in the characteristic of weight. Leather is a term used when the outer part of the animal or reptile skin has the hair removed and is finished for production; the term suede is used when the inside is finished. Sheepskin and lambskin are skins with the fleeces unshorn. Skins from the same type of animal can vary in weight, thickness, handle and drape. Different areas of the same skin can vary, so that it is very important that the whole of the animal skin is examined carefully.

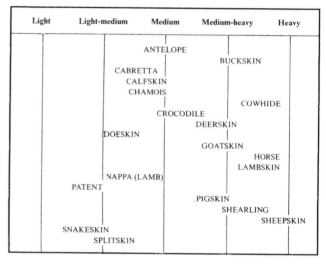

Types of fur

The fur or hair on the animal skin is retained, therefore the skins will vary in density and weight. However this variation will be mainly in the medium–heavy or heavy-weight category and so they are simply listed below for reference.

ASTRAKHAN	FOX	MUSKRAT	RACCOON
BEAVER	LEOPARD	OCELOT	SABLE
CALF	LYNX	OTTER	SEAL
CHINCHILLA	MARTEN	PERSIAN LAMB	SQUIRREL
ERMINE	MINK	RABBIT	

Interfacing

A range of interfacings is listed which can be used for increasing the structural characteristics of fabrics.

CRINOLINE	JERSEY (also fusible)
COTTON PLAIN WEAVE (also fusible)	MULL
	NET
DOMETTE (also fusible)	NON-WOVENS (also fusible)
ELASTANE (fusible)	
FELTS	PERMULL
HAIR CANVAS (also fusible)	PAPER TAFFETA
HOLLAND	SILK-PLAIN WEAVES
LAWN (also fusible)	TARLATAN
LINEN CANVAS (also fusible)	WADDING
	WOOL (also fusible)

Appendix two: major fabric finishes

All fabrics are finished to some degree; the finishes may have a marginal or significant effect on the finished fabric. The original characteristics of the fibre or the fabric structure may be suppressed, enhanced or distorted. A particular finish (example: embroideries, flocking, plasticised coatings) will make a substantial difference to the degree of change. The designer has to see and handle the fabric, and in many circumstances has to make an intuitive judgement of the fabric based on a fabric characteristic scale of assessment. The following finishes are the type of examples that can change the character of the fabric and need consideration when cutting patterns.

Some finishes are completed after the garment has been constructed. When this is the case, thorough fabric tests have to be made to identify the measure of the changes in the fabric so that the garment patterns can have the necessary allowances or adjustments made.

BEADED	EMBROIDERED	METALLIC	SCHREINERED
BLEACHED	EMERIZED (SUEDED)	MILLED	SEQUINNED
BRUSHED	FADED	OILED	SHOWERPROOFED
CREASE RESISTANT	FELTED	PATENTED	SILICONED
CREPE	FLAMEPROOFED	PLASTICISED	SOAPED
CRINKLED	FLOCKED	PLEATED	STONEWASHED
CRUSHED	GLAZED	PRINTED	TEFLONED
CURED	GRANITE	QUILTED	WADDED
DEVORE (BURNT OUT)	IRIDESCENT	RESINATED	WASHED
DISTRESSED	LAMINATED	RUBBERISED	WATERPROOFED
DYED	LACQUERED	SANDED	WAXED
EMBOSSED	MERCERISED	SANDWASHED	WRINKLED

Appendix three: measuring equipment used for the fabric codes recorded in this book

In the main section of the book, simple tests were devised for students to enable them to assess the five characteristics identified for coding the fabrics in this book. These tests are adequate; however, except for the drape test, more specialised equipment was used for coding the fabrics used throughout the book. These are illustrated on the following two pages.

Weight

Figure 12 The fabrics used in the book were weighed (20-cm square) on an accurate TANITA Cal-Q-Scale which calculated to 0.1 gm.

Thickness

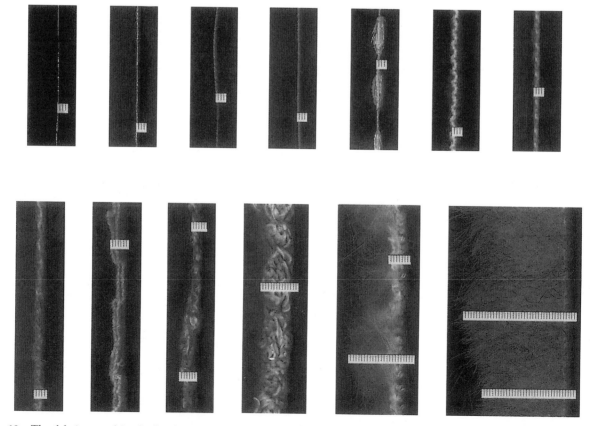

Figure 13 The fabrics used in the book were hung vertically and scanned on a A4 SHARP flat-bed scanner at 300 dpi. It was then possible to see the thickness of the fabrics and make accurate visual comparisons because the textural density was apparent. If comparison of compressibility was required for making up, a digimatic caliper was used manually to obtain general comparisons.

Shear

Figure 14 The fabrics used in the book were attached to two bars. The first bar was fixed; the second bar could be moved under tension in a shear direction. The shear measurement was the amount that the fabric would shear before ripples began to appear on the surface of the cloth. The amount was recorded by marker peg holes at 0.5 cm intervals along the sides of the instrument. The amount of recovery could also be measured.

Stretch

Figure 15 The fabrics used in the book were attached to two bars. The first bar was fixed; the second bar could be moved to stretch the fabric to the extent at which the fabric was still visually acceptable; the amount could be recorded by pegging holes at 0.5 cm intervals along the sides of the instrument. The low-stretch fabrics would not stretch to the measure 0.5 cm; therefore, in pattern cutting terms, low-stretch means virtually no stretch.

Appendix four: tests for practical characteristics of fabrics

This book has focussed on the characteristics of fabrics that have to be considered before pattern cutting (weight, thickness, weave structure, drape, stretch), but many practical characteristics have to be taken into account when developing a garment style. Whilst fabrics made from a particular fibre source or sources might be expected to have the same properties, different yarns, fabric structures and finishes can suppress or enhance particular characteristics. Therefore, as well as assessing fabrics for their use in creating garment shapes, designers should examine each fabric individually to assess its 'fitness for purpose'. Some considerations are listed below.

Abrasion resistance, absorbency, colour fastness, crease recovery, dimensional stability, durability, dye affinity, exposure resistance, extensibility, flame resistance, fungi resistance, hygral expansion, insect resistance, oil resistance, permeability, reaction to chemicals, shower resistance, shrink resistance, soil resistance, static resistance, strength, thermal conductivity, thermoplasticity, washability, water resistance.

BS, EN and ISO fabric tests

Many textile laboratories work to the British Standard (BS) tests which describe suitable instruments for the objective measurement of fabrics. Their major use is the comparison of fabrics of similar type where accurate calculations are required. Although there is some controversy about the efficacy of some of the tests, most companies and laboratories use them for the comparison of fabric properties. A standard from the European Committee for Standardisation (EN) is recognised in Europe, and a standard from the International Standard Organisation (ISO) is usually recognised internationally, although America sets most of its own standards, which may differ.

The BS, EN and ISO tests that relate to the five characteristics used in this book are listed below. However, the tests have a different aim; they are for the comparison of fabrics or to test quality against some set norm for quality control purposes. It is useful for students to know of these tests but they are not directly relevant for assessing fabrics for the purpose of cutting pattern shapes.

Weight	BS 2471 (2005) Textiles. Woven fabrics. Determination of mass per unit length and mass per unit area. BS EN 12127 (1997) Textiles. Fabrics. Determination of mass per unit area using small samples.
Thickness	BS EN ISO 5084 (1997) Textiles. Determination of thickness of textiles and textile products.
Shear	BS 2819 (1990) Methods for determination of bow, skew and lengthway distortion in woven and knitted fabrics.
Drape	BS 5058 (1973) Method of assessment of drape of fabrics. BS EN ISO 9073-9 (1998) Textiles. Test methods for non-wovens. Determination of drape coefficient.
Stretch	BS 4952 (1992) Methods of test of elastic fabrics.

BS EN 29073-3 (1992)   Methods of test for non-wovens.
BS EN 14704-1 (2005)   Determination of the elasticity of fabrics. Strip tests.

Laboratory tests for fabric 'hand'

Equipment is available to cover all kinds of tests for the suitability of fabrics for their purpose. However, a principal concern of researchers has been to seek a set of measurements that would analyse fabric 'hand' for particular manufacturing processes. Some of the work is contentious.

KES-F test (the Kawabata Evaluation System for Fabrics)

The Kawabata system was developed by Sueo Kawabata of Kyoto university and Masaka Niwa of Nara Women's University in Japan.[1] Kawabata claims that the important property of fabric 'hand' can be measured objectively; the system was based on the properties required for men's suits, the method started to spread into industry around 1975. As tailoring moved from the tailor's shop to the mass produced engineered garment, it was felt that a reliable system of measuring fabric 'suitability' was required. Fabric 'hand' was judged by 'experts', then summarised and categorised into primary hand values (PHV). Total hand values (THV) are developed for specific types of fabrics used for particular products. He believes that the mechanical properties that test tensile, sheer, bending, compression, surface and fabric structure are related to the subjective assessments of fabric handle. Kawabata developed four instruments which measure properties related to: tensile strength, shear, bending, compression, friction, roughness. Sixteen fabric measurements are plotted on an HESC data snake chart; comparisons of finishes or weave changes can be assessed.

FAST test (Fabric Assurance of Simple Testing)

The FAST test, developed by CSIRO of Australia, has been adopted by many companies as a reliable measurement of the mechanical properties required for the fabrics used in men's suitings. Its aim is to determine the measurements of the qualities required to 'move' fabrics to create moulded shapes; it is claimed by many manufacturers to be a simpler system, and a better predictor of tailorability, than the KES-F system. It also comprises four pieces of equipment: compression meter, bending meter, extensibility meter, dimensional stability meter.

Fabric weight	mass per unit area	FAST-1
Compression	fabric thickness fabric surface thickness relaxed surface thickness	
Bending	bending length	FAST-2
Extension	warp extensibility weft extensibility bias extensibility	FAST-3
Dimensional	relaxation shrinkage hygral expansion	FAST-4

Criticisms of tests of fabric 'hand'

The main criticisms of the KES-F system have been that:

(1) the instrument costs are too high;
(2) they are too sophisticated and require high-cost technical staff;
(3) there are too many measurements, some of which overlap;
(4) they are too sensitive;
(5) the results are too many and difficult to interpret;
(6) the range of fabrics (men's suitings) which 'experts' assessed was small and any human assessment is subjective and culture based.
(7) there is a simplistic assumption that a record of individual measureable properties can also measure a complex subjective tactile concept.

The FAST system is much less expensive but it is still not affordable by many textile laboratories; a number of scientists and researchers argue that simpler equipment can be used to get viable results. For example, many of the properties listed can be measured on an INSTRON tester with suitable extensions.

The justification for the accurate measurement is the move to automation and garment engineering that wishes to eliminate estimation and judgement from the process; zones of acceptabilty are required that can provide consistency in the manufacturing process. However, more fundamental criticisms state that it is unrealistic to assume that the different feel in the subjective handling of fabrics of different structures can be measured in individual property differences.[2] There are also problems of interpretation and also what they are measuring; machine measures of bending movement or shear deformation do not necessarily correspond with subjective tactile experiences. The optimum properties for garment manufacture may be at odds with those for garment end use. Concentrating the fabrics to fit machinery, where stability is paramount, can mean that many interesting fabrics are only used by small adaptable manufacturers. A large retail chain has stated that its design quality would suffer enormously if it did not have access to this type of flexible company that adapted to the requirements of the fabrics chosen for the range.

The reliability of even defining fabric 'hand' has been questioned, even a consensus of terms to be used is difficult. One method used in research studies is that of 'polar opposites' (examples: thick/thin, pliable/stiff). However, one study found that people use more than a 100 words to describe 'hand'.[3] Another study found that few people could agree on the polar opposites for describing the fabric handle of plain knit tee shirts.[4] Great care was taken to select unambiguous polar opposites for the characteristics which were to be used in this book.

Appendix five: permitted generic names for fibres

It is an offence to sell, or offer for sale, fabrics which do not label the product with the fibre content by generic name and the percentage of each fibre. The permitted generic names for fibres have been regularised by both European directive and internationally. The Statutory Instruments from HMSO are: SI 1988 No. 1350 and the amendments SI 1998 No. 1169 and SI 2005 No. 1401. A basic list of generic names and some codes for man-made fibres are given below.

(1)	Wool	
(2)	Alpaca, llama, camel, cashmere, mohair, angora, vicuna, yak, guanaco, beaver, otter, followed or not by the name 'wool' or 'hair'	
(3)	Animal or horsehair, with or without an indication of the kind of animal (e.g. cattle hair, common goat hair, horsehair)	
(4)	Silk	
(5)	Cotton	
(6)	Kapok	
(7)	Flax or linen	
(8)	Hemp	
(9)	Jute	
(10)	Abaca	
(11)	Alfa	
(12)	Coir	
(13)	Broom	
(14)	*	
(15)	Ramie	
(16)	Sisal	
(16a)	Sunn	
(16b)	Henequen	
(16c)	Maguey	
(17)	Acetate	CA
(18)	Alginate	ALG
(19)	Cupro	CUP
(20)	Modal	CMD
(21)	Protein	
(22)	Triacetate	CTA
(23)	Viscose	CV
(24)	Acrylic	PAN
(25)	Chlorofibre	CLF
(26)	Fluorofibre	PTFE
(27)	Modacrylic	MAC
(28)	Nylon or polyamide	PA
(28a)	Aramid	AR
(28b)	Polyamide	PA
(28c)	Lyocell	CLY
(28d)	Polyactide	PLA
(29)	Polyester	PES
(30)	Polyethylene	PE
(31)	Polypropylene	PP
(32)	Polycarbamide	
(33)	Polyurethene	
(34)	Vinylal	PVAL
(35)	Trivinyl	
(36)	Elastodiene	ED
(37)	Elastane	EL
(38)	Glass fibre	GF
(39)	Name corresponding to the material of which the fibres are composed, e.g. metal (metallic, metallised), asbestos, paper, followed or not by the word 'yarn' or 'fibre'	

*Entry no 14 has been deleted.

Appendix six: using *Adobe Photoshop* to reproduce full-size blocks with A3 or A4 printers

NOTE Only use this method if you are familiar with the use of the program. The blocks can be printed in sections and joined together matching the grid lines. The blocks will have heavy lines because of the printout resolution. The close fitting block on page 202 is used as an example.

Scanning the block pages

Using a scanning program, scan the required block page at 600 dpi in greyscale (example is the close fitting block).
1. Save it as a TIF file. Name the file CFBLOCK.

Using Adobe Photoshop *with an A3 or A4 printer*

(1) In the FILE menu select OPEN to open the TIF file CFBLOCK.
(2) In the IMAGE menu select the option ADJUST. Select the BRIGHTNESS/CONTRAST option and use the sliders to remove unwanted shadows from the image.
(3) In the IMAGE menu select the option IMAGE SIZE and alter the Resolution box to 120 dpi. Make sure that the Resample Image box is empty.
The block will print out full size at this new resolution.
(4) In the FILE menu select SAVE to save the file.
(5) In the IMAGE menu select DUPLICATE and duplicate the file to the number of pattern pieces in the block (example: for CFBLOCK duplicate two more images).
(6) From the Toolbox select the marquee and draw a rectangle closely around a separate pattern piece (example: the back). In the IMAGE menu select CROP (example: the back pattern piece is now a separate file image; save the file as CFBACK).
(7) Repeat this procedure to create the other two pattern pieces; name them CFFRONT and CFSLEEVE.

Printing the files on an A3 printer

The squares on the block pattern sheets in the book are divided into 5-cm squares. An A3 sheet of paper will show:
Portrait: 7 squares vertically, 5 squares horizontally
Landscape: 5 squares vertically, 7 squares horizontally.

Back and front pattern pieces
(1) In the FILE menu select PAGE SETUP and select the LANDSCAPE option and select the SIZE option to set the paper size to A3.
(2) Use the marquee to select closely the left section of the back pattern piece CFBACK (select up to 7 squares horizontally).
(3) In the FILE menu select PRINT. In the PRINT RANGE option select the SELECTION option.
(4) The printer will print out the left section of the back.
(5) Use the marquee to select closely the right section of the back pattern piece (select up to 7 squares horizontally but make sure that you overlap the previous back section).
(6) In the FILE menu select PRINT and the printer will print out the right section of the back. Close the file CFBACK.
(7) Using the file CFFRONT repeat the procedure to print out the front piece.

Sleeve
(1) In the FILE menu select PAGE SETUP and select the PORTRAIT option.
(2) Use the marquee to select closely the left section of the sleeve pattern piece CFSLEEVE (select up to 5 squares horizontally).
(3) In the FILE menu select PRINT (check the SELECTION option is on). The printer will print out the left section of the sleeve
(4) Use the marquee to select closely the middle section of the sleeve pattern piece (select up to 5 squares horizontally but make sure that you overlap the previous back section).
(5) In the FILE menu select PRINT. The printer will print out the middle section of the sleeve.
(6) Repeat this procedure to select and print out the right section of the sleeve.

Printing the files on an A4 printer

On the blocks an A4 sheet of paper will print:
Portrait: 5 squares vertically, 3½ squares horizontally
Landscape: 3½ squares vertically, 5 squares horizontally.

Back and front pattern pieces
(1) In the FILE menu select PAGE SETUP and select the PORTRAIT option and select the SIZE option to set the paper size to A4.
(2) Use the marquee to select closely the left section of the back pattern piece CFBACK (select up to 3½ squares horizontally).
(3) In the FILE menu select PRINT. In the PRINT RANGE option select the SELECTION option.
(4) The printer will print out the left section of the back.
(5) Use the marquee to select closely the second section of the back pattern piece (select up to 3½ squares horizontally but make sure that you overlap the previous back section).
(6) In the FILE menu select PRINT; the printer will print out the second section of the back.
(7) Repeat this procedure to print out the third and fourth sections of the back.
(8) Using the file CFFRONT repeat the procedure to print out the front pattern piece.

Sleeve
(1) In the FILE menu select PAGE SETUP and select the LANDSCAPE option.
(2) Use the marquee to select closely the top left section of the sleeve pattern piece (select up to 5 squares horizontally).
(3) In the FILE menu select PRINT (check the SELECTION option is on). The printer will print out the top left section of the sleeve.
(4) Use the marquee to select closely the middle top section of the sleeve pattern piece (select up to 5 squares horizontally but make sure that you overlap the previous back section).
(5) In the FILE menu select PRINT and select the SELECTION option. The printer will print out the middle top section of the sleeve.
(6) Repeat this procedure to continue to print out the six sections of the sleeve.

Bibliography

This bibliography is a short list of books that supplement the information and ideas in this book; they are arranged in subject areas. Most of the books may be found in university or college libraries. R. D. Franks Ltd (Market Place, London) stocks a wide range of current fashion/textile books which are listed on their website: www.rdfranks.co.uk.

Books: fabric technology

Cresswell, Lesley (2002) *Textiles at the Cutting Edge*, Forbes Publications, London.
Denton, M.J. and Daniels, P.J. (Eds) (2004) *Textile Terms and Definitions* (11th edition), The Textile Institute, Manchester.
Elssagger, Virginia Henken (2005) *Textiles – Concepts and Principles*, Fairchild Publications, New York.
Humphries, Mary (2004) *Fabric Reference* (3rd edition), Pearson Prentice Hall, New Jersey.
O'Mahoney, Marie (2002) *Sportstech: Revolutionary Fabrics*, Thames & Hudson, London.
Slater, Keith (2003) *Environmental Impact of Textiles: Production, Processes and Protection*, Woodhead Publishing, Cambridge.
Trocme, Suzanne (2002) *Fabric*, Mitchell Beazley, London.

Journals and media: fabric technology

Elearning, Multi-media textile CD ROMS, Media Innovations Ltd., University of Leeds: www.elearning-textiles.co.uk.
Textiles, The Textile Institute, Manchester.
Textile Horizons, Benjamin Dent Publications, London.

Books: technical pattern cutting

Aldrich, Winifred (2006) *Metric Pattern Cutting for Menswear* (4th Edition), Blackwell Publishing, Oxford.
Aldrich, Winifred (2004) *Metric Pattern Cutting* (4th Edition), Blackwell Publishing, Oxford.
Aldrich, Winifred (2002) *Pattern Cutting for Women's Tailored Jackets*, Blackwell Science, Oxford.
Aldrich, Winifred (1999) *Metric Pattern Cutting for Children's Wear and Babywear* (3rd Edition), Blackwell Science, Oxford.

Books: historical pattern cutting references

The cutting of folk costume and the work of 20th century designers with a strong signature cut.
De la Haye, Amy (1994) *Chanel: The Couturiere at Work*, Victoria and Albert Museum, London.
Deschodt, Doretta Davanzo Poli (2001) *Fortuny*, Harry N. Abrahams, New York.
Deslandes, Yvonne (1987) *Paul Poiret*, Thames and Hudson, London.
Kirke, Betty (2005) *Madeleine Vionnet*, Chronicle Books, San Francisco.
Lacroix, Christian (1992) *Pieces of Pattern*, Thames and Hudson, London.
Martin, Richard (1998) *Cubism and Fashion*, Metropolitan Museum of Art, New York.
Pochna, Marie-France (2004) *Dior*, Assouline, New York.
Tilke, Max (2004) *Costume Patterns and Designs*, Dover Publications, New York.

References

Introduction

(1) Bunce, G. (1993) *An Investigation of CADCAM Possibilities in the Printing of Textiles*, unpublished Ph.D Thesis, Nottingham Trent University.
Bunce, G. and Phillips, P. (1993) *Repeat Patterns*, Thames and Hudson, London.

Appendix four

(1) Kawabata, S., Niwa, M. (1989) Fabric Performance in Clothing and Clothing Manufacture, *Journal of the Textile Institute*, **80** No.1, pp. 19–50.
(2) Munden, D.I., Objective Measurements of the Physical Characteristics of Knitted Fabrics, *Knitting International*, December 1990, pp. 94–95.
(3) Kim, C. J., and Vaughn, E.A. (1975) *Physical Properties Associated with Fabric Hand*, AATC Book of Papers.
(4) Fritz, Anne (1992) A New Way to Measure Fabric Handle, *Textile Asia*, July, pp. 59–72.

Printed and bound in the UK by
CPI Antony Rowe, Eastbourne